Managing and Leading People

2nd edition

Charlotte Rayner and Derek Adam-Smith

Managing and Leading People
2nd edition

Charlotte Rayner and Derek Adam-Smith

Chartered Institute of Personnel and Development

Published by the Chartered Institute of Personnel and Development,
151, The Broadway, London, SW19 1JQ

First edition published 2005
Reprinted 2006, 2007, 2008
This edition first published 2009

Typeset by Fakenham Photosetting Ltd, Norfolk

Printed in Great Britain by The Cromwell Press Group, Trowbridge, Wiltshire

British Library Cataloguing in Publication Data

A catalogue of this publication is available from the British Library

ISBN 978 1 84398 217 3

Chartered Institute of Personnel and Development, CIPD House,
151 The Broadway, London, SW19 1JQ

Tel: 020 8612 6200

E-mail: cipd@cipd.co.uk

Website: www.cipd.co.uk

Incorporated by Royal Charter.

Registered Charity No. 1079797

Contents

List of Figures

List of Tables

Acknowledgements

The compilation of an edited text such as this relies heavily on the expertise and co-operation of the authors of individual chapters. We are grateful to them for the patience they displayed with the editorial process. Thanks to Stephen Pilbeam, another colleague at Portsmouth, for his helpful advice on pedagogic features. We are grateful also for the support of our colleagues at the CIPD during the production of this book. We record also our gratitude to the anonymous reviewers of the first edition for their valuable comments. Finally, but no means least, we would like to record our thanks again to Jane Stewart, our Senior Departmental Administrator, for her humour and tolerance with us while providing invaluable help in completing the work.

Charlotte Rayner
Derek Adam-Smith
University of Portsmouth Business School
January 2009

Notes on the editors and contributors

Derek Adam-Smith is Head of the Department of Human Resource and Marketing Management at the University of Portsmouth Business School.

Dr Emma Brown is Senior Lecturer in Human Resource Management at the University of Portsmouth Business School. Her particular areas of research interest include managerial psychology, international perspectives on gender and management and managerial behaviour in the workplace.

Richard Christy is a Principal Lecturer in the Department of Human Resource and Marketing Management at the University of Portsmouth Business School. He teaches marketing strategy, market research and business ethics and is a member of the Market Research Society.

Dr Ray French is Principal Lecturer at the University of Portsmouth Business School. He has a particular interest in cross-cultural aspects of organisational behaviour and human resource management and is closely involved with undergraduate business courses taught in Asia.

Dr Sarah Gilmore is a Senior Lecturer in the Department of Human Resource and Marketing Management at the University of Portsmouth Business School.

Dr Mark Lowman is Senior Lecturer at the University of Portsmouth Business School and has 15 years' experience in the pharmaceutical industry. His research interests include innovation management and marketing in knowledge intensive firms.

Gill Christy is a Principal Lecturer in the Department of Human Resource and Marketing Management at the University of Portsmouth Business School. She teaches human resource management and business ethics and is a CIPD member.

Charlotte Rayner is Professor of Human Resource Management at the University of Portsmouth Business School.

Gary Rees is a Senior Lecturer in Human Resource Management at the University of Portsmouth Business School, and Course Director of Post-graduate Personnel Management Programmes. He is a Chartered Fellow of the CIPD.

Sally Rumbles is a Senior Lecturer at the University of Portsmouth Business School. Prior to this she worked for over 10 years as a HR practitioner, which included specialising in training and employee development.

Simon Turner is an organisation development specialist and teaches on human resource management programmes at the University of Portsmouth Business School. He has his own HR training and development consultancy and can be contacted at www.upturnassociates. com.

CHAPTER 1

Managing and Leading People in High Performance Organisations

Sarah Gilmore and Derek Adam-Smith

LEARNING OUTCOMES

After reading this chapter, you should be able to:

- understand the ways in which change is challenging organisations to find new ways of working
- assess the importance of management and leadership in the change process
- describe the characteristics of a 'high performance' work organisation
- understand the structure and key features of this book.

INTRODUCTION

In 2007, the Metropolitan Police were found guilty by an Old Bailey jury of breaking health and safety laws over the fatal shooting of innocent Brazilian, Jean Charles de Menezes. The jury found that London's police force had unnecessarily put the public at risk in chasing Mr de Menezes – who the police suspected of being a suspected suicide bomber – across London. The trial revealed a string of errors which led towards his death. These consisted not only of mistaken identity but involved a failure by senior officers to adhere to operational plans, the poor briefing of firearms teams and their faulty positioning in terms of their location. This combination of errors meant that it became impossible to effectively stop the suspected suicide bomber before he boarded a bus and headed for the Underground. However, these charges were denied by the Met, who claimed that commanders and officers did all they could to apprehend the victim and minimise risk to the public. In deciding on a penalty, the judge said he was aware that a heavy fine would result in a loss to the public purse and a reduction in essential policing. The Met was therefore fined £175,000 with £385,000 costs. Deputy Assistant Commissioner Cressida Dick, who led the operation, was cleared of any personal culpability in the death of Mr de Menezes. Sir Ian Blair, the head of the Metropolitan Police, also resisted calls for his resignation, retaining the support of the London Mayor as well as the Home Secretary.

In a different organisational context – in a private sector organisation – 2007 saw the first run on a British bank in 150 years, which caused the Bank of England to step in as lender of last resort to Northern Rock, one of Britain's largest mortgage lenders. The £25 million liquidity support facility given to prop up the bank came as the organisation experienced difficulties in financing its lending. These difficulties arose as an outcome of the bank's business model. Rather than going down the traditional route of building up a mortgage business gradually by funding it from deposits made by savers, Northern Rock took advantage of the booming growth in global debt markets. Customers' home loans were bundled together and sold to investors around the world as mortgage-backed securities in a process known as 'securitisation'. This accounted for three quarters of its mortgage business and the model was highly successful: Northern Rock went from having about 3% of the total mortgage market to 8% over a nine-year period. But although this growth won the grudging respect of its rivals in the UK's notoriously competitive mortgage market, some suggested that the company needed greater diversification in terms of its risk management strategy in order to avoid the kinds of eventualities that eventually unfolded with the onset of the global 'credit crunch' and the reluctance of lenders to lend to institutions who were perceived to be unreliable. Some senior bank figures resigned in the months following the crisis and large-scale staff redundancies followed in 2008.

Both cases raise interesting issues of managerial accountability as well as how very different organisations manage risk. What do you think the main points are here that emerge from these examples?

1.1 ACTIVITY

Consider the case of the 'missing' data disks lost by HM Revenue and Customs. The child benefit records of 25 million people – including their names, addresses, birth dates, National Insurance numbers and bank account details – were lost, and hundreds of people in police witness protection programmes were also put at risk by the loss of these records. But in the wake of this case, further instances of individuals' confidential details being lost by official bodies emerged. The Information Commissioner, Richard Thomas, said that a number of public bodies and private companies had contacted him shortly after the HMRC incident was revealed to confess that they too had lost data. However, he stated that it was unlikely that a single junior official could be entirely to blame for the HMRC blunder. For an individual to download and dispatch data on the scale involved, failings in procedures and technology must also be involved. He concluded that there was 'certainly more to come out in the wash'.

Look at the press coverage concerning this story. What lessons do you think there are to be learned? What does the story tell us about organisational processes, and their relationship to governmental policies and practices?

The three cases discussed involve public and private sector organisations. There may be other, more current, organisational examples you might want to contemplate too. While they clearly demonstrate that organisational failure can occur in any sector of the economy – from a bank to a major police force – what can we learn from such cases? What questions about management, leadership, organisations and processes of organising do they raise?

THE NATURE AND CHALLENGE OF CHANGE

It could be argued that these examples illustrate a problem with meeting the challenges thrown up by change: the increased fears concerning the security of the general public; the need for organisational viability to involve risk management; the problem involving the storage, exchange and management of sensitive information as well as the growing reliance on IT and its appropriate handling. The implications of management failure can be huge – indeed, as in the case of Jean Charles de Menezes, they can be fatal. The cases also raise the emotive issue of managerial accountability for decisions, whether related to operational issues or to longer-term business planning. They can also lead to a fracturing of trust by employees in their employer, customers to a particular company and the general public towards those who govern in their name. This has been illustrated by the work of a variety of academic authors on the various aspects of organisational trust (eg Lane and Bachman, 1998; Grey and Garsten, 2001; Sako, 1992). It has also been highlighted by the concept of the psychological contract.

As will be illustrated in Chapter 6, the concept of the psychological contract is difficult to define. It is usually expressed as being concerned with mutuality: the

1.2 CASE STUDY

REPRESENTATION AND CONSULTATION AT CACHE

During a period of reorganisation, direct face-to-face contact with senior management proved to be an effective method for reassuring employees that their interests and concerns were being sincerely listened to. At CACHE, an organisation with 80 employees, four elected representatives were chosen to participate in discussions with the senior management team. The role of the representatives was to act as a conduit for comments and information about the reorganisation process. These representatives had personal responsibility for keeping all staff updated with progress via email. The representatives were trained for the role by specialist consultants along with members of the HR team. HR took minutes of the meetings between the representatives and the senior management team and these were then circulated via email to all staff. The meetings were held during normal working hours. CACHE also placed a suggestion box at reception for staff who wished to contribute other ideas about the reorganisation at any time. These regular meetings with employees, coupled with question-and-answer sheets, served to break down fears about job security and mistrust of management during the change process.

CIPD (2005)

To think about ...

- To what extent do you think initiatives such as this assist in protecting the psychological contract during a period of change?
- What else might HR suggest the senior management do to bolster it?

common and agreed understanding of promises and obligations that the respective parties to the employment relationship (ie the employer and employee) have made to each other about fundamentally important issues such as pay, work, loyalty, flexibility, job security and career progression. Unlike contracts of employment, the psychological contract is unwritten. It is a set of expectations and is usually never discussed or negotiated and therefore has no formal status (Rousseau, 1995; 1998; 2001; CIPD, 2005; Herriot and Pemberton, 1995). But this contract can be damaged – sometimes irreparably – by the behaviour of one of the parties. Research focus in this area has tended to concentrate on the implications of such a breach on *employees*, with such fractures in the contract often stated as being more likely to occur as an outcome of organisational change. Given the increasing dynamism companies continue to experience in their operating environment, managing the processes of change in ways that can maintain the psychological contract has assumed heightened importance. This sets a major challenge for the HR function. Does this have parallels with your own experience of change at work or that of your colleagues and friends? How do you think HR could maintain the psychological contract during a period of uncertainty?

TRIGGERS FOR CHANGE?

Since the 1970s, it could be argued that UK organisations experienced major environmental upheavals – with all sectors of the British economy having seen radical change during the 1990s (Buchanan *et al*, 1999). The pace and scale of these changes seem unlikely to alter and are continuing to trigger a complex multiplicity of overlapping, concurrent initiatives which in turn are radically altering existing structures, cultures and technologies (Eisenhardt and Bourgeois, 1988; Hambrick *et al*, 1998). But why has such major change occurred? What might be some of the main triggers or contours of change over the past 15 years? For example, to what extent is your organisation affected by changes in workforce demography? Are you seeing a declining number of school-leavers and young employees entering your company and a growing number of staff aged 45 and over? There is also the issue of continuity being experienced within processes of change – the Activity below might assist in the process of identifying prompts for change experienced by an organisation, along with those that have remained less volatile or essentially stable (Kolb, 2003; Leanna and Barry, 2000; Pettigrew, 1985; Scarbrough, 1998).

1.3 ACTIVITY

Think about your own organisation or one with which you are familiar. Which developments within your company, sector or industry in recent years (or longer) have been pivotal, and why? What changes have occurred as a result of these developments? What impact have these had on the way the organisation is managed, and what have been some of the major implications for staff? Are there areas that have remained stable? Why were they unaffected by these developments? Do you think that the focus on fast-paced change is overplayed?

ORGANISATIONAL RESPONSES TO CHANGE

Responses to these 'high velocity' transformational change contexts have seen organisations introducing new working practices such as total quality management, business process re-engineering, continuous improvement, teamworking, lean production methods and culture change (many of which will be referred to in the following chapters). But what philosophies or assumptions underpin these new working practices? What ideas about people and organisation support them? Go back to your responses to the Activity above: did your organisation instigate any of these practices or bring in others? Two key ideas will be highlighted below and they will reappear at certain points in the book because of their recent significance concerning the value and the role employees have to play within their organisation. They concern the idea of employees being the key to an organisation's strategic advantage in the market within which it operates – and as such possess talents that need to be maximised and focused to achieve organisational objectives. They also involve the belief in a link between what are termed 'high commitment' or 'high performance' practices and improvements in organisational performance. These ideas are important ones for HR because they place the HR function and its work at a pivotal strategic position for the company; a role the CIPD has argued it needs to fulfil.

EMPLOYEES AS STRATEGIC ADVANTAGE

During the 1990s, it was increasingly stated that the development of unique institutional knowledge that could not be replicated by other organisations created a strategic advantage within the market. This sustained competitive advantage emanates from a firm's internal resources, and in order to sustain ongoing advantage these resources must have four qualities: they must add value; be rare or unique; be difficult for competing organisations to replicate; and be non-substitutable – for example, not replicable by technology (Barney, 1991; 1995; 1997; Boxall and Purcell, 2003). As noted by Storey (1989) human capital resources can fulfil this demanding list of criteria very well and can embody intangible assets such as unique configurations of complementary skills, tacit knowledge, customer or market knowledge.

One aspect of this can involve a re-visiting of institutional, team and individual knowledge because organisational learning can often underpin the explicit extension of the strategic position occupied by the company's internal resources as the primary source of strategic, competitive advantage (Nonaka and Takeuchi, 1995; Senge, 1990). One key framework here is the work of Prahalad and Hamel (1990) and their notion of 'core competencies', which consists of a configuration of skills and technologies that allow an organisation to provide its customers with particular benefits. It is not product-specific: it represents the sum of learning across individual skill sets and organisational units. Most importantly, it is competitively unique and thus represents a 'broad opportunity arena' or 'gateway' to the future.

In brief, Prahalad and Hamel argue that companies need to create the future not just by focusing on organisational transformation and competition for market share but also by regenerating strategies and competing for opportunity share. So creating the future involves strategy being seen as learning, positioning, and planning as well as foresight, and strategic architecture. Organisational strategy therefore goes beyond the notion of 'fit' with its environment to achieving 'stretch' and 'resource leverage'. This means that the ability of employees to learn, combined with their existing knowledge base, becomes crucial; as does the recruitment and retention of knowledge workers who possess the configuration of skills and knowledge needed for this regeneration to occur. However, will this strategic model apply universally? To which sectors or industries does this concept pertain most directly, and what percentage of the workforce would therefore be affected?

THE HR FUNCTION

The work of David Ulrich has been significant here (Ulrich, 1997; 1998; Ulrich and Brockbank, 2005). In his highly influential work, he has proposed a framework which incorporates five roles which the function needs to incorporate in order to bring value to the organisation. These are: HR leader, strategic partner, human capital developer, functional expert and employee advocate. The first function involves HR practitioners leading their own function as well as facilitating the development of other leaders in the company. As a strategic partner, they have to bring knowledge and expertise concerning business change in order to partner managers in reaching their goals through strategy formulation and direction. This has arguably been the role that has most captured the imagination of the HR profession as well as other stakeholders such as the CIPD (Francis and Keegan, 2006). As human capital developers, HR has to recognise people as critical assets and develop their potential via the provision of learning opportunities so that employees and the organisation can be successful in the future. The last two roles involve the function servicing the needs of the organisation efficiently and effectively – mainly working as a support function but with a reduced opportunity to enhance organisational performance or provide significant competitive advantage. For many, it is the first of the two roles that illustrates the ways in which the function adds value and through its enactment can provide a means by which HR becomes able to contribute to the corporate planning process.

Unsurprisingly, Ulrich's work seems to have found favour with many in HR and find their echo in the CIPD's Professional Standards which emphasise two key roles that HR professionals must play within their companies: that of the thinking performer and the business partner. Business partnership is attained by engaging in value-adding activities; by making a contribution, directly or indirectly, to organisational profitability; by facilitating organisational survival when experiencing crisis; by assisting the attainment of organisational vision and strategic goals; by working in alignment with the organisation's mission; by enacting customer-focused continuous improvement; and by being personally flexible when reacting to and stimulating change. The process of adding value is enacted through operating as a business partner, which for the CIPD (2004, p.4):

> represents a model to which CIPD professionals should aspire. In future,

roles will not exist for people who are not able to add value to the business objectives of the organisation for which they work.

It also occurs through building cohesive relationships with line and strategic-level managers – necessitating an understanding of business objectives and operations. The CIPD goes on to say that the business partner therefore has to be a 'thinking performer' – engaging in thinking 'which is both operational and not limited to their current organisational level, and with an appreciation of the organisation strategy' coupled with 'operational capability at a business unit level' which constitutes the definition of 'performer'. Thus it can be argued that the practice and focus of HR is primarily concerned with the advancement of organisational goals – something that is often presented as integral to the concept of HRM and the concept of high performance working.

HIGH PERFORMANCE WORKING (HPW)

This is one response to meeting the demands of change and the increasing needs faced by many organisations (although not all) of mass customisation and fulfilment of individual customers. These may relate to the issues of change you might have noted when performing Activity 1.3. There is no precise definition of HPW and more organisations are likely to be working towards attaining this status than considering that they have achieved it. However, an Organisation for Economic Co-operation and Development (OECD) definition of high performance working refers to flatter, non-hierarchical structures, moving away from reliance on management control, towards teamworking, autonomous working based on high levels of trust, communication and involvement. Workers are seen as being more highly skilled and having the intellectual resources to engage in lifelong learning and master new skills and behaviours.

According to the CIPD (2004) prerequisites for HPW necessitate a vision based on increasing customer value by differentiating an organisation's products or services and moving towards the customisation of its offering to the needs of individual customers; embracing both market objectives and organisational dimensions. As cited by the International Labour Organisation study (http://www.ilo.org) most organisations made use of various performance benchmarks. These have their echoes in the CIPD's concepts of 'performance infrastructure' and 'performance differentiators' which relate firstly to the activities all organisations need to engage in to secure operational activity, and secondly to those actions which provide the means for strategic leverage. It could be argued that moving towards HPW will assist in developing the 'performance differentiators' needed to innovate and secure the future.

The main characteristics of HPW involve:

- decentralised, devolved decision-making, made by those closest to the customer in order constantly to improve the offer to customers. Most organisations therefore move from traditional hierarchies towards self-managed teams. Projects are used as a major focus for learning – thus making a strong link to performance and work organisation

- development of people capacities through learning at all levels, with particular emphasis on self-management, team capabilities and project-based activities – to enable and support performance improvement and organisational potential
- performance, operational and people-management processes aligned to organisational objectives – to build trust, enthusiasm and commitment to the direction taken by the organisation. There are issues connected with performance management and systematising change. But this is accompanied by the development of a culture within which people are prepared to embrace change in work methods, skills, relationships and even employment
- fair treatment for those who leave the organisation as it changes, and engagement with the needs of the community outside the organisation – this is an important component of trust and commitment-based relationships both within and outside the organisation. There is also the promise that better relations between management and employees will help improve productivity. However, although employee involvement systems have been shown to be of importance and working through and with trade unions can provide underpinning support, legitimacy and partnership for the changes involved, the key issue has more to do with the psychological contract and relationships than with structures and systems.

LINKS BETWEEN THE PRESENCE OF HR PRACTICES AND POSITIVE FINANCIAL PERFORMANCE

Much of the interest in the HPW concept has also come from the links made by various studies in both the UK and USA concerning the uptake of HPW and improvements in 'bottom line' results for those organisations (see Huselid, 1995, for example). In the UK, the Work Foundation's (2003) report concerning its research into organisational strategy, management practices and track record found that high-performing firms were those that adopt a joined-up approach to managing across five performance categories: customers and markets, shareholders, stakeholders, employees, and creativity and innovation – outlined above in relation to HPW. This emerged from how well firms scored on a High Performance Index, constructed from performance on each of these individual categories. Firms scoring highest on the index are found to be over 4% more productive than those at the bottom, with the average UK business around 25% less productive than those at the top. A 1% increase in the index score stimulates 2.5% extra sales per employee and gives a 1% boost to the profitability of a business. In a study conducted by the DTI in association with the CIPD (Sung and Ashton, 2005), they found that those organisations operating more of the 35 HPW practices identified by the study as being significant are more likely to be effective in delivering adequate training, motivating staff, managing change and providing career opportunities. Those adopting more of these practices have more people earning over £35,000 and fewer people earning less than £12,000.

It is findings such as these (see also Wood and de Menezes, 1998; MacDuffie, 1995) – exploring the positive relationship between the presence of HR practices and positive financial performance – that are of interest to managers,

1.4 THEORY TASTER

JEFFREY PFEFFER AND BEST PRACTICE

Two books by Jeffrey Pfeffer have been the focus for discussion for those interested in best practice models. In his 1994 book *Competitive Advantage Through People*, Pfeffer proposed 16 practices. These were: security of employment, recruitment selectivity, high wages, pay linked to incentives, employee ownership, information-sharing, participation and empowerment, teams and job redesign, skills development and training, cross-utilisation and cross-training, symbolic egalitarianism, wage compression, internal promotion, a long-term perspective, measurement of these practices, and an overarching philosophy.

Clearly, several of these overlap (such as information-sharing and empowerment) – and criticism of his proposal ensued.

In 1998, Pfeffer reviewed the 16 practices in the context of another book, *Building Profits While Putting People First*, and suggested seven practices. These were: security of employment, selective hiring, self-managed teams or teamworking, high pay linked to company performance, extensive training, reducing status differences, and sharing information.

Pfeffer's work has been useful in so far as it demonstrates the extraordinary complexity of attempting to disaggregate and specify 'success' parameters across, for example, different markets, and organisational types and sizes. As is evident in today's climate, many organisations would find the first item in both lists (providing employment security) challenging.

Pfeffer has, however, helped to open up considerable debate on the content of best practice models and their practical use. Boxall and Purcell (2003) provide an introduction to that debate, which includes the definition of 'best practice' (ie 'best' for whom?), and how far various stakeholders such as trade unions are included in analyses. This is a fundamental issue at the core of the notion of 'differentiators'. For example, how far might any identified 'best practice' be dependent on the existence of other practices? How might these change between working and economic contexts, and also over time?

The answers to such questions may be elusive, and some might suggest that attempts to find solutions are futile. Others would be convinced that the process of attempting to understand such broad categories is useful, even if such attempts do not lead to the final recipe for success.

underpinning as they do the CIPD's research agenda (eg Patterson *et al*, 1997; Guest, 1999; CIPD, 2001b; Purcell *et al*, 2003) as well as its Professional Standards. But these studies have been heavily criticised (for example, Godard, 2004; Godard and Delaney 2000; Legge 2001). Some of the main arguments here are that there is no consensus on what practices constitute a high commitment approach, the specification and measurement of business performance are often somewhat rudimentary and studies generally rely upon responses from managers who, unsurprisingly, offer a biased and partial perspective and may know little of how the practices they identify are interpreted in the workplace (Gilmore and

Williams, 2003). More significantly, the existing evidence suggests that the take-up of such practices is far from universal (Kersley *et al*, 2006; Cully *et al*, 1999). Indeed, Kersley *et al* (2006: 282) in one of the most up-to-date and nationally representative surveys of the state of employment relations in British workplaces concluded that 'any gains in employment relations climate arising from high involvement management practices are uncertain, at least from a management perspective'. This debate will undoubtedly continue because key stakeholders within organisations and professional bodies such as the CIPD have found important mechanisms by which to secure their professional and organisational advantage.

CONCLUSION

The first part of this chapter has sought to locate the management and leadership of organisations within environments that have experienced varying degrees of change over the past decades, while implicitly trying to challenge the idea that all companies have experienced exponential change. The three cases which open the chapter illustrate a few changes that various organisations sought to deal with (but they all ultimately failed), showing at least that the activities of management and leadership are difficult – yet as recent research has shown, effective front-line management engagement with the transmission of HR practices can have a positive impact on employee commitment and lead to better aspects of job experience (Purcell and Hutchinson, 2007). The following chapters will elaborate on these kinds of challenges while offering some solutions as to how they can be met.

But to close, we would like to raise the point that many accounts of managerial work and leadership (including our own here) rely on rationality and cause-and-effect thinking. Although not abandoning it, we also need to remind ourselves that much of management and leadership involves emotion – our own as well as that of others: the irrational, the illogical and the political.

OVERVIEW OF THE BOOK'S CONTENT AND PEDAGOGIC FEATURES

Since the early part of the last century we have been subjected to a battery of advice on how best to manage and lead employees in order to improve organisational effectiveness. Some of these ideas have failed and been confined to the rubbish bin of history. Others have become part of the subconscious process of management, so hidden that we are often not aware of their influence on day-to-day practices. One central theme that retains currency is that organisations must be led and well managed if they are to meet their business objectives, whether they are private, public or voluntary concerns. From this, it is argued, a range of practices may be utilised to ensure that staff contribute effectively and efficiently to the organisation's purpose. The role of the human resources function is thus to assess the relevance of these techniques and advise on their application to the individual business.

This text aims to provide a concise introduction to those established and more contemporary themes that are of concern to both HR professionals and line managers. In producing this contribution we have sought to avoid prescriptive 'how to do it' accounts. Rather, we explore both the practical value of the concepts we present, but also provide a critical evaluation of them. Our contention is that organisations need to choose the practices most suited to their own circumstances, product or service, market and, importantly, the type of staff they employ.

The skills, knowledge and attitudes of employees needed by an organisation, and how staff are to be led and managed, are heavily influenced by its business objectives. In Chapter 2 we explore the nature of organisational goals and strategies and how these influence human resources' policies and practices. In some cases – for example, local government – many of the organisation's objectives are prescribed by law. In larger private sector businesses they may be publicly communicated, while in smaller firms knowledge of objectives may be confined to a small group of senior managers. Whatever the circumstances, human resource managers must be able to discern and interpret them in order for effective people management decisions to be made.

There is an increasingly held view that the achievement of organisational goals can be enhanced if employees are made aware of them and involved by managers in the decision-making process. The issues surrounding schemes of employee involvement and participation are therefore explored in Chapter 3. The extent to which such practices are given credence by organisations is closely related to the style of management within them. Thus we turn, in Chapter 4, to the longstanding debate over the 'best' way to manage staff, and whether management differs from leadership, and if so, in what ways.

In Chapter 5 we consider the ethics of business and how we might define ethical business behaviour. These ideas are then applied to the management of people, and in particular, to the recent emergence of diversity management, which is claimed to be both ethical and of benefit to businesses. It is commonly suggested that in order to be competitive, however that is defined, organisations will benefit from a flexible labour market. The meanings attached to 'flexibility' are explored in Chapter 6 and their implications for the psychological contract – the largely informal but, it is argued, powerful relationship between the employer and employee.

The need for employee commitment to the organisation's goals has been encapsulated in the growing interest in performance management. How this may be characterised, its relationship to motivation theory, and how organisations may develop appropriate reward policies for effective performance by employees is examined in Chapter 7.

The next three chapters consider well-established, but still important, functions of human resource management. Chapter 8 deals with the contemporary debates around the design of jobs and how this may lead to improved job satisfaction and effective employee performance, while the next chapter examines practices that may assist in the recruitment and selection of employees who will contribute to the achievement of organisational goals. In Chapter 10 we turn our attention to training and development. Here, we not only consider traditional job training but, as the chapter title implies, how an understanding of training and the appropriate application of development strategies can provide organisations with the capacity to thrive in turbulent environments. In the concluding chapter we return to the themes outlined in the first part of the introduction, and offer a summary of what the evidence presented in this book means for managing and leading people.

Each of the main chapters begins with a set of objectives that indicate what it is seeking to achieve. Throughout the chapters (including this one) are boxed Activities, mini-case studies and illustrations which are designed to assist in the application of the ideas presented to practical situations. These are complemented by end-of-chapter discussion questions to aid the reader in consolidating his or her understanding of the main issues that have been covered. Where the text refers to a body of theory that is not explained in detail, we have provided a boxed summary of the topic. The aim of this short book is not to provide a comprehensive account of the topics covered but to highlight the main themes and debates. Each chapter ends, therefore, with guided further reading.

In addition to being of interest, the material presented will we hope both challenge commonly held assumptions and assist in the effective management of people.

1.5 DISCUSSION QUESTIONS

1. What are the key triggers of change in organisations, and what is the impact of these changes on employees and the HR function?
2. What is meant by 'high performance working'?

EXPLORE FURTHER

An interesting text exploring the role of HRM in improving business performance is David Ulrich's book (1997) *Human Resource Champions: The next agenda for adding value and delivering results*. Boston, MA: Harvard University Press.

How HR value is defined and can be achieved is the subject of a more recent book by Ulrich and Wayne Brockbank (2005) *The HR Value Proposition*. Boston, MA: Harvard Business Press.

A more critical account of this debate in the UK context can be found in Legge, K. (2001) 'Silver bullet or spent round? Assessing the meaning of the high commitment management/performance relationship', in Storey, J. (ed.) *Human Resource Management: A critical text*, 2nd edition. London, Thomson Learning.

CHAPTER 2

The Strategic Context

Richard Christy and Gill Christy

LEARNING OUTCOMES

After reading this chapter, you should be able to:

- discuss the idea of business strategy as the means through which organisations realise their goals
- understand how strategy development can also help public sector organisations to achieve their objectives
- choose models that help an organisation to analyse and understand its environment
- analyse an organisation's competitive advantage by reference to its key resources, including human resources
- discuss the general strategic choices that are available to organisations
- understand how a choice of strategy must permeate everything an organisation does, changing the value of its resources
- discuss the implications for people management of particular strategic choices.

INTRODUCTION

In January 2007 Marks & Spencer made a public announcement about a £200 million investment programme. The programme, known as Plan A, was described by the BBC business editor Robert Peston (2007) as a 100-point five-year plan by which M&S would 're-engineer itself to become a carbon-neutral, zero-waste-to-landfill, ethical-trading, sustainable-sourcing, health-promoting business'. A year later, Chief Executive Sir Stuart Rose appeared on BBC Breakfast News to explain one of the more visible signs of this plan: the introduction of a 5p charge for plastic bags in the food retail area of all stores on 6 May 2008.

For M&S this was an important announcement about a major shift in the way that the company does business. The plan represents a significant development in business strategy, and will affect every part of the operation. Why has M&S put its credibility on the line in this way? As the company website declares (Marks & Spencer, 2008):

> We're doing this because it's what you want us to do. It's also the right thing to do. We're calling it Plan A because we believe it's now the only way to do business. There is no
> Plan B.

Plainly, M&S expects to strengthen its relationship with its existing customers, to its competitive advantage in the high street. But the company also believes that these developments should be pursued anyway – to some extent it is expecting to persuade its customers to reduce waste by making it easy for them to do their bit to help the environment. Similar commitments are being made by more and more high street names in the UK, meaning that sustainability is now a major strategic consideration.

This chapter considers the importance of an organisation's strategy: what it is trying to achieve and how it intends to achieve it. These are fundamental decisions for any type of organisation, all the more so for business organisations which are in competition. Strategic decisions provide the backdrop for virtually every other choice made by an organisation: its marketing, operations and finance, and also its people. The strategy will allow the organisation to determine how many and what sort of people will be needed. The gap between this ideal and the present array of human resources may lead to decisions about recruitment, training, development, redeployment and sometimes redundancy. Human resources managers will often (and should) be actively involved in the development of an organisation's strategy and an understanding of the strategic context is essential for effective human resource management (HRM).

The ideas reviewed in this chapter have mainly emerged from the world of business and specifically from shareholder-owned companies in competitive markets. The significance of competition is that it can be said to increase the selective pressure on an organisation by rewarding and reinforcing a successful strategy and punishing strategic mistakes. However, non-business organisations without direct competitors also benefit from strategic management, because it helps them to align organisational resources of all types with their longer-term goals. The aims of organisations such as local governments are not always as simple as the aims of a business. As Wilkinson and Monkhouse (1994, p.16) point out:

> In public sector organisations, however, those in executive positions often have their power constrained by statute and regulation, which predetermine, to various degrees, not only the very purpose of the organisation, but also their levels of freedom to diversify or to reduce, for example, a loss-making service. The primary financial driver in these organisations is not profit, but to maximise output within a given budget [...] and, while elements of competition do exist, it is much more common to think of comparators rather than competitors.

As Worrall, Collinge and Bill (1998) discuss, political developments have required local government organisations to take a more overt interest in the concepts of strategy and strategic management. They warn, however, of the dangers of directly importing private sector strategy models into the public sector environment. Local government and the public services are qualitatively different and the business ethos may not be appropriate or helpful in some areas. As they point out, 'customers' and 'citizens' may often be the same people, but it is a mistake to consider the relationship between local government and citizen in purely market terms. Also, the relationship between officers (regular, paid employees) and elected members (often councillors) in local authorities represents a key difference between government and business organisations (*ibid*, p.479):

> This difference reflects the nature of government, its concern with needs, the public interest and with objectives that go well beyond simplistic business measures such as the rate of return on capital. It also reflects the accountability of local government to politicians who have power because they are chosen by – and can be removed by – the electorate.

Applying business-derived models to the strategy of public services requires care and thought. In a review of the applicability of marketing concepts to public sector services, Butler and Collins (1995) discuss the special characteristics of public service 'products' (which may actually be the administration of constraints, duties or facilities, such as collecting local tax), organisations and markets. In process terms, a significant proportion of public service 'new products' may emanate from the political process, outside the service-providing organisation (eg at national level) and, of course, many public services are provided free at the point of use.

Despite these important special factors, however, most people will be able to distinguish effective local government organisations from ineffective ones, and that judgement is likely to be grounded on some sort of purpose-based assessment of what the organisation has achieved. Organisational purpose and strategy also have important connections to the ethics of an organisation's conduct, as we shall examine in Chapter 5.

ORGANISATIONAL STRATEGY AND GOALS

In an organisational strategy, it is useful to distinguish between the organisation's mission, goals and strategy. These definitions are not always the same in the substantial literature on strategic management, but for the purpose of this chapter:

- an organisational mission is a general description of what the organisation is for, its purpose, or its business (eg 'ABC plc manufactures and distributes premium quality ice-cream')
- strategic goals are the intended results of pursuing the mission over a fixed time period (eg 'in five years' time, ABC plc intends to become the market leader in premium ice-cream in the UK')
- a strategy is the means through which the strategic goals are to be achieved (eg 'ABC's goals will be achieved by major investments in new product development, brand awareness and online customer ordering').

One observation to make at this stage is that mission, goals and strategy are all to some extent matters of choice for the organisation. Intelligent choices, when effectively implemented, will lead to success, while inappropriate choices will lead to failure and perhaps even the end of the organisation as an independent entity. Effective strategy development is about analysis as well as creativity, since the organisation needs to understand itself and the world in which it operates before it can make effective strategic choices. And since most organisations have to operate in fast-changing environments it follows that the strategy itself must be dynamic in order to adjust to changing circumstances, and to ensure that the organisation continues to exploit the opportunities available to it.

ANALYSING THE ORGANISATION'S ENVIRONMENT

Developing a successful strategy requires a good understanding of an organisation's external environment – the source of opportunities and threats – and also its internal environment. Understanding the internal environment allows an organisation to assess its strengths and weaknesses and to identify the resources and capabilities that will allow it to achieve its strategic goals. This section outlines some of the more familiar analytical tools that have been developed to assist in this part of the strategy process.

For more than two decades, Michael Porter's contributions (Porter 1980; 1985) to the field of business strategy have been influential. The most familiar frameworks are those of the five forces model (for analysing the attractiveness of an industry), the generic strategies framework (for determining the strategic approach to be adopted) and the value chain (for elaborating the practical implications of implementing the strategy). The five forces model suggests that the 'attractiveness' of an industry – in effect, the ease with which a profit margin may be achieved by those competing in the industry – will depend on five main forces:

- within-industry rivalry
- the power of suppliers to the industry
- the power of customers over the industry
- the threat of new entrants to the industry
- the threat of substitutes, or alternative ways of delivering the same value to customers.

Thus an industry centred on weakly branded, fragmented rival firms, served by large, powerful suppliers, with concentrated industrial customers, low entry barriers and a real threat of substitutes will be relatively unattractive. This will be relevant to the firms competing in that industry, of course, who may find it relatively difficult to identify profitable investments in that industry, but also to any potential rival contemplating entering the industry. Most industries are a mixture of attractive and unattractive factors: those supplying major supermarkets in the UK will appreciate the effect of very strong buyer power on their ability to make a margin. Similarly, postal services are well aware of the substituting effect of email on their businesses.

Any business will understand the importance of understanding customers, monitoring competitors and the other day-to-day aspects of the business environment. The 'PESTEL' framework provides a checklist of other important factors that can affect a business over time:

- Political factors: how will expected political changes affect this industry?
- Economic factors: what assumptions should be made concerning the big economic indicators (Gross Domestic Product growth, inflation, interest rates, exchange rates etc)?
- Sociological factors: what demographic assumptions should be made and how do they affect the industry? How will emergent social trends change the business environment?
- Technological factors: what opportunities and threats may result from expected technological changes, for suppliers, competitors and customers?
- Environmental factors: how might changes to the natural environment and changes to environmental practice affect the industry?
- Legal factors: what changes are expected, and what impact will they have on the organisation and its industry?

This framework can be used to identify specific factors in the HRM environment. For instance, political factors might include such items as the introduction of the National Minimum Wage, its extension beyond the initial age groups affected, and the level and timing of increases in the rates. Economic factors such as changes to the rate of inflation might generate compensatory pay claims, and new laws about smoking might need to be reflected in organisational disciplinary policies and practice.

In analysing and understanding its own capabilities and position, a range of techniques may be deployed by the organisation. A commercial organisation may review the distribution of its revenue and profit by product group, market and customer, for example. It will also consider the position of its various businesses in terms of industry life-cycles. Plainly the demands of managing a business in a high-growth market will differ significantly from those of a business in a mature market. Softer information, such as customer satisfaction indicators, may also be considered. Portfolio planning models can be used to review the general investment needs of the various businesses of a large corporate group as if they were the components of an investment 'portfolio'. One of the most familiar is the 'Boston box', developed by the Boston Consulting Group in the 1970s. This model categorises each of the corporate group's businesses on the basis of two elements:

- the growth rate of the market in which the business is operating (which is a simplified way of asking how attractive the market is)
- the relative market share of the business (which is a simplified measure of how well the business is doing).

The resultant four categories are as follows:

- High-share businesses in high-growth markets are called Stars and deserve cash investment, in order to keep up with the growth of their markets and not lose share.

- Low-share businesses in high-growth markets are called Question marks: they might deserve cash investment to boost their share, but the business must first identify winners. To do this a thorough analysis must be made of the prospects of each Question mark.
- High-share businesses in low-growth markets are called Cash cows: they need to be maintained, and are net generators of cash, which can be invested elsewhere in the portfolio.
- Low-share businesses in low-growth markets are known as Dogs and the logic of the model is that dogs must be disposed of: they are less deserving of cash investment than other types and are sitting on resources that could be reassigned. Obviously, this must be done with caution. For example, a dog business may provide important services to other businesses in the group or may serve one of the group's major customers in some small but significant way.

This four-way classification of business types is certainly a simplification of real-life situations, but experienced human resource managers may also recognise that these four types of business (or stages in the life of a business) will represent different human resource challenges – for example:

- Star businesses will need to recruit rapidly, in order to grow. Since high-growth markets are also associated with uncertainty (about the exact nature of future growth, for example), the human resources of a star business need to be flexible in both size and character, implying an important set of human resource development needs.
- Question mark businesses, if they are to be selected for conversion into stars, need to grow, but that growth will only be possible after identifying what has constrained their growth so far. This may result in the need for different types of human resources, as well as general growth in resource levels to match business expansion.
- Cash cow businesses have low or zero growth rates and address markets characterised by stability: customers are familiar with the products, most of the distribution infrastructure is in place, and so on. At the same time, however, competition is at its fiercest: only large, powerful organisations remain in the market. New custom can only be gained directly from other players, as there is no market growth. Human resources (as well as all other types) will have to be deployed as effectively and efficiently as possible, in order to maintain competitive value for money in the marketplace. High-quality and reliable customer service is likely to be pivotal, with clear implications for staff training, motivation and rewards (Legge, 2005). It will also affect the organisation's choices about the nature of the labour market(s) from which it seeks to recruit staff.
- Dog businesses have reached the end of their useful life in the organisation's portfolio: a dog business may live on after it has been sold to another owner (who

may be better able to manage it profitably), but in most cases, the HR issues will centre on redeployment and redundancy.

The Boston box model is characterised by strong internal logic, but the simplifying assumptions that are embodied in the concept mean that the outputs should be treated with caution: as an input to the strategic discussion, rather than an end product.

Attempts have been made to adapt the Boston box model to public sector organisations (Montanari and Bracker, 1986; Johnson and Scholes, 2002) in order to provide a similarly straightforward framework for discussion of government service provision. This model cross-references the level of public need and support for a particular service (ie how easy it is politically to persuade taxpayers to contribute) with the ability of the organisation to serve that need effectively. This results in a similar set of four types of service:

- The golden fleece service, which is delivered very effectively, but for which the public has relatively low levels of need. There is the risk, therefore, that such services could be seen as a drain on resources and reduced or closed down without great political damage. An example might be public library provision in the UK.
- The public sector star, which is very necessary and largely supported as a government-run service, but which is also delivered effectively. The fire service might serve as an illustration here.
- The political hot box, where need is great, or suddenly becomes so, but governmental ability to deliver this service effectively is challenged. The NHS is one such controversial service which attracts regular political debate, almost all of which is focused on the relative lack of performance in relation to high levels of public funding. An illustration of a government activity which suddenly became high-profile as the result of unexpected events would be the British government's work in respect of food safety after the discovery of the scale of the BSE epidemic in the mid-1990s. This in turn led to the formation of the Food Standards Agency.
- The back drawer issue, which is the equivalent of the 'dog' and which gets little support from the public, together with a general lack of effectiveness. Logic suggests that it should be dropped if possible. An example was the now-abandoned dog licensing system. Controversial areas may well fall into this segment, such as public support for the arts, particularly those perceived as being somewhat elitist (eg opera).

The adaptation of this business-derived model could be said to suggest a parallel between market forces and the democratic will. The strategic implications for public sector managers working in services which fall into these different categories are outlined by Montanari and Bracker (1986) in relation to the way in which the profile and public perception of such services can be enhanced, particularly those in the vulnerable categories of 'back drawer' and 'golden fleece'. Here strategic concerns would involve moves to develop a strong support base for the service and attempts to enhance its public appeal. 'Hot box' issues have to be managed in the full glare of public debate, and in such a way as to fulfil expectations, which may be a long-term process. Plans to increase the number of doctors and nurses qualifying and working in Britain to expand NHS provision cannot be realised quickly, and so managers in some NHS trusts have often turned to overseas recruitment as a means of increasing staffing levels and reducing waiting lists.

Once again, the people management implications for operating in any of these areas can be related to such things as recruitment, training and pay/reward matters, but also motivational issues. Public sector workers are often under much more overt scrutiny by virtue of their employment, and the level of interest which can be legitimately taken in their terms and conditions of service by the press and tax-paying public.

2.1 ACTIVITY

Using a variety of press sources, identify two or three recent disputes in the public sector involving either pay, terms and conditions of service or both. What appear to be the key issues in these disputes? Are there any common features? Are they linked to any strategic changes in the way in which the service is provided? How are they reported in different parts of the media?

RESOURCE-BASED VIEW

More recently, strategic development has been based on a different perspective: the resource-based view, which characterises the task as that of identifying and/or developing key resources that can be used to develop profitable competitive advantage in chosen markets. As Hooley *et al* (1998) argue, this view of strategy does not necessarily contradict that of market orientation (looking outwards at what customers need, rather than inwards at what the company can do). Organisational resources and capabilities are built up over time as a result of past decisions and choices made by the organisation; the availability of these resources determines what an organisation can realistically aim to achieve in serving its markets, as shown in the quotation below.

Collis and Montgomery (1995, p.119) state:

> The [resource-based view] sees companies as very different collections of physical and intangible assets and capabilities. No two companies are alike because no two companies have had the same set of experiences, acquired the same assets or skills, or built the same organizational cultures. These assets and capabilities determine how efficiently and effectively a company performs its functional activities. Following this logic, a company will be positioned to succeed if it has the best and most appropriate stocks of resources for its business and strategy.

Hooley *et al*'s (2008) typology of resources demonstrates the breadth of the resource-based view: potentially, everything in the organisation can contribute to (or, of course, impede) the chosen strategy. In this typology, an organisation's resources consist of:

- marketing assets, which may be customer-based (eg relationships or brands) or based upon internal support assets (such as information systems or patents), alliances (eg to give access to technology or markets) or supply chain assets
- marketing capabilities, which deploy the assets to produce competitive advantage (a particular capability in product management, for example)
- dynamic marketing capabilities, which allow the company to renew its array of assets to respond to a changing business environment. These capabilities may be 'absorptive' (to do with market sensing and learning), adaptive (in terms of targeting and positioning), and/or innovative (ie new products and services).

This approach to business strategy also opens the door to the consideration of people as one of the internal resources of a business which can be a source of sustainable competitive advantage. The knowledge, skills, motivation and behaviour of employees can be linked to operational efficiency, and thus to organisational capability. As Allen and Wright (2007) suggest, the resource-based view is beginning to be applied to research about HRM, and while the links are as yet untested, further exploration of this area may provide important evidence about the relationship between HRM and successful business strategy.

2.2 ACTIVITY

Choose a business sector that interests you. Using published sources, such as corporate and other websites, select three suppliers within that sector that appear to have different competitive strategies. Identify those strategies, on the basis of the frameworks discussed in this chapter. From the published evidence, how does the chosen strategy of each of the three seem to influence:

- their marketing communications (the intended message and the way it is presented)
- their range of products and services and the specification of these offerings
- the target market segments to which they are seeking to appeal?

STRATEGY AND PEOPLE MANAGEMENT

It is clear from the above typology that employees and their abilities are critical to many of these resources. Sometimes, an organisation's human resources may actually amount to the competitive advantage itself. Effective HRM itself may be a key capability for an organisation, allowing the organisation to attract, retain and motivate key people more convincingly than its competitors and thus affording a basis for competing. Certainly Karami, Analoui and Cusworth (2004), in a survey of British manufacturing industry, found positive associations between human resource capabilities and the performance of the firm and also between human resource involvement in strategic management and organisational effectiveness.

More simply, strategy is about looking for a match between what the organisation is especially good at – its 'distinctive capability', as Kay (1993) puts it – and a part of the market that is prepared to pay a high price for such capability, because it represents a particularly good match with their specialised needs. These concepts provide excellent candidates for 'differentiators' from a CIPD perspective (CIPD, 2007).

For a group of competitors in a sector at a given point in time, there may be a set of resources (assets and capabilities) that might be described as basic (ie necessary to participate at all) which the CIPD would term as 'infrastructure' elements. These can be compared to those that are potentially distinctive (ie that provide an organisation with a superior basis for attracting customers through enhanced products or lower costs). This is certainly an important distinction for the short and medium term: if a company allows a basic resource to fall into disrepair, for example, then it is likely to lose business to better-managed competitors. In dynamic competitive environments, however, some care is necessary with this idea:

- Strategic choices are so fundamental for an organisation that they have implications for all resources, not just the ones that distinguish an organisation from its competitors. Implicit in Porter's (1985) value-chain model, as well as the Mathur and Kenyon (2001) framework described below, is the notion that strategic choices must impact on the design of the whole business system.
- Allowing oneself to become accustomed to the idea of sets of basic and distinctive resources and capabilities runs the risk of missing the threat represented by discontinuous technological change and new market entrants. These new organisations may arrive with very different capabilities and practices (large supermarkets and financial services, for example). Organisations in the past that took for granted the basic importance of prime high street sites in CD and book retailing, the necessity of expert insurance brokers for motor insurance sales and the importance of strong relationships with travel agents in the airline industry might have been slow to notice the arrival of Amazon, Direct Line and easyJet respectively.

However, as Christopher *et al* (1991) point out in their discussion of relationship marketing, an organisation is not only involved in customer markets. They suggest that a further six types of market or quasi-market will be important to a company, notably including the organisation's participation in recruitment markets (as a buyer) and in internal 'markets' (the dialogue with its own employees). While most customer markets are highly dynamic and turbulent, it could be argued that recruitment and employment markets are less turbulent in nature. The CIPD distinction between 'infrastructure' and 'differentiator' factors is a useful way of thinking about how to be an effective employer – ie one that is successful in attracting and retaining the talent that the company needs. For example, some essential people management requirements are effectively determined by the ever-growing set of employment laws and regulations. Being able to manage the application of these rules efficiently and reliably is surely a basic managerial competence for any employer, whether in a competitive market or not. Getting high levels of commitment and performance from staff, for example by the creative and strategic use of employment practices which may be related to the objectives of employment legislation, requires a more visionary approach.

2.3 CASE STUDY

B&Q

The UK DIY retailer B&Q has become well known for its progressive employment practices, particularly regarding the employment of experienced older people, whose skills as advisers are specially valuable in the stores. The organisation's website (http://www.diy.com) describes its policy as being to:

implement procedures to eliminate discrimination and promote equality of opportunity in employment so that age, gender, colour, ethnic or national origin, culture, religion, disability, marital status, political affiliation or sexual orientation are not barriers for anyone who wants to work and shop at B&Q.

Readers will note that this represents a differentiating strategy based on human resources. B&Q's television advertisements featuring real members of staff is further evidence of the organisation's commitment to this policy and its value as a competitive strategy.

CHOOSING A STRATEGY

Strategy is about how an organisation proposes to achieve its goals in the environment it has to navigate. For a business, the key questions are which markets to participate in, and within each of those markets, how to compete.

Porter's Generic Strategy Framework (Porter, 1985) provides a familiar classification of strategies: an organisation competes by:

- differentiation – doing especially well something that is valued by customers

  or

- cost leadership – achieving the lowest unit cost

  or

- focus – concentrating on serving a particular part of the market (usually in effect a small-scale version of a differentiation strategy).

These alternatives can be illustrated by considering the market for within-Europe air services in the UK. In this market, BA is an example of competing through differentiation: it offers a high-service package, for which its prices are generally higher. Ryanair's strategy, by contrast, is based on cost leadership: the service provided is deliberately designed to be basic, in order to be able to offer very low prices. Focused businesses in this area are proving risky; some, like Eos and Silverlink, have concentrated on executive jets between the London and the United States; others, like the Channel Islands-based service Aurigny, are geographically focused. All have experienced financial problems, and Aurigny was bought by the States of Guernsey in 2003. At present, the decision to operate a 'no frills' strategy seems to predetermine the range of services that can be offered: it is plainly much more realistic to apply this strategy to short-haul rather than longer-distance services. These contrasting strategies are much more than different advertising campaigns by the relevant organisations: the effect of the strategic choice is felt through the whole of the organisation. BA and Ryanair, in order to deliver the very different service promises that they are making, have to design and run business systems that match the strategy, with implications for operations, finance and HRM.

A rather different perspective on competitive strategy choices is provided and elaborated by Mathur and Kenyon (2001). In an earlier article, Mathur (1992) suggested that thinking about competitive strategy had not yet taken full account of the fact that competition is about persuading customers to choose one way rather than another. Competitive strategies should therefore be analysed from the point of view of what customers can see when they are making their choices (rather than from the point of view of factors that are internal to the firm and not seen by customers). The basic framework envisages any marketing 'offering' (the whole package that is considered by customers) as comprising:

- the 'merchandise': the main product or service
- the 'support' element: added-value services that accompany the merchandise.

Both merchandise and support may be undifferentiated (ordinary) or differentiated (special), resulting in four generic forms of differentiation:

- the commodity-buy, in which customers choose an ordinary product or service with basic support (eg a business offering cheap flights and basic chain-hotel stays over the Internet)
- the service-buy, in which customers choose an ordinary product with special, differentiated service (eg a fuller-service version of the commodity-buy business, to include airport pick-up, transfers, guided city tours, etc)
- the product-buy, in which customers choose a special product or service with basic support (eg a business specialising in booking deluxe flights and stays at expensive hotels, booked from home over the Internet)
- the system-buy, in which both product and support are differentiated (eg a travel agency business offering tailor-made holidays, with full itineraries, specialised services, etc).

None of these strategies is 'superior' to any of the others: each potentially represents a profitable way of serving a particular part of the market. Because the different levels of added value tend to appeal to different parts of the market, all four approaches may co-exist in a market. Naturally, the four different types of offering will command different prices, and what is good value for some parts of the market will be of little interest to other segments.

In people management terms, the four generic forms of differentiation, flowing directly from the organisation's strategic decision about what value to offer to which parts of the market, each set a different agenda for the HR manager. A business promising high levels of service to its customers will obviously need to recruit, train and retain enough sufficiently qualified people to fulfil that promise. Conversely, a commodity-buy business makes less of a promise to its customers and must offer a low price in order to compete, which results in a very different HR context. The organisation's ability to pay its people depends on the willingness of customers in the targeted part of the market to pay for the value that they add. If target customers do not value the extra service very highly, or if they are unable to pay for it, then the strategy is unlikely to be successful. There would be a fundamental mismatch between what the organisation has chosen to offer and what the target segment is interested in buying.

Non-business organisations also have to make strategic choices, but the methodology for evaluating and comparing one possible strategy against another is likely to be more complicated than for a business. Because a business has a basically simple purpose – to make money for its owners – it is conceptually simple to evaluate a proposed strategy by examining how much money it is likely to make (in practice, forecasting the effects of a strategy can be complex and difficult, of course). But non-business organisations often have more complex, multiple purposes, making the strategy evaluation process conceptually more difficult. As Butler and Collins (1995, p.94) observe, financial and quantitative measures are generally inadequate to measure the success of public services: more imprecise qualitative measures must also be considered, often in respect of multiple and conflicting goals. However, it is still clearly important for non-business organisations to do this, not least because any expenditure involves opportunity cost – money spent on one thing is no longer available for anything else.

2.4 ACTIVITY

Choose two contrasting public sector (non-business) organisations: eg a local government organisation and a public university. On the basis of their published information (for example, on corporate websites), assess the extent to which their decisions about resource allocation seem to be guided by a clearly articulated organisational strategy.

In what ways are the more complex aims and objectives of public sector organisations (in comparison to businesses) evident in the strategic choices made by these organisations?

MAKING A STRATEGY HAPPEN

Developing and refining a strategy can be intellectually and creatively demanding for an organisation's management team. However, making a strategy happen requires far more effort: detailed planning and implementation over a long period, often with the need to respond to unexpected developments.

For an organisation to be successful, everything it has and does should be tested against the question 'Does this help us to pursue our chosen strategy?' The news item at the beginning of this chapter may provide an example of this process – the company is reviewing the detail of its operations against the strategy it is pursuing and is changing a number of these operations in line with the five 'pillars' of 'Plan A.' There are likely to be implications for its human resource needs and practices during implementation; for instance, one of the pillars is 'health.' The company expects to recruit and train 1,500 health advisers who will work in stores to provide direct advice and support for both staff and customers about healthier eating and lifestyles. This has clear HRM implications in terms of specifying the job role, recruiting and selecting appropriate candidates, identifying the necessary knowledge, skills and attitudes as the basis for training, determining their levels of pay, and so forth.

2.5 ACTIVITY

In a particular sector, select one example of an organisation that is competing on the basis of superior quality and one that is competing on the basis of low cost. From the published information that is available – eg corporate websites – examine the apparent differences between the HRM policies of the two organisations (in respect, for instance, of recruitment, training, promotion and reward policies). To what extent does a different business strategy seem to result in a different HRM policy?

One important implication of strategy development is that the value of an organisation's resources depends in part on the strategy adopted by that organisation. Implementing a strategy involves developing a programme to bring all of its resources up to maximum utility for the new strategy:

- investing in and maintaining the important skills and assets
- developing the low-value resources, where that investment is likely to be profitable
- disposing of the resources of low or negative value that cannot be viably transformed.

If the strategy changes, then new resources may suddenly be needed and the company's HRM priority must be that of locating and securing those resources. For example, a decision by an airline to move towards online marketing and booking involves a clear need for a set of new resources: the website, the call-handling facilities, the IT and communications infrastructure, and so on. At the same time, previously valuable resources may become less important and thus literally less valuable to the organisation. A company has no business to maintain resources that are not needed for its strategy, meaning that the resources in question must be modified or disposed of. To extend the example, an airline's decision to move towards online booking may reduce the value of its existing distribution channel assets: the retail facilities and staff, or the business relationships with intermediaries.

For some, this re-evaluation and reconfiguration of an organisation's resources behind new strategic priorities may seem heartless and inhuman. Certainly, the economic consequences of abrupt changes in investment levels – whether as a result of proactive strategy or of competitive failure – can be highly disruptive to human lives. Enthusiasts for free markets, however, point out that this process of perpetual realignment, tearing down and renewal is an important part of how a market economy manages to deliver increasing levels of choice, comfort and affluence over time. Those who value the benefits of modern necessities like mobile phones, affordable DVD players and cheap foreign holidays are enjoying the effects of a perpetual competitive struggle between powerful competing companies to make money for their owners.

At this point, some may be reflecting on the possible implications of the commonly used metaphor 'human resources': should these resources, too, be subject to the market-driven process of relentless renewal and reassignment? This is a very important question, to which we return in Chapter 5. This type of decision is not, however, simply a business one. Governments will always be involved to some extent in employment markets, both as participants and regulators, and the way they regulate will reflect broader cultural and political concerns about what is socially desirable.

Grahl and Teague (1991), for instance, identified a continuum of political and governmental approaches to the need to balance national competitiveness in a global labour market on the one hand, with attempts to ensure social inclusion and prosperity on the other. The core of this issue is seen as the degree of flexibility and adaptability of the workforce to both new patterns and new types of work. At one end of this continuum are largely de-regulated labour markets, such as those of the USA, which experience what they term 'competitive flexibility'. This is characterised by 'at will' employment, and essentially places the emphasis on the individual to remain employable (and employed) by taking responsibility for updating their own skills. At the other end is 'constructive flexibility', which is found in a number of European labour markets, where employment protection is much greater than in the USA, and employers are therefore required to maker longer-term commitments to their workers, and also expected to make greater contribution to training and re-training them as skill needs change. Indeed, they are obliged to be more creative because it is much more difficult either to initiate redundancies or to take other measures designed to reduce employment costs (Rodgers, 2003).

CONCLUSION

Whether one operates in the public, private or voluntary sector, the need to align business goals with HR strategy and the tasks of managing and leading people is accepted. All organisations are subject to pressures from the external environment as events beginning in the financial sector in 2008 have demonstrated. Currently, an increasing range of skills are becoming globally available, and market competition forces businesses to consider ways of reducing labour costs. In the 1980s and 1990s international outsourcing was mostly concentrated in the manufacturing sector; more recently it has become common in 'white-collar' work, especially customer service call centres and the information technology sector; and in the future it is likely to reach deeper into areas usually termed 'knowledge work' (research, design and development, for example). Such trends will continue to affect both organisational strategies and consequently organisational approaches to HRM issues. It is impossible to identify any single route to be successful in terms of economic performance – but the issue is obviously central to the choices available to businesses in determining their HRM strategies and practices in managing and leading people.

2.6 DISCUSSION QUESTIONS

1. Public service organisations differ from businesses in a number of important ways. Can the ideas of business strategy be satisfactorily adapted to these organisations? What sort of adaptations to the concept need to be made?
2. Distinguish between missions, goals and strategies, by reference to an organisation with which you are familiar.
3. In what ways does an organisation's choice of strategy affect the value of its resources? Provide example to illustrate the points you make.
4. What are the 'five forces' that determine the attractiveness of an industry? By reference to a sector of your choice, explain how the five forces operate in that sector.
5. What is the resource-based view of organisational strategy? Can an organisation's human resource be analysed in this way?
6. Compare and contrast the approaches to strategic choice in the models by Porter and Mathur discussed in this chapter. Apply these models to a sector of your choice and review the results of this analysis.

EXPLORE FURTHER

For a comprehensive review of the whole area of corporate strategy, go to the well-established text: Johnson, G., Scholes, K. and Whittington, R. (2007) *Exploring Corporate Strategy: Texts and cases*, 7th edition. London: FT/Pitman.

An interesting application of the shareholder value concept to marketing strategy is provided by Doyle, P. (2000) *Value-Based Marketing*. Chichester: John Wiley.

Good overviews of the issues related to strategy and Human Resource Management can be found in Legge, K. (2005) *Human Resource Management: Rhetorics and realities*. Basingstoke: Palgrave Macmillan; and in Boxall, P. and Purcell, J. (2008) *Strategy and Human Resource Management*, 2nd edition. Basingstoke: Palgrave Macmillan.

CHAPTER 3

Employee Involvement and Participation: Contemporary Theory and Practice

Emma Brown

LEARNING OUTCOMES

After reading this chapter, you should be able to:

- explain why organisations may adopt employee involvement and participation practices
- explain the relationship between management styles and the adoption of involvement and participation techniques
- recognise the importance of national cultural differences in the successful implementation of such practices
- recognise the role that psychological factors play in the communication process
- identify practical examples of involvement and participation schemes and their application in organisations.

INTRODUCTION: DECISION-MAKING AND EMPLOYEE INVOLVEMENT AND PARTICIPATION

In simple terms, employee involvement (EI) is a process usually initiated by management to increase the information given to the employees in order to enhance their commitment to the organisation and its business objectives.

In this context, employee participation (EP) refers to collective rather than individual processes, which enable employees and/or their representatives to influence decision-making processes in the organisation.

Employee participation may be described as an involvement process designed to provide employees with the opportunity to influence and take part in decision-making. This notion is relatively fresh. Such involvement primarily relates to matters that specifically affect relevant members of the workforce. A potential business benefit of EI is that the employees are more committed to the organisation and its objectives. However, what is not always clear is the degree to which employees are actually involved in the processes. This could be viewed as a matter of business rhetoric versus the reality of organisational operations. If employees believe they are to be involved in the relevant processes but in reality are not able to influence outcomes, then the enhanced commitment outcome may well be undermined.

In an ideal scenario, organisations need to increase employee commitment and motivation. If such increases are achieved, they could in turn support the principal business goals of beneficial cost control and/or profitability. In practical terms, this positive-outcome ideal may be easier to achieve where suitable decision-making processes have been followed. Such decision-making processes may include consultation, implementation and evaluation mechanisms. Figure 3.1 illustrates a simplified view of the interrelationship between EI/EP and the organisational decision-making processes.

Figure 3.1 Involvement and participation in decision-making

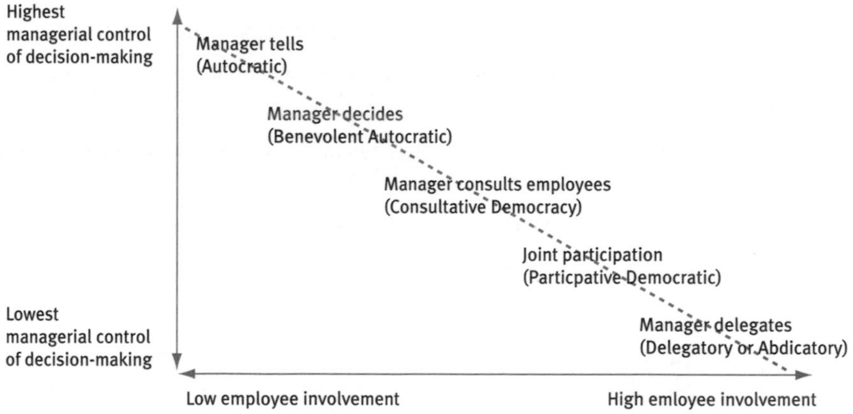

Source: adapted from Brown, E. J. (2001)

The degree of involvement may be pivotal to the notion that higher worker involvement and participation will, all things being equal, lead to increased employee motivation, mutual commitment and, by implication, increased stakeholder value. Sun *et al* (2000) support the underlying idea that the presence of EI is positively linked to performance via total quality management mechanisms. However, there is some indication that the link between EI and performance is not always positive. Wood and Wall (2007, p.1366) suggest that with contemporary attention being placed on performance imperatives in organisations this may in effect 'squeeze out employee involvement'. The issue of quality management and EI will be considered later in this chapter. In real or operational terms, increases in motivation and commitment have to be balanced by the reduction of costs, be they human, financial or opportunistic in nature.

Bakan *et al* (2004) propose that not all the effects of EI lead to productive outputs in terms of employee attitudes and related decision-making. This could for example be due to a perceived lack of mutual employee understanding about the value of EI and its place in organisational development. Conversely, it may also be considered that an absence of attention to EI issues could, *in extremis*, promote greater detriment than benefit.

The behaviour of managers is inherently connected with EI/EP. The willingness of managers, be it subconscious or otherwise, will affect the effectiveness of EI/EP in practice. The motivation for managers to involve employees in appropriate organisational practices is also a matter for consideration. In practical terms it may be assumed that the fundamental business reasons underlying EI and EP initiatives are usually connected with improving employee development and adding organisational/stakeholder value. In reality, the reasons may not always be altruistic.

The idea of increased EI giving rise to increased organisational commitment is transactional in nature and may be seen as improving the psychological contract between employer and employee (see Chapter 6). In practical terms there could be a difference between what Townley (1994) describes as the expectation and deliverance of work. Put simply, the human resource realities of EI may not be reflected by the operational realities (Sisson, 1994).

3.1 ACTIVITY

Consider an organisation you are familiar with.

* Describe how the decision-making process operates in your chosen organisation.
* Describe the extent to which employees are able to influence the decision-making in your chosen organisation.
* Briefly, comment on how the employees feel about the level of their involvement.
* What lessons could be learned by both the management and the non-management employees?

COLLECTIVE AND INDIVIDUALIST ISSUES

The notions of EI and EP may be viewed from a collectivist and an individualist perspective (Torrington, Hall and Taylor, 2008). Both perspectives have had some substantive impact on employee relations practices in many countries. Operationally, related impacts may be strongly but not exclusively related to direct hard or technical business factors such as profitability achievement and cost control. Examples of positive soft or human impacts may include the promotion of low or non-confrontational employee relations and an enhanced employee understanding, acceptance and adoption of organisational change.

It is important to consider the practical managerial implications, particularly where a softer or individualistic approach is being used in the organisation. In practice, it is likely that a blended approach using both hard and soft techniques is used by managers. The principles of EP and EI theory are applicable to any organisational setting but the reality may be different for various operational and socio-psychological reasons. For example, in a country where there is a strongly individualist national culture, employee acceptance of a collective organisational culture may be difficult, if not impractical, and may increase the potential for conflict in some form. As Hofstede (2001, pp240–1) states: 'Management in individualist societies is management of individuals ... management in a collectivist society is management of groups.' If it is assumed that contemporary businesses operate within an increasingly global market, both the organisational and cultural or social-psychological notions are increasingly important considerations for the success of international human resource management.

The wider adoption and use of collective/individualist approaches have implications for local and national government, technical and environmental innovation (eg the adoption of 'green' production methods, and recycling improvements) and legislative instruments/frameworks (eg Environmental Information Regulations 2004 and the Freedom of Information Act 2000). Often the consideration of involvement incorporates both operational and employment relations matters with the latter including conflict, and corporate and legal governance. Purcell and Sisson (1983) consider the collective or employee relations perspective together with some of the managerial implications.

3.2 THEORY TASTER

INDIVIDUALISM AND COLLECTIVISM: THE BASICS

Fons Trompenaars sums up individualism and collectivism as 'The conflict between what each of us wants as an individual, and the interests of the group we belong to ... Do we relate to others by discovering what each one of us individually wants and then trying to negotiate the differences, or do we place ahead of this some shared concept of the public and collective good?' (pp55–6). He goes on to discuss this at a cultural level: 'If we look at Anglo-Saxon literature on the subject it seems that the manager is undoubtedly an individual hero rationally designing the willed future. This is in sharp contrast to many Asian managers [for whom] strategy is ultimately a group process that is decided through a painstaking process, in which many colleagues are involved until consensus is reached about the course to follow' (p.56).

Source: Trompenaars (1996)

The behaviour of managers in the workplace may be due to a varying combination of intrinsic behavioural characteristics or extrinsic or non-behavioural factors such as managerial/hierarchical level and the degree of formalised job responsibility. The nature and culture of the business climate within which managers operate may have a substantial effect on their behaviour and, by implication, the employees for whom they are responsible. Individualist and collectivist environments are broad-category examples of organisational cultures within which the prevailing management behaviour may be affected or indeed adopted.

Figure 3.2 Collectivist and individualist behavioural and management styles

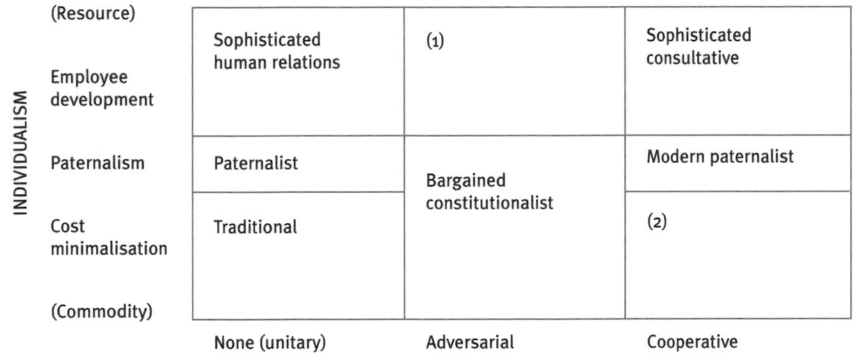

INDIVIDUALISM			
(Resource) Employee development	Sophisticated human relations	(1)	Sophisticated consultative
Paternalism	Paternalist	Bargained constitutionalist	Modern paternalist
Cost minimalisation (Commodity)	Traditional		(2)
	None (unitary)	Adversarial	Cooperative

Source: Kessler, I. and Purcell, J. (1995) 'Individualism and collectivism in theory and practice: management style and the design of pay systems', in Edwards, P. (ed.) *Industrial Relations Theory and Practice in Britain*. Oxford: Blackwell

Figure 3.2 illustrates the relationship between certain specific socio-culture employment relations factors and (consequent) styles of management. The matrix allows individualism to be considered along a simplified continuum where at one end employees are viewed as a resource and at the other as a commodity, while collectivism is viewed as a co-operative notion through to a unitary one. The resulting pattern identifies the organisational management style. For example, paternalism combined with co-operative collective relations produces a 'modern paternalist' style.

The model identifies two unstable management styles. These are shown as (1) and (2). In the former, it is difficult to see how managers can view employees as a resource while maintaining adversarial relations with the representatives. Similarly, in the latter, pursuing co-operative relations with unions when employees are seen as a commodity may be difficult to sustain. The second situation may arise where, for example, management may encourage performance-related pay to minimise company-wide pay increases, while collective interests may be to increase employee wages on a company-wide basis. Purcell and Sisson (1983) offer similar descriptors of observable management styles used in the process of employee relations.

The classical or 'adversarial' style of employee relations seems incongruent with EI initiatives. Historically, trade unions in the mid- to latter 1900s undermined the power of many managers by using collective power in a relatively forceful manner in order to achieve union and union members' goals at the expense of those of the organisation. In effect the unions undermined the right of the managers to manage. The wider implications for this movement were profound in organisational, social and political terms. The power of this development in employee relations, albeit a very extreme example, was seen on a national scale where widespread collective action in the early 1970s contributed substantially to the fall of the Conservative Government in 1974.

3.3 THEORY TASTER

CONFLICT IN ORGANISATIONS

Many of the prescriptions that are offered to managers as a means of improving organisational performance imply that employees will accept the implementation of these ideas with little or no resistance, provided the need for them is clearly explained. It is true that employees and employers have some shared interest in the success of the organisation. If the organisation does not meet its objectives, there could be job losses with serious consequences for workers and their families.

However, it is important to note that employees may not accept all change willingly, and may resist management efforts and contest the rationale for management's proposals. The consequence may be overt or covert expressions of conflict, including strikes, labour turnover and absenteeism. One framework that tries to explain the possibility of conflict between managers and employees is that of the frame of reference.

Those who believe that there is a complete sharing of organisational objectives between managers and employees are said to hold a unitary frame of reference. Here, employees willingly accept their role in the organisation, and the legitimacy of managers to decide how work should be organised. Conflict is, then, something that is abnormal, and the result of misunderstandings, or troublemakers stirring up discontent.

Others, however, see that there will be times when the needs of workers and the plans of management will conflict. An example that is often used to illustrate this is that of pay rises: employees will seek to maximise their increase, while managers will be concerned with controlling costs. Those that see conflict as inherent in organisations are termed pluralists. From this perspective, the role of management is to recognise this potential and manage the conflict in such a way that seeks to accommodate employees' legitimate interests in the decision-making process.

Employee involvement techniques are typically considered to draw from the unitary perspective since they leave final decisions with management. Participation, on the other hand, is seen as part of the pluralist approach as it provides for employees (or, more often, their representatives) to have a direct say in the decision that is made.

A more detailed explanation of the idea of frames of reference and the ways in which employees may seek to contest and challenge management can be found in Williams and Adam-Smith (2005).

It may be argued that in contemporary employment, employees are granted a substantial degree of autonomy through high involvement/participation practices (eg empowerment), and that this process represents a significant shift in the management of human resources. It appears to display a greater focus on employees as resources, capable of being developed as a source of competitive advantage. The objectives of increased autonomy may be to increase the value of the organisation both in human and fiscal terms. However, one notable danger of over-involvement is that the authority of managers may be undermined, albeit unintentionally. In an extreme case employees may perceive they have undermined managerial authority through their collective action rather any actual delegation of managerial authority. In basic terms, the employees could become the dominant decision-making power.

In simple terms EI has two facets. The first relates to organisational motivation, the underlying aim of which is to achieve improvements in terms of 'employee commitment and organisational communications...', for example (Torrington and Hall 2002, p.487). It is, however, pertinent to consider the second facet, which relates to the employees' motivation to be involved. An employee's desire to be involved is an important part of the practical process of organisational operations. For the benefits of involvement to be felt there has to be a high degree of employer/employee motivational congruence.

The potential benefits for productive involvement and participation are outlined in Table 3.1.

Table 3.1 Potential involvement-based benefits

Employees appreciating the opportunity, if not the practice, of being involved in operational initiatives
• Operational initiatives, improvements promoting organisational commitment
• Increased likelihood of employees accepting organisational change
• Increasing levels of job satisfaction
• Decreased levels of job-related stress
• Reduced staff turnover
• Potential reductions in staff training and development costs

Source: adapted from Torrington and Hall (2002), p.487

DEFINING EMPLOYEE INVOLVEMENT AND PARTICIPATION

In order to better understand EI and EP, it is useful to define the paradigms of participation and involvement. This can be achieved using various theoretical sources, examples of which are outlined later in this section. In practice, considering the implications can be problematic. This may be partly because the notions of EP and EI could be considered interchangeably and/or separately and partly because of definitional inconsistency and lack of precision (Price, 2004). A lack of consistency may also be due in part to the varying sources of business and academic interest. For the purposes of this chapter the concepts are referred to jointly unless specified and simple contextual definition examples are offered.

Mullins offers a simple definition of EI: 'the degree of commitment by members to the organisation' (Mullins, 2005, p.844). There is an implication thus that the business relationship is uni-directional in that it is the employees who show commitment to their organisation. In real terms the relationship may be to a degree more bi-directional. Mullins elaborates his notion of EI by considering Etzioni's (1975) notion of three sub-types of involvement (see Mullins, 2005, p.844). The resultant three characteristics offered by Mullins may be considered indicative of the prevailing culture by virtue of the expected employee behaviour or characteristics. Potentially the manifest characteristics exhibited by members of an organisation may also indicate the prevailing management style of an organisation and vice versa (Brown, 2001).

A variation of Mullins's adaptation of Etzioni's perspectives is illustrated in Table 3.2.

Table 3.2 Employee involvement and managerial style: relational issues

Involvement category	Characteristic	Indicative organisational culture/management
Alienative involvement … occurring where members are involved against their wishes [implying a strong negative orientation towards the organisation] Higher adversarial and/or authoritarianism	Calculative involvement … occurring where attachment to the organisation is motivated by extrinsic rewards [implying either a negative or a low positive orientation towards the organisation] Transactional and/or benevolent authoritarianism	Moral involvement … which is based on the individual's belief in, and the value placed on, the goals of the organisation [implying a strong positive orientation towards the organisation] Higher co-operative and/or participation

Source: adapted from Mullins (2005), p.844

Involvement may be described as a management-driven process, the aim of which is to increase commitment to the organisation. While this again implies a more uni-directional influence, Guest (1986, p.687) suggests a slightly more mutual relationship where EI is 'considered to be more flexible and better geared to the goal of securing commitment and shared interest'. This suggests that EI is a softer form of employer–employee relationship than EP. Employee participation may be referred to using two perspectives (Bratton and Gold, 2003 p.361). The first is labelled as direct participation, referring 'to those forms of participation in which individual employees, albeit often in a very limited way, are involved in decision-making processes which affect their daily routines'.

The second perspective is labelled as indirect participation, referring 'to those forms of participation in which representatives or delegates of the main body of employees participate in the decision-making process' (*ibid*). This latter perspective offers a clearer picture of the relationship to the collective employee relations process including trade union interests. Indirect EP may take the form of informal or formal talks between parties and is often referred to as employee consultation, which is considered later in this chapter.

When considering organisational performance, EI may be described as 'a range of processes designed to engage the support, understanding and optimum contribution of all employees in an organisation and their commitment to its objectives' (Learning and Teaching Support Network, 2004). When viewed as a separate notion, EP may be broadly defined as the process whereby a person or group's business activities are determined by another person or group. The Learning and Teaching Support Network (2004) suggests EP may be described as:

> a process of employee involvement designed to provide employees with the opportunity to influence and, where appropriate, take part in decision-making on matters which affect them.

The practice of EI and EP has evolved in recent years due to both business and social pressures. It can be argued that contemporary theory and practice in human resource management (HRM) has moved from a hard to soft HRM emphasis (Storey, 1989). Hard HRM has been described as a human capital-based approach which is arguably associated with some specific worker attributes (see Schultz, 1961 and Bontis *et al*, 1999). Hard-based worker attributes may well differ from those demonstrated by workers operating in a soft environment where commitment is emphasised with the underlying objective of promoting the mutual achievement of both personal and organisational goals. This latter notion implies an emphasis on integrated and congruent working practices. In addition, the apparent move from hard to soft HRM may also reflect a transition from a collective organisational and sociological mind-set to a more individualistic one. This reflects the notion that contemporary HRM has shifted focus from trade union- or collective-related practice to more individualist working practices.

3.4 ACTIVITY

Consider

- to what degree EI is a reality in an organisation with which you are familiar
- in what ways EI could add value to your business:
  - in human terms
  - in non-human terms (eg in shareholder value).

Arguably, the concepts outlined above are relatively new and this may in part be due to the changes in contemporary employee relations practice. Farnham (1993) notes the appearance of EI literature around the beginning of the 1980s. Following its emergence, the practical use of the concepts became more apparent. As Farnham outlines, the CBI published guidelines on EI around this time (Confederation of British Industry, 1979). It has been suggested that involvement processes were, in part, used in the 1980s as a managerial tool to increase potential for employee input in some organisational processes (Marchington, 2001).

This offers some support to the notion that contemporary interest in soft HRM techniques and business 'values' broadly equate to the relatively high levels of individualism in current working practice. By implication the greater inclusion of employees, who are not necessarily managerial by job description, could be viewed as a lever against collectivism and the power of the trades unions. In practice this has, in part, led to reduced trade union activity and presence (Morehead *et al*, 1997). Any reduction in collective or trade union activity and power may thus give rise to increased managerial ownership of decision-making processes.

LEVELS OF INVOLVEMENT AND PARTICIPATION

Involvement and participation by employees may be considered from both theoretical and practical standpoints. In this section two examples of a level- or factor-based view of EI and EP are offered. The first example is a generalised organisational view using a theoretical outline incorporating examples of a more practical nature. The second example is operational, non-hierarchical and sector-specific. Both help illustrate how EI and EP are related to organisational decision-making processes.

The first example is based on a five-level principle:

- The first level is at the job level where the employee is involved in relation to his or her own specific job rather than, say, decision-making at the organisational level. Company appraisal systems may be viewed as job-level involvement mechanisms since, at this level, the employee has the opportunity to be directly involved in decisions relating to himself/herself, such as personal development.
- The second level is the management stream where a group of managers may make operational decisions which affect both themselves and the employees they manage. In practical terms, such decision-making may be based on a consensus approach and relate to (a geographical) area of business units but be without a policy-making element. It may be argued that the locus of control has shifted to the organisational managers but not necessarily to the exclusion of non-managerial employees and groups. One potential practical consequence of employee exclusion could be the creation or development of an internal power imbalance. Simply put, an imbalance may lead to an increase in internal conflict, while conversely an increased degree of employee inclusion may help reduce conflict (Lewin, 2001).
- The third level relates to policy-making and may have some operational similarity to the preceding stream but there are two practical differences. The first is the organisational level of the activity. It is likely that it will be at the upper hierarchical level of the business. Such a level may well incorporate a board of directors or equivalent. The second practical issue is that actual policy-making is relevant. Thus the consequent communications may be categorised as more downwards and thus uni-directional in nature.
- At the fourth level, the owner(s) of the organisation will have vested interests in the business. It is reasonable to propose that one of the overriding concerns

will be fiscal in nature. By extension the fiscal concerns of the owners will incentivise them to have an interest in participating in business operations such as logistics, marketing, operations and HRM. The HRM factor may well be of particular note where financial decision-making is necessary as a result of poor or falling market value.

- The final level relates to relevant union/representative interest. This stream is less clear in the sense that it may be argued that a union as a body is not within the organisational sphere of actual ownership/influence. Despite this, the collectivist element may be a considerable influence on areas of business operations. Trade unions play an active role in influencing many decision-making processes at policy level and beyond. Practical examples may include influencing or moderating financial decision-making particularly in relation to staff employment and remuneration, working practices and health and safety matters. Importantly, trade unions offer the scope and opportunity for employees to express their collective perspective or employee voice (Armstrong, 2006).

The second example of EI is sector-specific. For the purposes of this outline, the sector chosen is a local authority social services department. This example shows a more practical application for levels of EI/EP where the primary illustration is the relationship between the employee and the 'end consumer'. Here the emphasis is not on generalised groups of participants but on levels of technique. Nevertheless, there is still an EI/EP element to the decision-making processes. This model also informally incorporates a behavioural element and in practical terms relates to styles of management, examples of which were introduced earlier in this chapter. The levels for this case are illustrated in Figure 3.3.

Figure 3.3 Focus on practice: a social services ladder of participation

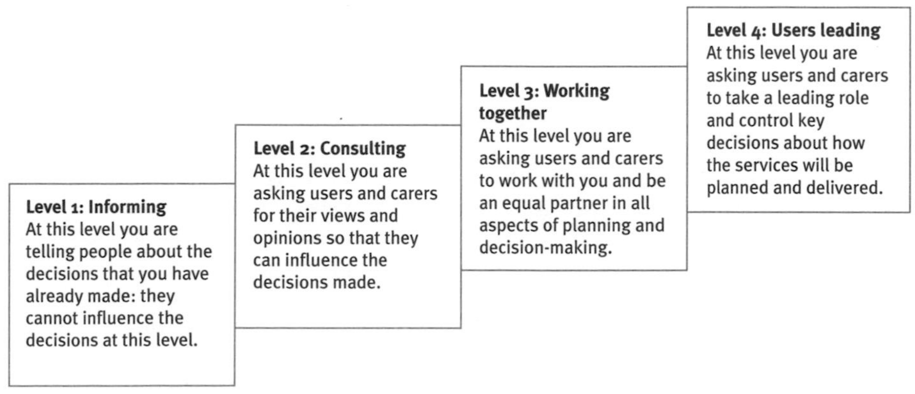

Source: http://www.worcestershire.gov.uk

The consideration of alternative and potentially complementary perspectives on EI and EP help to effectively interpret dynamic business relationships which can range from the strategic to the end-consumer.

PROCESSES AND FORMS OF PARTICIPATION AND INVOLVEMENT

Employee participation is to a large degree dependent on efficient communications. Such communications are a fundamental foundation of organisational operations and this is becoming more evident with the changes in the scope of contemporary working practices. Over the last few decades such changes may in part have been due to organisations extending operations to include networks and subsidiaries outside their home countries. Arguably, the value of EI schemes is dependent on the context and degree of employee inclusivity (Shapiro, 2000). Shapiro suggests that there is a relationship between the success of EI initiatives and the degree of inclusivity of the *whole* workforce. For example, if full- and part-time employees are involved equally in a process, they may perceive themselves to be treated fairly and by extension such perceived fairness may increase the effectiveness of an EI scheme. Equity theory (eg Adams, 1963; 1965) is, in practical terms, about employees' perception of fair and equitable treatment. One example that is often considered is the relationship between pay and performance: the idea of a 'fair day's work for a fair day's pay'. There is some evidence to support the notion that an increased perception of being treated fairly is positively related to increased commitment (Sweeney *et al*, 1990). In a similar vein to Shapiro's work considering the degree of employee inclusivity, the type of employee involvement and participation (EIP) may be viewed as having two contextual approaches. The first is direct EIP involving individuals in an organisation, and the second is indirect EIP involving perhaps team-based groupings, for example (Cox, Zagelmeyer and Marchington, 2006). It may be

3.5 THEORY TASTER

EQUITY THEORY

Stacy Adams is one of the key theorists in proposing equity theory as an explanation of motivation. Equity theory is one of the *process* theories of motivation (see Activity 7.4).

The principles behind this idea are that we each make a judgement about the effort we put into doing a job and the rewards, in terms of pay, promotion opportunities, etc, that we receive in return. We then compare this with the effort and rewards of others. When we feel that we are treated equitably with others, that is, the ratio of inputs to outputs is the same, we are motivated. However, if we perceive that others get greater rewards than us for the same or less effort, or we are having to put more into our jobs compared with others who get the same reward, we become demotivated.

Feelings of inequity, it is argued, can have important effects on work behaviour. Staff may adjust their input to the same level of others who are seen to be getting the same level of reward for less effort, for example, by reducing the time spent on activities, being absent from work, or reducing the quality of their work. Alternatively, we may seek to influence others to reduce their outputs. If inequity persists, employees may choose to leave the organisation, and find another job where they believe equity in effort and reward will be found.

argued that these categories may parallel the individualist and collectivist notions discussed earlier.

The practical issue of active communications may be considered from a number of perspectives. Various factors have a bearing on the presence of effective EI/EP in an organisation and the level of commitment to it from all parties. Existing mechanisms will have a direct bearing on employees working efficiently. Figure 3.4 illustrates factors which have a bearing on the presence and effectiveness of EI/EP. Two generic categories are used alongside a description of factors underpinning and supporting effective EI/EP.

Figure 3.4 Relating employee involvement and participation to organisational communications

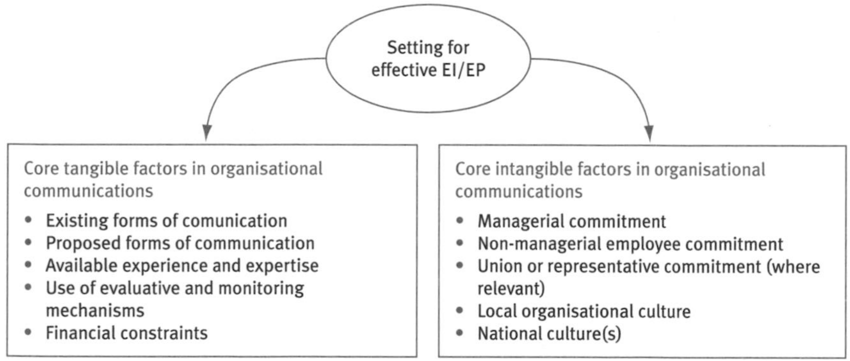

Tangible factors are actual (for example, visual) in nature. Practical examples would include memos and letters involving input from the relevant parties, or budgetary/forecast documentation originated by senior management but involving input and feedback from employees. Those factors which are not readily quantifiable, measurable or always consistent in nature are 'intangible'.

Commitment, or the lack of it, may be judged by its effects rather than any apparent evidence. For example, the supposed commitment of an individual may be suggested by the evidence of non-verbal and verbal indicators, but those indicators may not, in fact, reflect the individual's real position. Such 'realities' may be inconsistent between individuals within a work-group or team and potentially between an individual and the norms and values of an organisation. Care therefore must be taken to consider a balanced view of intangible indicators and to consider them in association with other tangible factors. As an illustration, consider a candidate at interview consciously thinking about how good he or she will be in the job. Subconsciously he or she may well hold a belief inconsistent with that which might appear in tangible evidence. In an ideal world the conscious and subconscious beliefs will be consistent, thereby reducing potential subconscious conflict (eg stress). This is somewhat like an individual's own version of rhetoric (conscious) versus reality (subconscious). At interview, individuals sell themselves in order to get a job but are making decisions based in part on both conscious and subconscious consideration. Non-verbal and verbal indicators may be evidenced by an enthusiastic voice and action. Evidence of subconscious beliefs are not so easy to discover or judge. Within work, tangible technical performance measures may suggest that an individual is performing well. In isolation they do not provide evidence that individual is happy, engaged, or involved in his or her work while achieving the relevant goal(s). Other, softer qualitative techniques can help in assessing the latter facet. Expertise assumed, the use of observational techniques such as body language analysis as a practical HRM tool may help to judge another's subconscious behaviour in the workplace. So while each of the techniques provides useful but limited information, used together they can potentially provide a more rounded and accurate picture of an individual.

One of the potential benefits of an increased knowledge of the employee status is that issues identified can be communicated to the relevant levels and parties within the organisation. The issues can then be discussed and, where relevant, prioritised, actioned and (re)evaluated with a view to improving organisational performance. There are occasions where organisational communications are downward in nature but this is by no means always the case. While the form and nature may adapt, inherent human communications are generally a two-way process. In business settings, two-way communications are frequent and a necessary part of working life.

Operationally, however, there is some credence in the notion that the communication of decision and policy-making is downwards. This may be particularly true of some bureaucratic organisations, particularly where an autocratic management style prevails. As organisations have evolved to address changes in contemporary activities, alternative or additional mechanisms have been used which actively incorporate two-way communication as a means of enhancing EI and EP. Though admittedly simplistic, this idea does provide some support for the notion that contemporary organisations are less bureaucratic and top-down-driven.

3.6 ACTIVITY

EIP and organisational communications

- Identify the factors required to reduce the potential for inaccurate information circulating in an organisation from
  - an organisational perspective
  - a managerial perspective
  - a non-managerial perspective.
- Briefly outline the potential consequences of poor organisational communications on EI/EP.
- Outline potential methods to gain and use EI/EP to increase an organisation's performance and value for stakeholders.

INVOLVEMENT AND PARTICIPATION MECHANISMS

The previous sections have dealt with various theoretical perspectives on EI/EP. In this section some complementary perspectives will be introduced. Within the last section, communication issues were introduced. This section will expand on the practical relationship between EI/EP and organisational communications.

Upward problem-solving refers to a suite of mechanisms making use of two-way communication rather than the more traditional downstream techniques. Often two-way communication is between managers and their own specific staff. The mechanisms used may be considered at various levels. Examples include the job/role task level, a consultation/representation level and the financial level. The potential alternative techniques used in upward problem-solving may incorporate appraisal systems, attitude surveys, quality circles, suggestion schemes and consultative committees. The appraisal system is a fundamental tool for employee development. Where there is genuine two-way communications, both the employer and the employee may see a developmental opportunity, partly through the process of mutual learning.

The use of attitude surveys allows employees to express their perceptions on matters relating to the organisation and its operations.

The practical mechanisms of this method may be quantitative and/or qualitative in nature. Specific techniques used may include questionnaires, interviews, a blended approach of these two and focus groups. These methods require a degree of structure and clear statements of confidentiality. Table 3.3 describes some potential benefits of using an attitude survey.

Table 3.3 Attitude survey: potential benefits

Provides particular information on the preferences of employees
Gives warning of potential problem areas
Diagnoses the cause of particular problems
Compares morale in different parts of the organisation
Obtains views about processes such as job evaluation, pay determination and performance management in order to assess their effectiveness and the degree to which employees believe they are fair
Obtains views of personnel policies and how they operate in such areas as equal opportunities, employee development, involvement and health and safety
Evaluates training
Assesses how organisational and other policy changes have been received to observe the effects of policies and actions over a period of time
Provides a basis for additional communication and involvement, especially if the survey includes two-way feedback with employees on their attitudes and what actions they would like the management to take.

In practical terms, one issue of notable importance is the availability of individuals with the skills, experience and expertise to facilitate such processes in a manner promoting a bias-free set of results. Through the use of such techniques, valuable additional information can be gained to help increase the effectiveness of both practical and strategic HRM planning. One of the main objectives for the use of attitude surveys is to identify and devise strategies to close the gap between an individual's identified needs and the extent to which the needs are being met. The satisfaction of such needs on a workforce basis can increase the potential for business improvements thereby adding value to the organisation.

Quality circles are another form of upward problem-solving in that smaller groups of five to 10 volunteer employees meet to discuss issues which may have a bearing on the performance of the company. Such meetings are normally led by a trained team leader. The meetings are normally structured and focus on issues which are within the participants' sphere of work. It is assumed that the benefits of involving employees in the quality circle approach goes beyond the literal 'quality' improvements for the organisation. EI theory has suggested that employees who are given the opportunity to show their knowledge, skills and experience in a non-confrontational setting may become more committed to their organisation. In this case, employee commitment may in part be a consequence of their feedback to the management, where it is seen to be valued. For the management there could be an opportunity to gain an understanding and awareness of organisational difficulties that may have been hidden. In common with many facets of EI and EP, commitment to the processes from both employees, managers and, where relevant, trade unions is a key to success.

Suggestion schemes can provide a valuable means for employees to participate in improving the efficiency of the company. One employee benefit is that their suggestions may bypass the normal channels of communication which could in themselves be a barrier. Usually, participants are directed to avoid areas outside their usual scope of duties. The process should be conducted in a productive/ positive manner at all times. The success of suggestion schemes depends upon an established procedure for submitting and evaluating ideas, the merit of which is judged by a representative number of interested parties. The composition of the representative group is important. Persons who may have a strong vested interest in blocking or actively opposing suggestions for change, for example, could be excluded. Similarly, a case could be made to exclude those who have an obvious lack of interest in and comment on the process. Reward mechanisms may be used to encourage productive EI. Confidentiality may be an issue under some circumstances and will have to be appropriately addressed.

Joint consultation, which may otherwise be known as employee consultation or representative participation, is another form of EP. The aim is, in simple terms, a transactional one where both parties benefit. Topics for discussion may be varied. Potential topics could include predominantly non-negotiable matters such as working methods, matters of practical and procedural organisation, health and safety, working conditions, employee facilities, and work rules. Consultation committees may be operated by formal bodies such as a joint consultation committee (JCC), labour management committee (LMC) and European works council (EWC). The decline in the number of workplaces with JCCs is noteworthy. Their incidence has reduced from 34% in 1984 to 29% in 1998 (Millward *et al*, 2000). In part this decline may in fact be due to increases in other forms of EI.

Bratton and Gold (2003, p.375) propose alternative JCC models which, to a degree, illustrate a change in approach:

- The *marginality* model accords with the notion that consultative committees, often using union-based representative, became less influential in the 1980s due to the financial uncertainties of the time.
- The *complementary* model suggests consultative committees are complementary to collective bargaining processes rather than confrontational, as often assumed. The notion is that they operate as a facilitating body alongside collective bargaining, which seeks to determine pay and other terms and conditions.
- The *revitalisation* model proposes the notion that consultation committees are now increasing due to, or alongside, the increased interest in EI practices.

3.7 ACTIVITY

Consider an organisation you are familiar with and address the following questions:

- What forms of EI have been used?
- What benefits did they provide for the organisation and the staff?
- What were their weaknesses/limitations?
- In what way(s) were the barriers to EI dealt with?

CONCLUSION

Employee involvement has emerged in recent years as a key lever for organisations seeking to increase worker identification with their business objectives, and to utilise more fully the skills and experienced possessed by staff. At the same time, it offers employees some scope to influence the way they are managed in the workplace. For those workers interested in issues beyond their immediate role, EI may offer a route to improved job satisfaction. The success or failure of such techniques can have profound implications both for the organisation and the employees. However, this is a complex process. Underlying the concepts of EI and EP are the notions of mutual or reciprocal trust and respect (see Sanders and Schyns, 2006), which in turn underpin the psychological contract between employee and employer. In Chapter 6 we will consider the nature of the psychological contract and the implications for both employee and employer.

3.8 DISCUSSION QUESTIONS

1 You have been asked by the organisation for which you work (or one with which you are familiar) to introduce EI or participation schemes. Which ones would you recommend, and how would these improve organisational performance?

2 Why have EI practices become more prevalent in recent years within organisations?

3 What factors within organisations can inhibit the effectiveness of EI techniques?

EXPLORE FURTHER

Gennard, J. and Judge, G. (2005) *Employee Relations*. London: CIPD. This mixed-level text considers various aspects of work process and infrastructure including EI. It is also relevant to CIPD-taught courses.

Legge, K. (2005) *Human Resource Management: Rhetorics and realities*, 2nd edition. Basingstoke: Palgrave Macmillan. This incorporates EI and participation issues within the HRM context.

Leopold, J., Harris, L. and Watson T. (2005) *The Strategic Managing of Human Resources*. Harlow: FT/Prentice Hall. The specific treatment of EI and EP are part of a suite of materials which also include detailed strategic and international issues.

CHAPTER 4

Leadership

Gill Christy

LEARNING OUTCOMES

After reading this chapter, you should be able to:

- understand the similarities and differences between management and leadership
- explain the characteristics of the various theoretical frameworks that have been developed for the study of leadership
- relate those frameworks to examples within organisations
- assess the importance of leadership and management to organisational performance.

INTRODUCTION

This chapter focuses on leaders in a business or organisational context, and views leaders as key players in both devising and implementing organisational strategy. It considers how existing theories and frameworks help to address the question of what exactly makes a leader effective in a business or a working environment. Some concepts and models clearly derive from, and apply to, other areas of human activity such as politics, sport and warfare. The notion of leadership provides an enduring fascination – not only to academics such as psychologists and political or social scientists, but also to journalists, biographers, authors, dramatists and film-makers for whom it provides a rich source of material both factual and fictional. As we shall also see, many terms and metaphors associated with the study of leadership derive from sporting and military contexts. However, when we enter the more usual organisational arenas – businesses, public sector and governmental organisations, non-profit-making organisations such as charities – we tend to encounter the term 'manager' more frequently than the term 'leader' as the one to describe such key players. It is therefore important to start by considering how far these two related concepts, leadership and management, overlap.

MANAGEMENT OR LEADERSHIP?

There seems to have been a certain revival of interest in the concept and application of leadership in recent years. Two decades ago, ambitious candidates for top-flight jobs in the world of business and public affairs might have enrolled on programmes to become 'Masters of Business Administration' or to take diplomas in management studies. Today there is a burgeoning market in postgraduate degrees such as leadership studies, or business development and leadership. The Management Standards Centre (MSC) included the term in its revised National Occupational Standards for Management and Leadership, and in 2003 Investors in People UK launched its supplementary 'Leadership and Management' model, discussed further below. Similar thinking has also led to the development of the CIPD's own Leadership and Management Standards, now integral to the professional development and qualification programme. So an initial question to consider is why there is such renewed interest in the concept of leadership, and how this fits with traditional ideas about organisational management. Perhaps part of the answer is to do with changing patterns of organisational life and similar changes in social expectations within the working environment.

Traditional organisations with strongly hierarchical structures are becoming rarer, and newer forms of both commercial and public sector organisation tend to be more flexible and task- or client-focused. What Handy (1976) described as 'matrix' organisations are generally considered to be more effective in a highly fluid commercial or operating environment; and the 'shamrock' style of organisation (Handy, 1989) charts the move towards further operational flexibility. As we discuss in Chapter 6 this type of organisational flexibility was also described by Atkinson (1984) in his model of the flexible firm, which disaggregates different organisational requirements and builds in a further form of organisational flexibility by outsourcing or subcontracting a number of its activities. This kind of articulated organisational structure works against the maintenance of strong hierarchies based around position (or legitimate) power (Mullins, 2007), and often requires individual managers to exercise a different form of authority from that conferred simply by virtue of status or rank. Similarly, wider social attitudes towards authority have changed and, as in other walks of life, people generally expect to be consulted and involved in their work rather than simply instructed. In some circumstances these expectations are now supported by the law – for instance, through the Information and Consultation of Employees (ICE) Regulations of 2005 which now apply to all businesses with more than 50 employees. Together, these trends may have renewed the interest in leadership as an important skill for those attempting to 'get things done through other people'.

Mullins suggests that there is a close relationship between the two concepts (management and leadership) and recognises that at least some authors and commentators dislike attempts to separate the two (*ibid*). Other writers, such as Hollingsworth – someone with both military and commercial experience – and Kotter (Bloisi *et al*, 2003; Huczynski and Buchanan, 2007) make a very clear distinction. Kotter describes leaders as those who set a direction, align people to the vision and motivate them – whereas managers plan, organise, control and resolve problems. In Hollingsworth's model, leadership involves innovation, development, a focus on people, inspiring trust, having an eye on the horizon and 'doing the right things'. By contrast, management is associated with administration, maintenance, systems/structure, control, paying attention to the bottom line and 'doing things right'. This distinction is also reflected in the National Occupational Standards for Management and Leadership, which appear to show a transition between operational and/or supervisory levels of management at levels 2 and 3, and a more strategic approach at levels 4 and 5 (Management Standards Centre, 2005). It is therefore a useful means of organising further discussion of the subject in terms of organisational people management practice.

For the purposes of this chapter, *strategic* leadership is taken to mean the activities involved in the initial creation of an overall business or organisational strategy, then directing and energising organisational resources towards the achievement of that strategy. Insofar as it then relies on others to carry out the strategy it may involve some management, but it is primarily about business vision and mission. This means 'doing the right thing', creating the differentiators which, in people terms, involves becoming an employer of choice, an organisation which is able to encourage outstanding performance from its workforce and thus achieve superior results. On the other hand, *managerial* leadership is taken to mean activities surrounding the creation, maintenance and development of an appropriate infrastructure for business operations, including that which involves organising the work of other people. It means creating a working environment that can help a business or other organisation to achieve its objectives. In this sense management *includes* leadership to some degree: it is about 'doing things right'.

STRATEGY AND LEADERSHIP

We have already defined strategy as being the way in which an organisation seeks to pursue its purpose or achieve its objectives. A prominent view of business strategy is 'resource-based' – that is to say, mainly to do with identifying the key resources that give the organisation a distinctive capability and finding ways of applying those capabilities to parts of the market that offer the best prospects (Johnson *et al*, 2007; Legge, 2005; Boxall and Purcell, 2003). Following from this, the key tasks in the strategic planning process could be said to be:

- analysing the organisation's environment and the changes that are expected over the plan period
- identifying and evaluating the organisation's key resources: those that are distinctive (by comparison to competitors) and those that are also important to delivering value to customers, taxpayers or client groups
- considering strategic options: ways of matching organisational resources to particular parts (segments) of the market, looking for the approach that is forecast to create maximum
 added value for shareholders, or to achieve the most effective use of public or

donor
money

- choosing the preferred strategic option
- re-aligning the organisation's resources (human and others) behind the chosen strategy: acquiring new resources, modifying existing resources and getting rid of those that cannot be economically reconfigured (which, of course, opens up questions about the ethical treatment of *human* resources)
- directing and energising those resources towards implementing the strategy
- responding to unexpected events during implementation.

4.1 ACTIVITY

Look up the following article by Sean Coughlan on the BBC business news website, http://news.bbc.co.uk

'MBAs must drop the Machismo' (28 February 2005).

This summarises some research carried out by Brunel University Business School.

- What light does this research shed on the changing nature of organisational leadership and management?
- What are the implications of this research for universities and business schools who deliver MBAs?

Most of these activities are focused at the higher levels of a business or organisation, and are often the province of a single individual (for instance, in a small business or owner-managed enterprise) or a small group such as a company chief executive and board of directors. In the public sector, strategic management will be in the hands of those who exercise political power and the professional experts who advise them and find appropriate means of executing political decisions. They are activities which are primarily about making informed strategic choices – in other words responding to the question 'What *is* the right thing to do?' They are also about convincing and energising others to put their effort behind the chosen strategy, and in this sense involve many leadership skills. In terms of people management, this level of leadership is about defining approaches to ensure that appropriate talent is recruited and motivated to achieve superior results.

MANAGEMENT AND LEADERSHIP

As mentioned earlier, in 2003 Investors in People UK launched its supplementary 'Leadership and Management' model, which seeks to help organisations create and maintain effective leadership skills amongst managers (Investors in People website: www.investorsinpeople.co.uk). This emphasises the important links between the two functions as well as indicating the increased significance of developing leadership within UK organisations. Leadership ability is defined as one of the attributes of the successful manager, along with the intellectual skills required for the assimilation of information, analysis and planning, technical and professional knowledge of the business area or sector, and a clear understanding of the specific organisation and its capacities.

Similarly, the Management Charter Initiative (MCI), which developed as a result of the recommendations in the Handy and Constable McCormick reports of the late 1980s, undertook a major analysis of the nature of management for the purposes of establishing a clear framework for managerial qualifications. Its work resulted in the adoption of a competency-based approach which quickly became highly influential in the field of management development in Britain (Frank, 1991). The 1997 edition of the occupational standard was based around four major components: managing operations, managing finance, managing information and managing people, only the last of which could be clearly seen as requiring leadership skills. More recently, the MSC has researched and developed a new set of standards, which also provide a functional map and set of units of competence which encompass the important knowledge and skill components of effective management. The significance of leadership is more clearly emphasised in the title of the new standards themselves: the National Occupational Standards for Management and Leadership. The six basic elements of the new standards, which can be viewed at the MSC website (http://www.management-standards.org), are:

- Managing self
- Providing direction
- Facilitating change
- Working with people
- Using resources
- Achieving results.

Leadership ability can be firmly associated with the second, third and fourth of these elements; and indeed the term 'working with people' has replaced 'managing people' in a way which might indicate the reducing emphasis on formal control and the increased need for collaboration in present-day work environments noted above.

The 2007 version of the CIPD Managing and Leading People Professional Standards recognises that soft skills are just as important as technical ones, and so these are better represented and thus reflect more fully aspects of leadership which are essential to good management practice. Nevertheless, these functions are qualitatively different from those required of strategic leadership which, as we have noted, appear at the higher levels or organisations. The majority of the standards are much more concerned with 'doing things right' in the sense of providing an effective structure within which people can achieve high levels of performance for their organisation.

It is now possible to turn to some of the concepts and theories about leadership, and to identify how well they might support the development of effective people management, either at a strategic or at more operational level.

LEADERSHIP: THEORETICAL FRAMEWORKS

It is useful at this point to remind ourselves of some of the key frameworks which have developed for the analysis and study of leadership. A summary of differing academic approaches to the subject is offered by several writers, including Mullins (2007), Bloisi *et al* (2003), Hersey *et al* (2001), Huczynski and Buchanan (2007), Kreitner and Kinicki (2001), and Yukl (2006). Most offer a framework for leadership studies which identifies the following main schools of thought (after Mullins, 2007, p.366):

- The qualities or traits approach
- The functional or group approach
- The approach which sees leadership as a behavioural category
- The leadership styles approach
- The situational approach and contingency models
- Transformational leadership
- Inspirational leadership.

Taking each of these approaches in turn, we can examine the general principles and models involved, and comment on their suitability in relation to either strategic leadership or managerial (operational) leadership. Some comments about the implications of each model for the development of effective organisational leaders are also included.

QUALITIES OR TRAITS APPROACH

This approach is essentially the 'great person' theory of leadership, and takes an approach which tries to identify the significant features of acknowledged leaders. Early approaches to the study of leadership (mostly undertaken before and shortly after the Second World War) dwelt on the personal qualities and characteristics of successful leaders in an attempt to isolate the 'magic ingredients'. They have not generally agreed on a common set of characteristics, although one or two, such as self-confidence and intelligence, did figure in a number of models (eg Kreitner and Kinicki, 2001). In fact, it is possible that the very act of selecting successful leaders for study introduces a form of bias which prejudices the results of any subsequent analysis. For instance, the absence of women from many research samples may well reflect the social constraints of the time rather than indicating that women lack innate leadership qualities. Indeed, it has been argued (Alimo-Metcalfe, 1995) that studies of women leaders actually identify a different range of effective leadership qualities compared with studies of men – and that it is important to (*ibid*, pp7–8):

> challenge the dangerous implicit assumption that identifying the criteria for leadership positions from groups of senior managers, all or most of whom (chances are) are male, may well lead to gender-biased criteria for the subsequent assessment process.

Alimo-Metcalfe's research also has relevance when considering the contrast between so-called 'transactional' and 'transformational' styles of leadership and is discussed further below.

Similarly, it is also important to note that the characteristics that have been proposed as significant may not be universally applicable. Cultural factors, for instance, may result in very different values being placed on a specific personal quality (such as willingness to take risks, to 'break the rules' in pursuit of an objective, or to act openly in pursuit of personal ambition) in different societies. Hofstede's model (1991) has identified dimensions of cultural difference, which he termed 'uncertainty avoidance', 'power distance', 'masculinity/femininity' and 'individualism/collectivism', and he described how combinations of these formed the characteristics of particular cultural environments. Clearly some cultures might accept and applaud qualities such as personal ambition and risk-taking where others would be more likely to value behaviours which support collective achievement or stability and a sense of social inclusion. The importance of cultural difference in relation to appropriate leadership styles and behaviours is developed more fully under the heading of situational or contingency theories of leadership.

As a result, we might consider that trait theories offer few pointers which can help aspiring managers assess their potential other than by trying to decide if they possess the appropriate qualities, or can develop (or even simulate) them. Trait theories offer little help in terms of suggesting how managerial leaders can prepare and adapt themselves to the reality of work to be performed. Furthermore, little connection is made with the variety of organisational circumstances where leadership needs to be exercised, including those circumstances where leadership shifts from the operational to the strategic levels of activity. The high public profile of both political and business leaders who operate at strategic level may well tempt us to analyse their qualities, but our information is imperfect (even about high-profile individuals) and of course the same individual can be both successful and unsuccessful during her or his career.

Adoption of the 'traits' approach also has implications for the role of people management in an organisation. If the development of successful organisational leaders is largely a matter of identifying those individuals who possess the desired characteristics and then offering the selected potential managers opportunities to develop and exercise these abilities, then the focus of people management will probably be on devising appropriate tests (such as psychometric or aptitude tests) which will help identify the 'right stuff', and devising systems of training and promotion which will support their development.

THE FUNCTIONAL APPROACH

The functional approach to leadership studies generally considers what leaders *do* to be effective, rather than examining what they *are*. One of the main exponents of a functional approach in the UK is John Adair, an author with a military background, and the influence of his theory of action-centred leadership (Adair, 1983) derives from its adoption by the Industrial Society (re-named the Work

4.2 ACTIVITY

Research and consider the careers of some prominent business leaders, for instance Richard Branson, the late Anita Roddick, Michael O'Leary, Sir Alan Sugar or Jacqueline Gold. Can you identify common traits? Have they always been successful?

Foundation in 2002) as a central plank of their management and leadership training programmes in the 1980s. He suggested that there are three main areas of managerial leadership activity: those concerned with building the team; those concerned with developing the individual within the team; and those directed at the achievement of the task. This type of approach has an important appeal in that it suggests that leadership skills can be acquired, and that pre-existing characteristics are less significant than the ability to learn how to act in such a way as to balance the three key areas of activity. From the people management perspective it places less emphasis on selection and more emphasis on training than trait theory would imply. It gives individuals a better framework for self-selection into managerial roles, and a clear set of development tasks to help them to create a successful infrastructure as managers. Adair's approach has proved highly successful as the basis for a robust and accessible system of training for supervisors and middle managers. However, it has little to say about the type of leadership that is involved in actually creating and driving organisational strategy. This is not to suggest that Adair himself has nothing to say about strategic leadership in other contexts (see, for instance, Adair, 2003).

The approach taken firstly by the MCI and now the MSC in their review of management standards is that of functional analysis, and the resulting functional map forms the basis for the 56 units which comprise the current standards. It is similar to action-centred leadership in the sense that it provides a general prescription, and one which has been thoroughly researched in a variety of sectors, for managerial competence. In terms of people management, yardsticks such as these have significant value in terms of setting required performance standards for supervisors and managers, identifying both individual and job-related managerial training needs, developing career structures, and of course can be used for selection purposes. What all functional approaches might fail to recognise sufficiently well, however, is the significance of such elements as tacit knowledge regarding effective performance: the sort of knowledge of and 'feel' for organisational context which generally only results from experience (Pilbeam and Corbridge, 2006). It is possible that leadership and management are more integrated a set of activities than competency-based or unitised approaches might lead us to believe. Leadership, and strategic leadership in particular, may be more than the sum of its parts.

THE BEHAVIOUR OF LEADERS

Behavioural theories extend the basis of study beyond the leader himself or herself, and have as their basis a consideration of the effects which leaders have on the actual performance of groups by examining leader behaviours and relating them to outcomes. The Ohio State studies and those of the Michigan Institute for Social Research in the 1960s and 1970s pioneered this approach and produced

4.3 ACTIVITY

Watch the opening scene of Ridley Scott's 2000 film *Gladiator*. It shows the preparation for a battle. Stop it when the first arrows are fired – about 8 to 10 minutes in. Analyse Maximus's behaviours during the pre-battle preparations using Adair's 'Task, Team, Individual' model of leadership.

If you aren't squeamish, watch the rest of the film. Then consider and analyse the different leaders (listed below) who emerge using ideas discussed in this chapter. You might consider situational factors, behaviours and characteristics.

- Maximus the general (played by Russell Crowe)
- Marcus Aurelius, the old emperor (played by Richard Harris)
- Commodus, the young emperor (played by Joaquin Phoenix)
- Gracchus, the 'republican' senator (played by Derek Jacobi)
- Lucilla, the daughter of Marcus Aurelius (played by Connie Nielsen).

remarkably similar results. Mullins (2007, pp370–1) summarises these as being leader behaviours concerned with task functions (the 'structure' dimension in the Ohio State studies and 'production-centred' supervisory behaviour in the Michigan one) and leader behaviour concerned with maintenance functions ('consideration' in the Ohio State term and 'employee-centred' behaviour in the Michigan one). He further relates them to McGregor's 'Theory X and Theory Y' managerial assumptions and the dimensions of concern for production and concern for people first proposed in Blake and Mouton's (1964) managerial grid and now revised and renamed the leadership grid (Blake and McCanse, 1991).

Behavioural studies have the advantage of offering would-be managers some options regarding behaviours which can be effective, rather than a single prescription for success. Whilst the studies concluded that there was no universally superior style, and that the circumstances of leadership might have an important influence on the effectiveness of one style over another, they did conclude that a balance between these two dimensions of behaviour seemed to be important in achieving success. In this respect they have much in common with situational or contingency theories, which have more to say about the *way* in which behaviours can be matched to circumstances. Once more, this type of approach offers a wider range of options for the use of training and development techniques as a means of encouraging managerial leadership capacity. In relation to strategic leadership, 'consideration' and 'structure' are both relevant to strategic tasks, but in general behavioural theories have little explicit to say about leadership at this level of organisational life.

LEADERSHIP STYLES

Approaches to the study of leadership which analyse the differences between leadership styles are generally focused upon the leader's attitude towards people and the resulting behaviours which they exhibit in their day-to-day dealings with members of the team. This generates a range of possibilities, and the resulting classifications usually identify a range of styles, perhaps most succinctly described by Tannenbaum and Schmidt (1973). They focused on the relative strength and power of managers and non-managers (ie subordinates) in terms of decision-making. At one end of the resulting continuum is 'boss-centred' (autocratic) decision-making where a manager largely decides what is to be done in a specific circumstance, and others accept and follow the decision. At the other end is joint (or democratic) decision-making, where a manager will define a problem or situation and then participate in the decision-making simply as a member of the team. This model recognises the need for an understanding of the relationship between specific managers and their teams from a basis of both leader and follower characteristics (such as personality, relevant knowledge and experience, sense of security, etc) and permits the inclusion of circumstantial considerations (organisational and societal factors, etc) in the equation. In this respect it bears considerable similarity to the contingency models discussed in the next section. Insofar as it examines the skills and requirements for leading a team, the approach is not prescriptive, and is an appropriate tool for analysing and identifying the range of successful managerial leadership styles. It also offers some important messages about the importance of flexibility in terms of managerial style. Like the behavioural theories discussed earlier, these approaches have significant value in terms of management development – but also have similar shortcomings when it comes to the consideration of strategic leadership.

SITUATIONAL AND CONTINGENCY MODELS OF LEADERSHIP

While traits-based and functional models of leadership concentrate on the leaders, and behavioural models examine the effect on the led, situational perspectives add a third dimension: that of the circumstances, both organisational and environmental, in which the leadership activity occurs. This allows the development of what is generally termed the contingency approach to leadership – in other words an approach that might answer the question 'What type of leadership actions and behaviours are appropriate?' with the phrase 'It depends on the circumstances.' Contingency approaches thus suggest a wide range of different but equally valid ways of leading and managing people. Some, such as Hersey and Blanchard's model of situational leadership (see Hersey *et al*, 2001), focus on the appropriate leadership styles for groups or individual followers who are at different stages of 'readiness' or 'maturity' to achieve a task – readiness being defined as a combination of both ability and willingness or confidence to carry out the task in question. As these vary over time, so the leader has to choose and use the most appropriate style to fit the circumstances. The four styles suggested in the situational leadership model are summarised from Hersey *et al* (2001, pp182–7) as follows:

- S1: telling – provides high amounts of guidance and direction but little supportive behaviour. This style is most appropriate for low follower readiness, including situations where followers are unable and/or unwilling. The leader structures the task and concentrates on step-by-step help and instruction.
- S2: selling – requires high amounts of both directive (task) and relationship behaviours. This style is most appropriate for low to moderate follower readiness, particularly when followers are willing but still not fully capable of performing. The leader encourages more dialogue to achieve 'buy-in' amongst the followers.
- S3: participating – shows high levels of two-way communication and supportive (relationship) behaviour but low amounts of guidance (task behaviour). This style is most appropriate for moderate to high follower readiness – in other words situations where followers are competent but inexperienced, or competent but demotivated. The leader should focus on discussion, encouragement and facilitation rather than instruction.
- S4: delegating – involves little direction or support – in other words low levels of both task and relationship behaviours. This style is most appropriate for high follower readiness – in other words situations where managerial intervention is largely unnecessary (unless there are significant problems) and can focus on monitoring.

For instance, a personnel assistant who is who is highly capable and confident about carrying out selection interviews would respond well to a delegating style of management in relation to this work. However, if they then find themselves in changed business circumstances and need to carry out redundancy interviews without having had much relevant experience, then a 'selling' style of managerial leadership might be more suitable, or possibly a 'telling' style if the individual was particularly resistant to carrying out the new task.

4.4 THEORY TASTER

CONTINGENCY APPROACHES IN RELATION TO CULTURE

There is evidence that contingency approaches to leadership have particular relevance when considering inter-cultural situations. Kreitner, for instance, suggests that national culture is an important contingency and that cultural analyses such as those of Hofstede can be helpful in identifying appropriate styles for the needs of different cultural groups (Hofstede, 1991; Kreitner, 2001; Kakabadse *et al*, 1997).

There seems, from Kreitner's research, to be some indication that the most widely applicable style is the participative one. It is well suited to many national cultures but particularly those such as that of the USA and Sweden where there is limited 'natural' respect for hierarchy and seniority: what Hofstede would term a 'low power distance' culture. Nevertheless, it can be successful in a wider range of cultures than the directive style. The latter is more specifically suited to 'high power distance' cultures where status automatically commands respect (Kreitner suggests French and Indian cultures), and where subordinates will generally expect their managers to have the answers by virtue of the expertise that has enabled them to achieve their status. The directive style translates poorly into 'low power distance' cultures or those where joint regulation or co-determination is the norm (for instance, the German one). He explains (Kreitner, 2001, p.613, emphasis in the original), however, that:

> Participative leadership is not necessarily the best style; it simply is culturally acceptable in many different countries … directive leadership turned out to be the *least* appropriate leadership style.

Moving more directly into the area of strategic leadership in a business context, Clarke and Pratt (1985) and Rodrigues (1988) both consider the importance of the stage of growth which a business has reached and suggest that this too can be an important contingent factor with relation to the choice of strategic leadership style. Taking a basic model of the business growth cycle such as the 'Boston box', which identifies four developmental stages of an enterprise – start-up, growth, maturity and decline (see Chapter 2) – these authors suggest that there are matching styles of strategic leadership: champion, tank commander, housekeeper and lemon-squeezer. The start-up organisation or venture needs a 'champion' style, a leadership style which is prepared to fight for the enterprise on a variety of fronts, thus suggesting the need for an energetic individual with a wide variety of technical management skills.

4.5 CASE STUDY

THE CHAMPION STYLE

An example of a 'champion' is the founder of easyJet, Stelios Haji-Ioannou. At the end of 2002, having developed this very successful low-cost airline, he stepped down as chairman in order to use his talents in what he considered to be the most effective manner, involving himself in new ventures, entrepreneurial innovation and similar 'no frills' developments in other markets. His easyGroup (see www.easy.com) has initiated a wide variety of new ventures including mobile phones, low-cost cinemas, car rental and, more recently, pizza delivery and rented office space in London. The skills of the champion relate closely to those of the tank commander, whose strategic role is to develop strong teams that can drive the business forward once it has entered a growth phase.

The housekeeper needs fewer entrepreneurial skills but needs to be able to achieve more in the way of planning, cost control and the formalisation of processes and organisational structures such as reward and training systems. The lemon-squeezer, who is trying to extract the best from a declining business and if possible turn it around, needs a range of skills which are more to do with taking tough and difficult measures as effectively as possible than fostering and encouraging growth. Possible examples of this type of leadership might include Sir Stuart Rose at Marks & Spencer between 2004 and 2006, and Justin King at Sainsbury's in late 2004–5. Such circumstances are common in business life: examples which came to prominence at the start of 2008 include the challenges faced by the new management of Northern Rock, and those at Tata following its purchase of the Jaguar and Land Rover brands from Ford. Clarke and Pratt consider that most managers have one primary style and are not necessarily suited to all stages of business development.

The contingency approach to leadership emphasises contextual factors as an important influence on leader success. Professor Joseph Nye, in a BBC interview ahead of the UK publication of his book *The Powers to Lead: Soft, hard, and smart* in May 2008, stressed the relationship between contextual knowledge and leadership power, explaining that contextual knowledge helps leaders to determine what balance they should strike between the use of what he terms 'hard' power (issuing commands) and 'soft' power (the ability to attract and retain followers). Contingency approaches remain highly relevant for the exercise of leadership in modern organisations, having perhaps two main implications for organisational leadership and its development. First of all, training for management and leadership skills must include the use of tools and techniques that can enable those in managerial and leadership positions both to identify salient circumstantial features, and then choose the right method to match those circumstances. It might also suggest that leadership can, and perhaps should, change hands in response to changed circumstances if one person's skills are more appropriate than another's, which clearly has implications for management structures and individual careers. It also has particular relevance for strategic leadership. Radical change in organisational circumstances might necessitate such a significant change in strategic direction that a leader who is firmly associated with the former strategy may be far less able to lead in the new direction (Rajan, 2002). High-profile examples of this phenomenon would be the changes in leadership of all three of the main political parties in the UK since 1980.

TRANSFORMATIONAL LEADERSHIP

Recent literature on leadership has noted the difference between so-called 'transactional' forms of leadership and 'transformational' ones. This contrast relates back to ideas about the nature of leadership in a society which no longer accepts 'authority' as the basis for command. If authority and 'position power' (French and Raven, 1968) no longer works, what are the alternatives? One approach is to bargain – in other words to appeal to the self-interest of the followers. So-called transactional forms of leadership rely on the leader's capacity to negotiate appropriate follower behaviours based on legitimate rewards or punishments, although there is, of course, an inherent assumption that the leader has the appropriate authority to offer such rewards or administer punishments. Alimo-Metcalfe (1995) notes the findings of Rosener (1990) that the men she studied were more likely than the women to adopt transactional styles, and suggests why women have tended to be more participatory (Rosener, 1990, p.124):

> The fact that most women have lacked formal authority over others … means that by default they have had to find other ways to accomplish their work.

This is contrasted with transformational leadership, which is a process by which leaders create high levels of motivation and commitment by generating and communicating a clear vision and, often, appealing to higher ideas and values amongst followers. Rosener (1990, p.120) defines it as motivating others by 'transforming their individual self-interest into the goals of the group' and by trying to make people feel part of the organisation. Whilst recognising this apparent gender difference, Alimo-Metcalfe (1995) warns against too close an association between female management styles and transformational leadership, suggesting that even here there are gender differences in the use of transformational techniques (such as empowerment). In her view, the 'female' version of transformational leadership is mainly focused on the creation of a sense of belonging, inclusiveness and connectedness with others in the organisation as well as its goals, whereas the same technique used by men is more focused on separateness and autonomy in pursuing organisational aims. Thus she suggests that a more general move within organisations to adopt such transformational approaches is not necessarily a means by which women can expect to achieve status and leadership positions more readily, despite an initial expectation that it might.

Legge (2005, Chapter 3) explains how this focus on a shared vision and personal commitment was, in the 1980s, part of a transformational leadership style which was characteristic of successful Japanese companies. It was re-integrated into American management culture (which was more focused on transactional leadership) via the work of the 'excellence' gurus like Peters and Waterman, or Ouchi. She charts the appeal of this style of leadership, and in particular its association with the 'American dream' and thus some of the 'soft' human resource management practices which facilitate the growth of an enterprise culture. She also offers a critique of this essentially paternalist and unitary approach to the management of people, which (when push comes to shove) will always prioritise business needs over individual or workforce needs, thus perhaps laying managers open to charges of hypocrisy when individual and corporate interests clearly do come into conflict. These, and related, issues are discussed more fully in Chapter 5 on ethics.

These concepts are clearly relevant to many strategic situations: for example, can an organisation that develops its own leaders respond effectively to discontinuous external change? Also, this set of ideas helps to illuminate the process of realigning the organisation's resources described above, as well as bringing new insight to the strategic analysis of the organisation's external and internal environments.

INSPIRATIONAL LEADERSHIP

Finally, it is impossible to discuss questions of leadership without considering the concept of inspirational leadership, which has regained some significant currency in recent years. In some ways this brings us back to concepts associated with trait theories, and in particular the characteristic usually described as 'charisma'. Inspirational leadership, we are told by Adair (2003) and others, is about creating and communicating vision, having a passion and a dynamism that drives both the leader and engages the enthusiasm and efforts of the led, even exhibiting unconventional behaviour and performing heroic deeds (Conger, 1999). It includes the ability to take a long-term view, to inspire trust and confidence which unlocks talent, enabling the organisation to achieve exceptional performance. A recent trend in the world of management training and development that reflects this renewed attention to the highly personal nature of leadership, and in particular strategic leadership, is found in the growing interest in emotional intelligence as a relevant and learnable management skill.

Mullins (2007) and Legge (2005) both sound notes of caution in their consideration of inspirational leadership and draw attention to some of its drawbacks. Certainly it is difficult to see how charismatic leadership can be developed effectively. This is not to deny that many business founders have been charismatic and inspiring individuals, but their skills have often been better described as those of the 'champion' which, as we have seen, relies on a wide range of business skills as well as the ability to protect and nurture a project. It is also less than wholly evident that inspirational leadership in itself results in significant benefits for organisational performance; in some cases it may be that the loss of the visionary results in the dissolution of the organisation. A specific attack on the cult of the inspirational leader was made by Beverly Alimo-Metcalfe at the HRD 2008 event, where she was reported (Evans, 2008) as saying that:

> Organisations shouldn't be choosing leaders who were 'charismatic and inspirational' because these qualities 'in the hands of some people can be lethal. People at the top who are charismatic get there through the demise of others – they emasculate everybody else along the way. This kind of leadership can be toxic.'

Adrian Furnham has also written about arrogance and egotistical leadership behaviour using the legend of Daedalus and Icarus (Furnham, 2005). Inspirational leadership relies on a certain degree of emotional manipulation, and so its ethical status as a general management strategy might be open to challenge. It may also inspire less desirable characteristics in the followers, such as a high level of individual dependence on the approval and support of the leader; a fear of 'going against the grain' or groupthink; and a degree of enthusiasm for the 'vision' which could encourage people to act in ways which stray beyond the boundaries of what might be considered ethical, or even legal (Conger, 2002). Inspirational leaders can be bullies as well as visionaries, and the more powerfully they communicate their values the less space there is for reasoned doubt or even opposition. For every Richard Branson there might equally be a Robert Maxwell.

4.6 ACTIVITY

Locate and read the following article by Rima Manocha: 'Who's really number one?', *People Management*, 14 October 2004, pp14–15.

- Analyse the comments using one or more of the theoretical frameworks for the study of leadership discussed in this chapter.

If you are studying with a group, you might organise your own competition. Ask everyone to present a short account like those given to *People Management*, and then vote.

LEADERSHIP: THE RESEARCH AGENDA

Writing in the February 2008 issue of *Impact*, Linda Holbeche, the CIPD Director of Research and Policy, noted the evolving nature of management and leadership, and suggested that some important new themes are emerging from current research. Amongst these are the challenges created by the need to lead in situations of increasing complexity, ambiguity and uncertainty; the idea of building 'communities of leaders'; and the influence of leader values in shaping the behaviour of those around them. These ideas have clear implications for HR practitioners, who are often charged with the responsibility for developing organisational leaders.

It is also evident that the question of leadership remains an important area for academic research. The growth of 'virtual' organisations and teams has led to an interest in the practice of 'e-leadership', and this is likely to be of growing significance as technology offers more and better opportunities for work to be organised using geographically dispersed expertise (Avolio *et al*, 2000). Ilze Zigurs has developed some ideas about the transfer of traditional team roles into a virtual environment, including that of leadership. If physical presence is an important means of signalling and reinforcing leadership in traditional teams, what happens when there is no such presence? The concept of 'telepresence' becomes relevant here – but as she explains (Zigurs, 2003, p.344):

> being telepresent is more than just keeping up a steady stream of email messages to team members. Leaders need to learn how to use the vividness and interactivity of media to make their presence felt in a positive way.

She goes on to suggest ways in which aspects of leadership – such as communicating vision, motivating, mentoring and building trust – can be transferred from face-to-face to virtual environments, and makes specific recommendations for leadership in virtual teams.

There is also significant focus on cross-cultural leadership, most notably in the continuing work of Project GLOBE (Global Leadership and Organizational Behavioral Effectiveness), which involves over 160 researchers working in 62 societies. An in-depth study of some of the Project's findings has examined culture and leadership styles in 25 of the countries under review, and uses Hofstede's (1991) model as the basis for comparative analysis (Chhokar *et al*, 2007). From other perspectives, the relationship between leaders and followers continues to generate new ideas and approaches, including developments based on the theory of 'leader member exchange' (LMX). This examines the two-way or dyadic relationships between a leader and a follower (rather than a leader and the group as a whole) – as described by Kang and Stewart (2007, p.532):

> LMX theory of leadership focuses on the degree of emotional support and exchange of valued resources between the leader and members. Thus, LMX leadership theory's main focus is to diagnose this relationship so a higher quality can be developed in this relationship, enabling improved performance.

Kang and Stewart highlight the significance of trust and empowerment in high-quality leader–member exchange, and suggest that LMX might have important implications for the practice of human resource development. Whether we are concerned with virtual, inter-cultural or traditional leadership, the academic field can offer the practitioner insights into accepted approaches, as well as extending the range of knowledge and understanding about effective leadership in new contexts and situations.

4.7 ACTIVITY

Locate and read the following article by Beverly Alimo-Metcalfe and Margaret Bradley about a recent research study into the link between leadership and employee engagement: 'Cast in a new light', *People Management*, 24 January 2008, pp38–41.

- What appears to be the most significant dimension of leadership in this study, and why?
- What are the implications of this research for organisational leadership development initiatives – for instance, the use of competency-based programmes such as the MCI?

CONCLUSION

It is clear that there is a renewed sense of the importance of good leadership amongst those most concerned with setting standards for today's managers, be they in business, the public services, or elsewhere. This comes from both social and political changes, which have encouraged more individualism and less obedience to traditional forms of authority. It also stems from the need, as Handy predicted in 1989, for organisations to become more federal than monolithic, and for new styles of management and leadership to emerge to suit the changed environment, including the virtual one. It reflects a growing public interest in the standards of behaviour of those who run businesses and direct our lives through political decisions, and their competence to carry out the tasks entrusted to them. In this respect it links firmly with discussion about ethical standards and organisational practices considered elsewhere in this book.

Personnel and HR professionals will be concerned to ensure good people management and leadership in their organisations, to improve both the performance of the organisation itself, and to enable it to attract and keep good staff. This means choosing appropriate frameworks for the selection of potential leaders, their initial training, managing the performance expected of them once in the job, appraising, developing, and rewarding them, facilitating their careers and, sometimes, removing them. A coherent, fair and equitable approach to these tasks is thus essential.

In terms of their applicability to managerial leadership, functional approaches, such as those developed by the MSC, have a lot to offer in terms of managerial leadership and professionalism. They are accessible to all, and can be used for a variety of organisational people management purposes. They offer a valuable way of ensuring that we 'do things right'. In terms of strategic leadership, and particularly when considering international and cross-cultural ventures, contingency theories seem to have more currency, offering a means by which those in charge of organisational strategy can ensure that they make the sort of choices which connect successfully to their business environments: 'doing the right thing in the circumstances'.

4.8 DISCUSSION QUESTIONS

1 What do you see as the significant differences between leadership and management? Must all good managers be good leaders? Do all business leaders have to be good managers?

2 Imagine you are in charge of devising a management development programme for a large commercial organisation. What would you include on the subject of leadership, and how you would teach this topic? How would you do things differently if you were designing a management development programme for a local authority? (You might like to consider one recently developed leadership and management training programme described by Rebecca Johnson in the 23 August 2007 issue of *People Management*.)

3 Think about someone you know who you would describe as a good leader, preferably in an organisational context. What makes them good in your view? Relate this analysis to the 'life-cycle' stage of the organisation or part of the organisation where they work. Have they shown leadership in a variety of different situations (growth, maturity, decline) or just one? Would the skills and attributes you identified earlier be suitable in all contexts?

4 Are you a member or leader of a virtual team? If so, try to analyse what sorts of leadership behaviour appear to be effective in this environment. If not, what challenges might exist for leaders of such teams, and how could an HR specialist help to identify them? You might like to consider if any lessons can be learned from the way in which virtual communities such as Facebook or Second Life operate.

EXPLORE FURTHER

Mullins, L. (2007) *Management and Organisational Behaviour*, 8th edition. Harlow: FT/Prentice Hall. This text offers comprehensive descriptions and discussion of all major conceptualisations of both management and leadership, including those relating to gender, as well as relevant case studies.

Yukl, G. (2006) *Leadership in Organisations*, 6th edition. London: Prentice Hall. Another comprehensive review of the nature of leadership in an organisational setting.

Adair, J. (1983) *Effective Leadership*. London: Pan Books. This text remains an important guide for the key processes involved in managerial leadership; highly readable and a good basis for a training programme.

A recent addition to the literature, *The Powers to Lead* (2008) Oxford: Oxford University Press, by Harvard Professor of International Relations Joseph Nye, considers leadership styles and skills, and also discusses the transferability of leadership between different arenas such as the military, politics and business.

Grint, K. (1997) *Leadership: Classical, contemporary and critical approaches*. Oxford: Oxford University Press. This text takes a critical tour around some significant academic thinking relating to the nature of leadership.

Avolio, B., Walumba, F. and Weber, T. (2009) in a forthcoming article provisionally entitled 'Leadership: current theories, research and future directions for the annual review' *Psychology* offer a summary of recent directions in academic leadership research.

Schneider, S. and Barsoux, J.-L. (2003) *Managing Across Cultures*. Harlow: FT/ Prentice Hall. This accessible text on cultural difference in a business context summarises the work of Hofstede and others, and contains a chapter on the implications of national culture for various aspects of organisational life, including leadership.

Electronic sources for further information

Information about Project GLOBE (Global Leadership and Organizational Behavior Effectiveness) can be found at the Project's website, hosted by the Thunderbird School of Global Management, and located at http://www.thunderbird.edu/wwwfiles/ms/globe/index.asp

John Adair's website: http://www.johnadair.co.uk

The easyGroup's website: http://www.easyGroup.com

Investors in People website: http://www.investorsinpeople.co.uk

MSC website: http://www.management-standards.org

BBC business news pages and archive: http://news.bbc.co.uk

CHAPTER 5

Ethics and Diversity in Human Resource Management

Richard Christy and Emma Brown

LEARNING OUTCOMES

After reading this chapter, you should be able to:

- understand the concept of business ethics
- explain the difference between the duties, consequences and virtues approaches to ethics
- comprehend what may be meant by an 'ethical dimension' to the management and leadership of human resources
- identify the link between ethics, equal opportunities and diversity management
- consider the implications for an organisation of diversity management.

INTRODUCTION

In Chapter 2, it was suggested that strategy could be understood as the way in which an organisation deploys its resources in order to achieve its goals. To be successful in a changing environment, an organisation needs to keep all of its resources aligned to the chosen strategy, which may involve acquiring new resources, developing existing resources and disposing of resources that are no longer of value to the organisation and its strategy. At the end of the chapter, the question was posed: is it acceptable for an organisation to treat its human resources in the same way as other non-human resources? If not, why not, and what rules should apply?

Thinking about these issues is important because the ethics of managing human resources will depend to some extent on the nature of the relationship between an employer and its employees. A firm's delivery van, for example, could be defined as part of its 'transportation resources'. This van is exclusively available to the firm, can be used (within the law) as the firm sees fit, can be rented out or sold when no longer needed or scrapped when no longer useful to the firm. Is the same true of the firm's human resources? Obviously not, but why not?

The first point to make is that employers do not actually own their human resources – otherwise, the word would be 'slavery' rather than 'employment'. The actual arrangement is a contractual one between two parties, who choose to take on certain rights and duties towards each other. It is quite true, of course, that human resources (employees) can be motivated and otherwise persuaded to act in the interest of the employer, sometimes to an astonishing degree, but they remain individuals who choose to act in that way. This aspect of the relationship, however obvious, is central to effective human resource management (HRM).

It is also usually true that the employment relationship is a continuing one. A continuing relationship brings benefits for employers, in terms of reduced transaction costs, such as recruitment and training. It also brings benefits for employees, for example by providing a more stable income stream. Furthermore, the employment relationship needs – from an ethical point of view – to be seen as different from other buyer/seller relationships because of the great asymmetry of power between most employing organisations and individuals. Employers are usually economically more powerful than individual employees and have ready access to far more specialised resources: it is perhaps not surprising that laws and other controls have emerged to provide special protection for the 'sellers' in employment transactions.

Above and beyond these practical points about people as employees, there is a strong sense that humans are special – that they have rights that other inanimate resources do not have, purely by virtue of being human (we will side-step the question of animal rights in this chapter). Humans are individuals and citizens as well as employees, meaning that they can reasonably demand to be treated in certain ways by employers, whether or not those rights are reinforced by law. Thinking about the nature and purpose of the employer–employee relationship helps to illuminate how that relationship should be conducted ethically (by both parties). Before examining how ethics can be applied to the main aspects of HRM, we review briefly the fundamental perspectives on ethics.

APPROACHES TO ETHICS

The study of ethics seeks a systematic and defensible understanding of good and bad. In Western philosophy, this is usually considered to have resulted in three main perspectives on ethics:

- Ethics seen as *duties* – things that should be done or refrained from, because they are good or bad in their own right
- Ethics seen as *consequences* – good acts are those that lead to good results, and vice versa
- Ethics seen as *virtues* – the desirable qualities or character traits that are possessed by good people.

For a long time, strong arguments have been made to support each of these main outlooks and most readers will recognise the role that each plays in day-to-day ethical reasoning. However, the question of what is good and bad in human behaviour remains complex and difficult, with the possibility of contradictory answers from the different perspectives.

Duty-based views of ethics (known as 'deontological' ethics) see goodness or badness inherent in the act itself, rather than in the consequences. If lying is bad, for example, it is because the act of deliberately saying something that the speaker knows to be false is bad in itself, plain and simple. Deontological ethical frameworks offer a set of duties or principles which must be respected, irrespective of the consequences. The German philosopher Kant (1724–1804) has been one of the leading voices in duty-based ethics: in his view, ethics are based on the duties that we owe each other as fellow members of a rational species. We should, for example, only act in ways that could reasonably be adopted by anyone in similar circumstances (which is close in meaning to the golden rule: 'Do as you would be done by'). Keeping promises, for example, is required, because not to do so would render the idea of a promise absurd. Also, people should always be treated as being of value in themselves, rather than simply used as a means (to achieving someone else's desires): people should be treated with respect for their equal status as moral beings and not subjected to degrading or humiliating treatment, coercion or abuse.

The general problems with an exclusively duties-based view of ethics involve:

- excessive rigidity, which can result from taking no account of possible consequences of following a principle or duty
- complexity – if principles are made more detailed in an attempt to deal with the wide range of real-life situations, then the resultant algorithms can become very unwieldy
- priority – which principles should take precedence over which others, and what is the principle that governs this precedence?

Those who see ethics only in terms of consequences look for good or bad in the results of the act, rather than in the act itself. A deliberate untruth, for example, is neither good nor bad in itself – it depends on the consequences. From this point of view, the ethics of stealing, or even killing, can only be judged by asking what happens as a result of the particular act. One familiar form of consequentialism is utilitarianism, which looks for the greatest good for the greatest number. In its original form, utilitarianism tries to assess the change in happiness for everyone affected by a proposed act (later forms sought to consider the consequences for those affected if the proposed action were to become commonplace). There are two main types of difficulty in an exclusively utilitarian view of ethics:

- methodology – while measuring changes to happiness may sound like a good idea, it is extraordinarily difficult to do so with any precision or consistency, as a moment's thought will confirm
- justice – as Mackie (1977) points out, the problem with this approach is that it can allow undeserved bad consequences for one group to be offset by good

consequences for another group, as long as the net change in happiness is positive. This can be potentially very bad news for minorities, in particular.

The contrasting views of duty-based and consequences-based ethics are reflected in the quote ascribed to Machiavelli: 'The end justifies the means.' 'Ends' are results and 'means' are principles or methods, and the argument between the two views has been running for centuries.

Virtue ethics is a separate way of thinking about good and bad. Virtues are desirable character traits, exhibited by good people. For Aristotle (384–322 BC), human virtues are those qualities that allow us to fulfil our highest purpose as humans: these qualities lie between undesirable extremes (as 'courage' lies between 'cowardice' and 'foolhardiness') and wisdom is required to recognise the virtuous approach. The virtues approach is about how people should live their lives, in order to realise their highest potential. This takes time and experience: rather than propose a series of rules or principles, the main way of becoming virtuous is to study the lives of good people and learn to imitate them.

5.1 ACTIVITY

Utilitarian thinking

In recent years, there have been many reports of financial services and other companies 'outsourcing' call centre or back-office work from the UK to lower-cost Anglophone locations such as India or Sri Lanka. This has led to controversy, since the outsourcing initiatives are often accompanied by redundancies in the UK.

This phenomenon provides an opportunity to explore the utilitarian approach to ethics. Imagine a hypothetical case of a large UK-based insurance company that is proposing to outsource its customer service call centre from a medium-sized town in the north of England to Bangalore. The UK centre is to be closed and there will be several hundred redundancies.

Make a list of the groups of people who will be affected by this initiative and then:

- describe the likely nature of the effects for each group, and
- take a guess at the likely size of each group.

How useful is this approach in illuminating the ethical implications of the proposal? Is it possible to judge the 'greatest good for the greatest number'? What difficulties would arise in trying to make this analysis more detailed and precise? Putting these methodological difficulties to one side, how satisfactory does the utilitarian approach seem to be as a way of assessing good and bad in this case? If it seems to be unsatisfactory or incomplete, what is missing?

ORGANISATIONS AND PEOPLE

How useful are these ethical perspectives in thinking about the ethics of managing people at work? Plainly, all three approaches have some relevance:

- Most would agree that there are some ways of treating employees that are just plain wrong, whether or not they are also illegal. Bullying and intimidation, for example, are plainly unacceptable. Duties-based thinking also underlies the establishment of employees' rights (and corresponding duties on employers).

- Similarly, an organisation can hardly avoid considering the consequences of proposed actions, for the organisation, for its employees and for third parties.
- Discussions of leadership often consider what are, in effect, virtues. Yukl (2002) describes the 'qualities' or 'traits' approach to understanding leadership and lists characteristics such as self-confidence, initiative and self-belief. These qualities are very like the idea of virtues – each could be seen as a desirable point between undesirable extremes, for example.

However, if we define business ethics as the study of good and bad in business conduct (an approach that can be extended to non-business organisations as well), then the ethical approaches that have been developed for personal ethics may not be adequate, because corporate businesses and other organisations are not people. They are, at the same time, different from completely inanimate objects for two reasons:

- they do behave with intent, in pursuing their objectives through strategies
- they are, from one point of view, groups of individual people, who singly or jointly make the organisation's decisions and who do so as human beings, with the ability to reason ethically. Employees generally do not leave their own values at the door when they go to work and they retain a capacity to imagine the effects on other people of the choices they make at work.

THE PURPOSE OF AN ORGANISATION

An important additional factor to consider when thinking about the ethics of HRM is that of the aims and purpose of the employing organisation. Organisational purpose relates directly to ethics in HRM because organisations can be taken to employ people primarily in order to pursue that purpose. The idea of organisational purpose is an important one in trying to understand the ethics of actions taken by an organisation: a business, for example, has a very different purpose (or set of purposes) from a university. Some types of organisation have multiple purposes: local governments, for example, have many different demands to satisfy, while others, such as small businesses, are in principle simpler.

Business organisations generally might be thought to have a simpler purpose, but this is a subject of some controversy. One school of thought defines the business purpose as that of maximising owner (shareholder) wealth, on the basis that this is the aim of shareholders in investing their money. There is therefore a duty on the directors of the company to pursue this aim in their running of the company. Friedman (1970) provides a succinct and often-cited summary of the view that the social responsibility of business is to make as much money as possible for the owners, within the law and the rules of competition. If this definition of purpose is accepted, then for a company to spend shareholder funds in ways that cannot be

5.2 THEORY TASTER

PERCEPTION: THE BASICS

Perception is a theoretical area that has immense importance for most aspects of human interaction and thus management and leadership. Theories in psychology are often based on the notion that stimuli in the external environment are received and filtered (or screened) and then interpreted and understood by an individual.

Several key components affect both the screening mechanism and also the method of interpretation. Context is fundamental and may affect both. For example, shouting in the restaurant kitchen may be 'normal' and as such screened differently from shouting in the dining area of the restaurant. Learning is intrinsically part of such processes where previous negative and positive experiences will affect how an individual is sensitised to certain stimuli (or not) and subsequently interprets them. For example, organisational restructuring will be perceived by some as threatening and by others as exciting, depending on their previous experience of restructuring, their career aspirations and their ability to find another job.

Issues to do with discrimination are often considered within perception. How far 'a person' is seen in his or her own right (whatever that might be) or through his or her membership of specific gender, race or other demographic group is the basis of discriminatory practice. Younger staff may be treated differently from older staff because colleagues perceive them differently *only on the basis* of their age and as such this is seen as unfair, because the *individual's* strengths (and weaknesses) are not taken into account. Such distortions of judgement can be found in stereotyping people according to a group. Conversely, perception can lead to over-emphasis on personal issues such as the 'halo effect' (positive regard) or 'horns effect' (negative regard) where an individual's previous behaviour prejudices the way in which they are perceived in the future.

Perceptual bias is present in everyone, because we bring different screening processes and interpretations to the information we receive in any situation. Learning can help us be better aware of our own perceptual weaknesses and the inaccuracies that might bias our judgement.

shown to be consistent with maximising owner wealth is unethical. This amounts to an ethical objection to what some companies do under the heading of corporate social responsibility (CSR), unless, of course, the CSR programme has the aim or effect of increasing or safeguarding the company's profit (see below).

Sternberg (2000) proposes a three-way test of business ethics, in which an action proposed by a business has to be:

- consistent with the business purpose (which is defined in a similar way to Friedman)
- consistent with the requirement of ordinary decency (eg not cheating, stealing, coercing, and so on)
- consistent with the requirement for distributive justice (that rewards should be proportional to contribution).

However, many define the business purpose much more broadly, suggesting that a business has a wider responsibility to the society in which it operates and that the task of a manager must recognise additional duties associated with the needs and claims of various stakeholder groups. In the original sense, stakeholders were disinterested individuals who safeguarded the stake in a bet, but the word has now become used to denote any groups with an interest in an organisation – those that may affect or be affected by the actions of the business. In business organisations, shareholders are one such group, but so are employees, customers, the local community, suppliers, and so on. The task of a manager, from this point of view, is to 'balance' stakeholder needs, which provides a very different ethical yardstick for a business than Friedman's view (and some practical difficulty in knowing when that balance has been achieved).

Donaldson and Preston (1995) discuss the various ways in which businesses can respond to stakeholder groups, pointing out that a company may decide to engage with stakeholder groups because it is a more effective way of making money for shareholders. Alternatively, a 'normative' approach to stakeholder theory recognises duties towards stakeholders that must be discharged even if those actions are not clearly consistent with maximising owner wealth. One example of the latter might be a company's involvement in local community projects, in which the expenditure cannot be shown to be maximising owner wealth. This is not to say that there will be no commercial benefits from this type of expenditure – customers may approve of the venture, for example, and so switch more of their purchases to the sponsoring company – but it may be very difficult to convert those benefits into forecast cash flows. In a normative view of stakeholder theory, an organisation will acknowledge duties to get involved in this way, even if the commercial benefits are partly unclear.

Since employees are one stakeholder group, the potential importance of this distinction should be clear. In the shareholder view, employees are one of the resources deployed by the organisation in its efforts to maximise owner wealth, usually in competition with other organisations trying to appeal to the same market. In the stakeholder view, the employee stakeholder group is one of many whose interests and needs are part of the organisation's agenda, to be balanced in some way with the needs of other groups. At first glance, the 'shareholder' approach to HRM may seem to require the lowest possible salaries, barely legal working conditions and a generally oppressive and exploitative approach to the management of employees. However, the first impression may be misleading: the shareholder-focused company can only make money for its owners by successfully developing and marketing products and services in competition with other suppliers. It will therefore have to find ways of attracting, retaining and motivating good staff, in order to stay competitive. A 'stakeholder' approach to HRM might make different claims about its motives, but on any given day might also look remarkably similar to the HRM practised by a shareholder-focused company.

As a special survey in *The Economist* pointed out (22 January 2005), CSR has become an accepted part of the corporate dialogue with the rest of the world. As Crook (2005, p.3) comments:

> It would be a challenge to find a recent annual report of any big international company that justifies the firm's existence merely in terms of profit, rather than 'service to the community'. Such reports often talk proudly of efforts to improve society and safeguard the environment – by restricting emissions of greenhouse gases from the staff kitchen, say, or recycling office stationery – before turning hesitantly to less important matters, such as profits. Big firms nowadays are called upon to be good corporate citizens, and they all want to show that they are.

Readers would be correct to infer from the sardonic tone of this quote that *The Economist* special survey raises some concerns about the way in which the notion of CSR is developing. Companies are now called upon to report according to a 'triple bottom line', in which economic results (profits) are joined by effects on the natural environment and on social well-being. This raises methodological difficulties – while there are clear conventions for measuring profitability, it is much more difficult to find general yardsticks for environmental protection or social justice.

5.3 CASE STUDY

CO-OPERATIVE BANK AND INNOCENT DRINKS

Some organisations seem to place a strong emphasis on ethical behaviour in their public faces. At the time of writing, an example of a large, established organisation in that category is the Co-operative Bank (http://www.co-operativebank.co.uk), while the Innocent fruit drink company (http://www.innocentdrinks.co.uk) provides an example of a smaller, more recently established company.

The Co-operative Bank designs its ethical policy in consultation with its customers. The bank 'will not invest in business that operate in areas of concern to our customers' (Co-operative Bank website [accessed 18 April 2008]).

A lighter touch is evident at the Innocent website [accessed 18 April 2008].Under the heading 'Our ethics', the company comments:

> We sure aren't perfect, but we're trying to do the right thing. It might make us sound a bit like a Miss World contestant, but we want to leave things a little bit better than we find them. We strive to do business in a more enlightened way, where we take responsibility for the impact of our business on society and the environment, and move these impacts from negative to neutral, or better still, positive. It's part of our quest to become a truly sustainable business, where we have a net positive effect on the wonderful world around us. Below you will find our strategy for, and our performance to date in, doing so ...

To think about ...

In each case, assess the information provided by the companies, perhaps also reviewing related press comment, and discuss the following:

- What, in your view, are the company's likely motives for making such a prominent point of its ethical conduct?
- What sort of problems will have to be managed by a company in implementing a strategy like this?

However, assuming that these methodological difficulties can be overcome in due course, concerns are also expressed about the principle of this type of CSR. Friedman's (1970) view about the purpose of business was discussed above. In addition to his concerns about the possible misuse of shareholder funds, he also expresses doubts that companies have the expertise to judge which non-business projects should be given priority, or to carry through such projects efficiently and effectively. In his view, social projects should be the domain of elected governments, rather than unelected boards of directors; society is better served by encouraging companies to get on with what they do best, in competition with each other. This perspective echoes Adam Smith's concept of the 'invisible hand', through which individuals pursuing their own interest are guided to benefit society even though they had no such intention. However, CSR in its broader sense is now the accepted orthodoxy: for as long as customers expect the firms they buy from to give an account of their effects on society and the environment, then prudent companies will be likely to comply. Many companies are genuinely seeking to do much more than toe the line in their CSR programmes, of course, with clear positive effects for many communities.

OTHER INFLUENCES ON BUSINESS ETHICS

In understanding the ethics of managing employees, organisational purpose and legal requirements are strong influences. Another important factor is the values of individual employees. As noted above, employees act as human beings when doing their jobs and must be expected to introduce their own values into the way they perform. Mahoney (1994) discusses the 'moral resources' that are available to organisations and employees, including external resources such as codes of conduct, the law and religion, together with internal resources such as conscience and personal moral development. Clearly organisations must be, to some extent, reliant on the good ethical sense of their employees: no code of conduct can cover every eventuality and no system of supervision can monitor everything. Sometimes, employees will experience conflict between their personal values and what their employer is asking them to do. This may be of a general nature, in which case it is possible that the employee is working in the wrong organisation. Sternberg (2000) points out that the way to avoid conflicts of this nature is not to work for an organisation that is foreseeably likely to produce them. Sometimes, however, where the company becomes engaged in something that causes ethical concern to an employee, the conflicts will be of a more particular nature. In this latter case, the issue is related to whistle-blowing and de George (1999) provides a clear discussion of the circumstances under which external whistle-blowing would be justifiable (and possibly even ethically obligatory).

The view that 'good ethics means good business' is one that would probably be shared by both shareholder and stakeholder-focused enthusiasts, although they might well differ on the precise meaning of 'good ethics', as discussed above. If this is so, then companies (and non-business organisations) have strong prudential reasons for promoting ethical conduct by their employees.

Codes of conduct are one way in which an organisation can signal to its employees the standards of behaviour it requires. Codes of conduct may be industry-wide, as in the case of the long-established Code of Advertising, Sales Promotion and Direct Marketing, published by the UK Advertising Standards Authority (ASA). The ASA includes representation from advertisers, agencies and media organisations and its code is an example of self-regulation, as opposed to compulsory regulation, eg by statute. Professional associations also publish codes that bind their members and which are often underpinned by possible disciplinary sanctions. The UK's Market Research Society provides one such example. Its main code of conduct aims to provide practical guidance to those involved in market research on issues such as responsibilities to respondents, responsibilities to clients, and professional standards.

Increasingly, companies and other organisations are developing and publishing their own codes of conduct, as can be seen on a wide range of corporate websites today. Besides providing guidance for employees about the expected standards, these published codes also send a clear signal to the outside world: 'These are the standards by which we are happy to be judged.'

To be effective, codes of conduct need to help users to find practical and relevant solutions to real-world problems. Codes that are either impossibly idealistic on the one hand, or purely platitudinous on the other are much less likely to play a useful role in fostering ethical conduct. From the point of view of ethical theories, codes of conduct are certainly partly deontological in nature, since they will usually include principles or duties to be respected by those covered by the code. However, it is usually true that the principles in the code have been developed by senior members of the industry, profession or organisation, based on their extensive experience of the outcomes of different courses of action, which is an example of consequentialist thinking. One reason why a well-written code of conduct can be so valuable to employees is that, at any given time, it may be very difficult to forecast exactly which course of action is going to be in the best interests of the organisation, even for individuals who are strongly committed to acting in an ethical way.

5.4 ACTIVITY

Locate the CIPD's Code of Professional Conduct and Disciplinary Procedures (for example, from the CIPD website at http://www.cipd.co.uk).

Consider Section 4 – Standards of professional conduct, in particular. In what ways do these standards seem to reflect the influences of deontological (duty-based), consequentialist and virtues approaches to ethics?

As with any professional code of conduct, the CIPD code has to cover a potentially very diverse range of real-life situations. Read through the code and discuss the role these standards and requirements would be likely to play in helping CIPD members to identify ethical courses of action in their work.

Even the best codes of conduct, however, cannot possibly cover every possible situation that will arise, particularly when organisational environments are changing so quickly. Training and briefing in ethical decision-making is also very important in fostering ethical conduct by employees, as is the establishment of a clear commitment to ethical behaviour from the top of the organisation downwards. This clear commitment is not simply a matter of broadcasting to employees – feedback channels are also important. As Sternberg (2000) points out, good corporate governance should include the provision of effective communication channels, through which possible whistle-blowers can make potential problems known to those at the top of the organisation (ie those who are in a position to do something about the issue). The problems that worry potential whistle-blowers are of general public concern – damage to the natural environment, for example – but should also be of direct concern to the management of the organisation, not least because of the potential damage to the organisation's reputation.

Many corporations have established specialist ethics officers, who are responsible for fostering ethical conduct throughout the organisation and for providing guidance in difficult cases. This source of advice will often be a valuable part of an organisation's ethical mix, but it is most likely to work effectively in a culture that involves every employee in the organisation's ethical policy. Every part of an organisation has dealings with people (employees, customers, suppliers, and so on) and has the potential to act ethically or unethically. If corporate ethics is allowed to become the concern of a few specialists rather than the responsibility of all, then the risk of major problems will remain high.

5.5 ACTIVITY

Choose two examples from the last 10 years of cases of unethical conduct by businesses: these may be connected with health and safety, for example, or bad treatment of employees, customers, suppliers or the natural environment. Alternatively, an example may revolve around financial mismanagement or misbehaviour. Collect information about what happened from published sources such as news organisation websites (the BBC site, for example, at http://www.bbc.co.uk is particularly useful in this respect). Using the ethical perspectives discussed in this chapter, identify as precisely as you can what the wrongdoing was (for example, what was done or should not have been done) and discuss how, with hindsight, the problem might have been avoided.

EQUAL OPPORTUNITIES AND ETHICS

To discriminate means to distinguish between one thing and another. In its original sense, therefore, the word 'discrimination' is ethically neutral – indeed, HRM activities such as recruitment or promotion must entail discrimination (between the one that is to be appointed and the others, for example). However, discrimination has recently acquired a pejorative sense, alluding to the exercise of prejudice, which is clearly unethical, and often illegal. In this sense of the word, it is 'unfair' or 'irrelevant' discrimination that is objectionable: the introduction into the process of factors that have no connection with the work to be done. Discriminating against lazy or dishonest people is thus acceptable (and perhaps even advisable), but discriminating on the basis of gender, ethnic origin or age is unethical.

The principle of equal opportunity (EO) requires that people should be recruited on the basis of their ability to do the job, with no other factors intruding into the decision (see Armstrong, 2003). In what ways can this be said to be ethically desirable (ie whether or not it is also legally obligatory)? In this case, both duty-based and consequentialist ethical arguments can be made to support the equal opportunities principle. The duty-based ethics point is clear: to treat employees on some basis other than EO (for example, to allow racist or sexist sentiments to enter into decisions about them) is to fail to show respect for their equal status as fellow members of the moral community. As discussed by Boatright (2000), prejudice also treats people only as members of groups, rather than affording them the individual treatment that they should reasonably expect. And making recruitment, promotion or redundancy decisions on the basis of prejudice is manifestly unjust to those who are disadvantaged.

From the employer's point of view, a strong consequences-based case in favour of EO can also be made. Organisations that rule out candidates from a whole group on the basis of prejudice are depriving themselves of a significant pool of talent in the labour market. Other things being equal, they are likely to be less successful than their competitors in attracting and keeping the talent that they need to do business effectively. For these reasons, the prospects of such organisations will be damaged by the exercise of prejudice, irrespective of any legal penalties to which they may be exposed. However, anti-discrimination legislation is commonplace in modern economies, which suggests that the market-driven response to prejudice has been found to be inadequate. This may be because in real life some employers might perceive enough scope to exercise their prejudices without significant disadvantage, unless legal penalties were also in prospect. Also, not all employing organisations are subject to competition and thus, in the absence of prohibitive legislation, would suffer no penalty at all for unfair discrimination. Alternatively, a government may find that the theoretically purgative effect of competition is taking too long to eliminate unfair discrimination and decide that legislation is desirable for utilitarian reasons.

It would be wrong, however, to infer from these arguments that equal opportunities is the sole – or even the pre-eminent – ethical principle at play in contemporary HRM. In large numbers of businesses around the world, the owners or managers may regard it as perfectly normal and desirable to prefer to recruit or promote an acceptably competent member of the same family over a better-qualified stranger. This is not the place to debate the relative merits of the two principles, but rather to suggest that EO is often not the sole governing principle in HRM, however strong the deontological and consequence-based arguments in its favour.

Even in Western employing organisations, the EO principle is made more complex by the growing interest in two other ideas – diversity management (which is discussed in the last part of this chapter) and so-called 'positive' discrimination, in which measures are taken to improve the chances of a particular group that is seen as being disadvantaged. A moment's thought will show that these two ideas could each have the practical effect of diluting or directly contradicting the EO principle in some cases. This should not be surprising – EO is a proposition about justice in the *process* of things like deciding on job offers or promotions. However, both diversity management and positive discrimination make separate arguments about justice that begin from the observed *end result* of the process.

Arguments about positive discrimination have been going on for a long time. We review them briefly here because they provide an example of the complexity of ethical arguments in practice, and also because they seem to be becoming more prominent in some European countries, having been much more familiar in the United States up to now. For example, the Norwegian government introduced legislation to make it a requirement from 1 January 2008 that 40% of main board seats in public companies should be held by women. This rule, first announced in 2003, had been virtually completely met by the deadline: by contrast, the average proportion of women board directors for Europe as a whole was reported as just 8% (BBC, 11 January 2008). In the UK, the government announced a forthcoming Equality Bill in June 2008 (BBC, 26 June 2008), whose aim will be to allow positive discrimination in certain circumstances in the interests of increased equality. In each case, these measures seem to envisage cases in which some groups will be given preferential treatment of some sort, in order to address end distributions that are seen as lastingly unfair: in effect, EO in the process of appointment has to be modified or even suspended in some cases, in order to have an end result that is more satisfactorily equal.

Respectable ethical arguments can be made to justify this type of discrimination. Boatright (2000) reviews three main types of argument in favour:

- *Compensation* – Some groups have been unjustly discriminated against for a long time and this injustice calls for the compensation that positive discrimination can offer.
- *Equality* – Where distributive injustice has been entrenched for a long time, the gap between the majority and the disadvantaged minority may require to be closed through legislative action, in order to allow EO policies to operate fairly.
- *Utilitarian* – Positive discrimination in some circumstances can be justified as a means of addressing urgent social problems.

However, the arguments against positive discrimination are also considerable: at the individual level, it can amount to unfair discrimination and each of the arguments about EO discussed above must apply. Those who are (rightly or wrongly) perceived to be 'filling quotas' in recruitment or appointment may also face the problem of unkind (if unspoken) assumptions about their individual abilities, and there may also be a risk of being seen to patronise the disadvantaged group as a whole. Perhaps the vexed question of which type of ethical argument should be given primacy over the others is one that is best left to the interplay of democratic forces in society.

By contrast, diversity management (DM) as an idea is not centrally concerned with the arguments for and against positive discrimination. The idea of DM is mainly about organisational performance. As one definition (Hays-Thomas, 2004, p.12) explains:

> we will use the term 'diversity' to refer to differences among people that are likely to affect their acceptance, work performance, satisfaction, or progress in an organisation. When we speak of 'managing diversity', we mean the purposeful use of processes and strategies that make these differences among people into an asset, rather than a liability, for the organisation.

As the same author later observes (p.26), a policy context of affirmative action (such as has applied in the USA since 1965) is relevant to DM, since it will have the effect of increasing the diversity to be managed. However, the idea of DM is that diversity is to be desired by an organisation *in its own right*, irrespective of any legislative context. The DM proposition is essentially instrumental – learn to promote and manage diversity effectively and your organisation will perform better. The reason for this is that a diverse set of human resources will far better equip an organisation to sense, understand and respond to changes in its business environment, with benefits in terms of successful innovation, better risk management and greater resilience to environmental turbulence. As such, the proposition seems to be irresistible to a business – who would not want the bottom-line benefits that are seen as the reward for effective DM? Some caution must be exercised with this simple equation, however: for example, effective DM is likely to require far more than just lip service and to take time to achieve. This may be one reason why the evidence of bottom-line benefits is sometimes mixed, as suggested by von Bergen *et al*, 2005. We should perhaps not be surprised to find that the DM task is complex and that success is unlikely to be instantaneous. In terms of ethical human resource management, DM is a proposition that is mainly justified in terms of its beneficial *consequences*, although the more respectful treatment of individual employees that can result from effective DM is also desirable from a *deontological* point of view.

DIVERSITY MANAGEMENT

The idea of diversity management (DM) is that it seeks to go beyond ruling out unfair discrimination because of legal or ethical considerations alone. Rather, it proposes that there are specific benefits to be gained by organisations which adopt this approach all with implications for managers and leaders and the HR function. We have reviewed that any organisation needs to satisfy stakeholders. For both public and private sector organisations, reducing unnecessary costs is likely to be important. Naturally the achievement of DM will incur direct costs – for example, in training on diversity awareness. These have to be balanced not only by the benefits of DM but also against the costs of *not* being a diversity-aware organisation (eg adverse publicity, cultural misunderstandings, consumer disapproval and the risk of litigation). However, diversity management is not solely concerned with money issues. When discussing the management of diversity, Pilbeam and Corbridge (2006, p.191) state:

> A managing diversity philosophy is founded on the acceptance and recognition that individual differences are to be valued and actively used in the pursuit of organisational and individual goals.

As the authors imply, in practical and strategic terms, financial issues are considered alongside other aspects, such as legislation, policy and procedural factors. If an organisation is seen as embracing diversity, its 'brand image' in the recruitment market may well be improved, such that it becomes an employer of choice. If employees feel alignment between their personal values and those of the employer, job satisfaction and commitment may be enhanced.

An organisation considering its own structural and cultural evolution needs to consider the fit between the prevailing cultural values and norms in the organisation and its own aspirations for greater diversity in the workforce. Workers who are new to a business where a different culture prevails, based for example on ethnic or religious groupings, could find themselves in a hostile work environment where victimisation, harassment, loss of dignity, bullying (Pilbeam and Corbridge, 2006), ignorance, prejudice, stereotyping and discrimination may arise (Chryssochoou, 2004).

With the increase in labour mobility, organisational workforces may become more diverse, whether or not the employer is actively pursuing a policy of increasing diversity. Hence employers may need to plan how to manage diversity anyway (Hunt, 2007). For example, a large international organisation is very likely to contain levels of diversity that result from multinational operations, tele- and remote working (including 'offshoring') and internationally mobile workers. As integration succeeds, national differences start to blur as the organisation becomes more thoroughly global in nature. Managers and leaders in such organisations have a key role in achieving DM.

5.6 ACTIVITY

When considering diversity management strategy and practices, the varied costs to an organisation may not be easy to quantify or even, in the short term, to identify.

- What might be both the financial and human costs of diversity management to an organisation?
- Are there any other cost factors that could influence the management of diversity?

How then do we structure a response for managers who seek to understand the challenge carried by DM? Dowling, Festing and Engle (2008) found the following categories affected international employee performance:

- the compensation package
- the task
- headquarters support
- the performance environment
- cultural adjustment.

Table 5.1 Performance factors

	Frontline/individual performance factors (high employee expectations)	In-line managerial performance factors: the manager as:	Organisational performance factors (high organisational expectations)
Reward focus	Individual reward expectations	A reward and financial controller	Financial effectiveness
Operations focus	Clarity of individual task	An initiator of operational task/ role synergy	Organisational role clarity
Communication focus	Interpersonal communication(s)	A communication hub	Organisational communication(s)
Cultural focus	Personal cultural norms and values	A spokesperson and cultural moderator	Organisational cultural norms and values
Cost benefit focus	Personal cost/benefit/risk	A general business cost/ benefit risk analysis and action	Organisational cost benefit/risk analysis and action (eg legal compliance)
Support focus	Employee support availability	A support moderator	Employer support offered

Source: developed from Dowling *et al* (2008)

Table 5.1 applies these categories to show the complexity of expectations at the individual, managerial and organsiational levels. Looking through the managerial column it can be seen that DM affects most managerial activity.

While the factors noted in Table 5.1 are not exhaustive, they help indicate the complexity of factors which may be important when managing diversity and 'maximizing the achievement of employees' (Pilbeam and Corbridge, 2006, p.209).

A successful DM process needs to recognise that some barriers to greater diversity may be obvious and overt, but that others may be harder to see. The process must therefore unfold over time, and much will depend upon the willingness of existing employees to support the policy, and links to ideas previously suggested around employee engagement and the reciprocal employee/employer relationship (Pilbeam and Corbridge, 2006) where together employees and the employer understand how to get the most out of difference and bring mutual benefits. While the organisation can become stronger, both in terms of being able to recognise and seize new market opportunities and also in being better able to respond to external challenges, individual employees are also likely to enjoy greater job satisfaction and a richer range of personal development opportunities.

Beyond the market and financial benefits, there are other organisational advantages to adopting and continuing strong diversity practice. We have been aware for many years of the problems related to 'groupthink' (Janis, 1970). Similar people in groups, while they tend to get on well together, may be uncreative in their thinking and, at the extreme, can make poor decisions as the group fails to engage in real debate about the issues at hand. Diversity thus helps creativity, mitigates against groupthink, and enables equality of voice for all members of the working community.

On an individual basis, a successfully diverse organisation whose rules and procedures are accepted as fair by all staff (including the majority groups) will enjoy the benefits of stronger and more confident working relationships. Arnold *et al* (2005) found that poor interpersonal relationships were characterised by poor listening, low levels of trust and little support, and that these increased stress levels for all staff. Low levels of trust in decision-making and relationships lead to lower levels of commitment, as well as higher levels of stress and a greater propensity to leave the organisation (Quine, 1999). Fundamental to contemporary interventions which achieve better psychosocial cultures is that of dialogue and 'bottom-up' approaches (Mackay *et al*, 2004), a state typical within well-managed diverse workforces. The synergy of shared knowledge, skills and attributes may arise, which again can enhance the working capacity and flexibility of the business.

What does one need to do to ensure that the management of diversity becomes a business success factor (Schneider and Barsoux, 2003)? The notion of competitive advantage being gained through positive diversity action is relatively new, as is a culture of diversity. Changing an organisational culture is always difficult: a culture that is resistant to change can be a barrier to DM. Diversity training can help to overcome such barriers. Robbins (2005, p.538) outlines the goal and function of diversity training as 'Participants learn to value individual differences, increase their cross-cultural understanding, and confront stereotypes.' Robbins refers to the behavioural awareness of diversity issues in the workplace as a tool to improve good practice and fit in diversity terms, as shown in Table 5.2.

People from diverse backgrounds may not be able to communicate easily at first as they have to discover their different norms and values, creating the potential for conflict. Managers need to have skills in managing conflict positively, so that those who are from different backgrounds learn to work together with respect for each other. Mediation skills and very clear communication will help managers and leaders assist their staff through the more difficult periods.

It is important to remember that all levels of the organisation need to commit to the diversity management process. It is interesting to note the emphasis Robbins places on recruitment and selection (see Table 5.2). Without doubt this is the correct starting point, as one needs to get diverse employees working inside the organisation. Readers might think about how their own organisation advertises (in

5.7 CASE STUDY

TESCO

An organisation that does pay attention to diversity issues may be seen, and indeed brand-marketed, as ethically aware. Recent in-store advertising by the Tesco organisation showed employees, who are from diversely categorised groups, advertising relevant services, but always promoting the Tesco brand. The lay customer may, albeit perhaps subconsciously, perceive the organisation as non-discriminatory and therefore ethically 'good'. The Tesco diversity statement reads:

Staff

Diversity benefits a business in many ways, including greater customer and staff loyalty ... We are committed to ensuring that at all times and in every aspect of employment, including recruitment, training and development, everybody receives the same treatment. Both internal and external applicants are considered on individual ability, regardless of factors such as gender, age, colour, creed, race, ethnic origin, disability, marital status, religion or belief, trade union membership or sexual preference and orientation.

Source: http://www.tesco.com

To think about ...

Consider the following questions:

- What are the potential advantages of an organisation actively considering such an approach to diversity management?
- What could be the potential barriers to the effective adoption of such an approach?
- How could these be constructively addressed?

the broadest sense of the word) vacancies and think through how effective this is from a diversity point of view.

The final frame within Robbins list is much harder to achieve – that of positively valuing diversity and dealing with the tensions which diversity in its nature creates. It may require organisations to redefine concepts of what binds employees together. These will have to include respect, trust, listening and fairness. Most would be happy to pay lip service to these ideas at an abstract level. However, they are hard to achieve in practice, and introduce a further complexity into the HRM field.

CONCLUSION

In this chapter we have outlined areas that are becoming of increasing urgency in the HR field and which relate to ethical practice generally and diversity specifically. These are not easy topics, and possibly require all staff to reflect at a deeper level than previously. An ability to demonstrate good ethical practice is an area which we suspect will increase in importance, and we have shown that there are conflicting 'rules' and a vast array of alternatives from which to choose. The HR practitioner will need to add knowledge of ethics and their implementation into their toolkit to assist managers across the organisation to change as these agendas develop. At an infrastructure level, all organisations will need to comply

Table 5.2 Diversity behaviours in the workplace

Embrace diversity	Successfully valuing diversity starts with accepting the principle of multiculturalism. Accept the value of diversity for its own sake.
Recruit broadly	When you have job opportunities, work to get a diverse applicant pool. Avoid relying on referrals from current employees since this tends to produce candidates similar to your present workforce.
Select fairly	Make sure your selection process does not discriminate. Particularly ensure that selection tests are job-related.
Provide orientation and training for minorities	Making the transition from outsider to insider can be particularly difficult for non-traditional employees.
Sensitise all employees	Encourage all employees to embrace diversity. Provide diversity training to help all employees see the value of diversity.
Strive to be flexible	Part of valuing diversity is recognising that different groups have different needs and values. Be flexible in accommodating employee needs.
Seek to motivate individually	You need to be aware of the background, cultures and values of employees. What motivates one employee may not motivate another.
Reinforce employee differences	Encourage employees to embrace and value diverse views. Accentuate positive aspects of diversity. Be prepared to deal with challenges such as mistrust, miscommunication, and lack of cohesiveness, attitudinal differences and stress.

Source: Robbins (2005) *Organisational Behaviour*, 11th edition. Adapted by permission of Pearson Educational Inc., Upper Saddle River, NJ (p.600)

with the law. However, we hope that we have also outlined benefits that the proactive organisation which is looking to be a high-performance differentiator will seize on and develop.

Perhaps one of the most important effects arising from employee awareness of a genuinely diverse workforce will be on the operational and emotional integrity of the psychological contract. This will affect how managers behave with their teams and also how all employees treat each other and make business decisions. Chapter 6 will now deal with the fundamental aspects of the workplace psychological contract.

5.8 DISCUSSION QUESTIONS

1 Thinking about an organisation with which you are familiar, provide practical examples of ways in which it is operating ethically. Can you relate these examples to the duty, consequences or virtue perspectives of ethics?

2 Discuss the view that an organisation that is providing good value products or services to its customers, paying its bills and treating its staff decently over a long period of time is acting as ethically as anyone can reasonably expect.

3 Look for examples of organisations that appear to be making special efforts to practise diversity in their HRM policies. On the basis of the available evidence, what seem to be the motives of these organisations for seeking diversity? If you were evaluating such a policy, what evidence would you seek in order to help you assess its effectiveness?

EXPLORE FURTHER

There are a number of well-written texts on business ethics. Crane and Matten provide a balanced and accessible discussion of the various viewpoints: Crane, A. and Matten, D. (2006) *Business Ethics*, 2nd edition. Oxford: Oxford University Press. For a strongly argued account of the importance of a purpose-based view of business ethics, see Sternberg, E. (2000) *Just Business*, 2nd edition. Oxford: Oxford University Press.

For further reading on the topic of diversity management, see Daniels, K. and Macdonald, L. (2005) *Equality, Diversity and Discrimination*. London: CIPD. This book offers a variety of perspectives from the consideration of diversity in an organisational context through to the prevention of discrimination and the promotion of workplace equality.

Kandola, R. and Fullerton, J. (1998) *Diversity in Action: Managing the mosaic*. London: CIPD. This provides a view of diversity incorporating various complementary perspectives which are claimed to add value to organisations.

Macdonald, L. (2004) *Managing Equality, Diversity and the Avoidance of Discrimination*. London: CIPD. This is a mixed-level textbook allowing both HR managers and practitioners to gain an increased understanding of contemporary issues, EO and diversity.

CHAPTER 6

Flexibility, the Psychological Contract, and Empowerment

Simon Turner

LEARNING OUTCOMES

After reading this chapter, you should be able to:

- identify the ways in which organisations seek to achieve improved employee and organisational performance through HR policies and practices
- understand the different meanings attached to the concept of flexibility
- evaluate the importance of the psychological contract as a key influence on employees' behaviour
- assess the ways in which employees might be empowered at work.

INTRODUCTION

This chapter aims to explore the connections between organisational performance and topics in the current human resource management spotlight: the policies of flexibility by which organisations respond to the need for continuous improvement, the slippery concept of multi-faceted psychological contracts which might help us to make sense of workers' attitudes towards the employer, and the drive for empowerment as organisations ask workers to become committed and to assume more responsibility for self-management.

There are connections between these themes. Commitment is seen as an element of the psychological contract, and the state of the contract in turn influences workers' attitudes towards providing flexibility. The concept of empowerment is partly intended to lead to the committed worker. Employers' desires for these concepts to be 'got', or controlled, are linked with the creation of HR policies designed to improve organisational performance. There is much debate in the HR field surrounding the approaches and activities designed to secure improvements in outcomes and performance, including recommendations by the Chartered Institute of Personnel and Development, the UK professional body. It has been observed (Marchington *et al*, 2005) that there is a tendency for these concepts to become conflated with the anticipated results, so that the descriptions become prescriptions, accepted as conventional wisdom.

And there are tensions within this field. The desire for organisations to integrate HR policies with business objectives may sit uneasily with the move towards Atkinson's (1984) flexible firm, with decentralised responsibilities and externalised workers. The client organisation in an outsourcing arrangement may find it difficult to manage, or influence, the policies of the supplier of labour, for example. It has been noted that in the HR management literature, the focus is on the remaining core activities and not on how non-core activities are provided (Marchington *et al*, 2005).

PERFORMANCE

Organisations seek to identify the link between people and performance (Purcell *et al*, 2003) and the concept of high-performance working (HPW) is introduced (CIPD, 2003b; CIPD, 2004a; DTI, 2005), characterised by references to flatter, non-hierarchical structures, moving away from reliance on management control, towards teamworking and autonomous working based on high levels of trust, communication and involvement. Whether the focus is on profit and shareholder value in the private sector, or on outputs and service levels in the public sector, performance is the current currency.

As we noted in the first chapter, there are claims that 'UK manufacturing companies that introduce HPW can expect to achieve a 20% increase in productivity and profitability' and that 'private sector service firms and public sector bodies could enjoy a similar boost to performance' (CIPD, 2004a, p.4). Workers are seen as being 'more highly skilled and having the intellectual resources to engage in lifelong learning and master new skills and behaviours' (CIPD, 2004a, p.3). It is noted that HPW practices can also be called human resource management practices or high involvement practices elsewhere.

Purcell *et al*'s (2003) study on the impact of people management on organisational performance was intended to show the way in which HR practices – or what the CIPD terms 'people management', meaning all aspects of how people are managed – impact on performance. The study was conducted within a framework which claims that performance is a function of people's ability (knowledge and skills), their motivation, and the opportunity they are given to deploy their skills (referred to as AMO). The authors concluded that a range of 11 HR policies and practices are required to turn this into action, and a model (see Figure 6.1) was devised, covering recruitment and selection, training and development, career opportunity, communications, involvement in decision-making, teamworking, appraisal, pay, job security, job challenge/job autonomy and work–life balance.

> These performance-related HR policies encourage people to exercise a degree of choice on how and how well they do their job. In other words, they help induce discretionary behaviour which makes people work better and

> improve performance. This happens because the HR policies and practices develop positive employee attitudes or feelings of satisfaction, commitment and motivation.
>
> Purcell *et al* (2003, p.ix)

Figure 6.1 The people and performance model

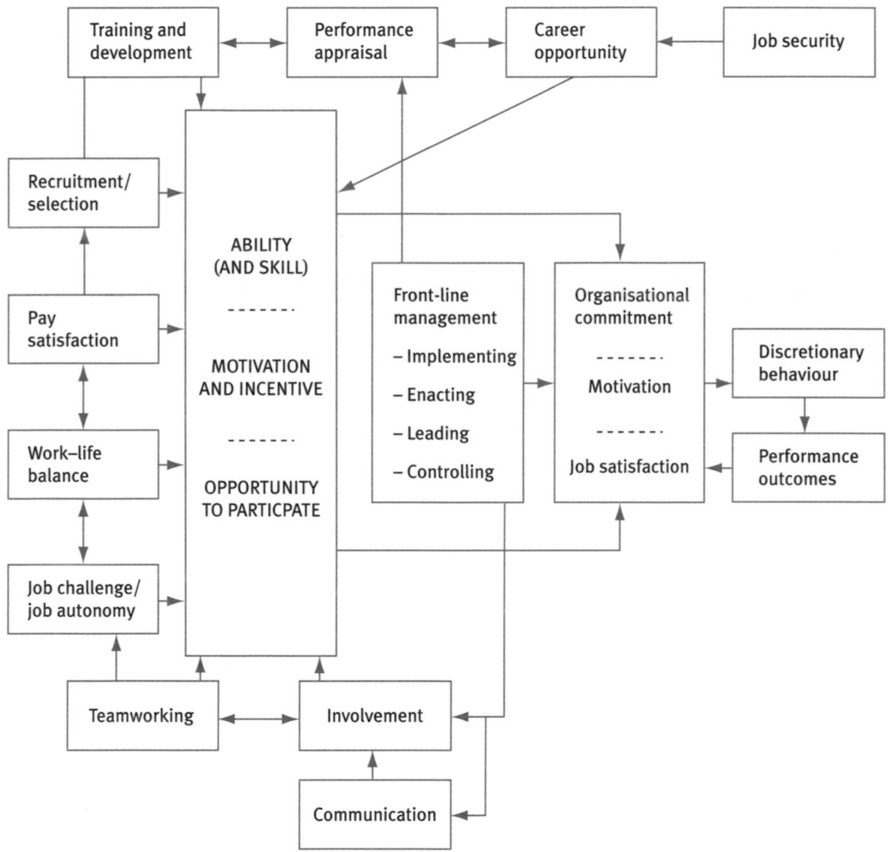

Source: This material is taken from *Bringing Policies to Life: The vital role of front-line managers in people management* by Sue Hutchinson and John Purcell, 2003, with the permission of the publisher, the Chartered Institute of Personnel and Development, London

Some HR policies and practices were shown to be particularly important in terms of influencing employee outcomes like commitment, job satisfaction and motivation. These were those concerned with career opportunities, job influence, job challenge, training, performance appraisal, teamworking, involvement in decision-making, work–life balance, and having managers who are good at leadership and who show respect.

In contrast to our discussion in Chapter 2, among the implications for HR policy and practice is 'operational measurement' rather than 'remote' measures of profit:

> Proving that HR contributes to performance is not a major issue, and measures which use profit or shareholder values are too remote from the practice of people

> management to be useful. What is important is operational measurement where a close link can be observed, and the regular collection of these measures covering people, operational, financial and customer areas is commonly done in the best firms, linking back to the logic of the balanced scorecard.
>
> Purcell *et al* (2003, p.72)

We can conclude that the responsibility for enacting the policies rests with front-line managers, since these are the people with whom workers theoretically interact. In Hutchinson and Purcell's (2003) framework, 'organisation process advantage' – the way these policies are implemented – is what makes a difference. Put another way, 'It's not what you do, it's the way that you do it.'

The CIPD (2004c) Standards for Leadership and Management are placed in the language of performance infrastructure ('critical failure factors') and differentiators ('critical success factors'). The former describes what is needed to do things right (efficiency) and deliver acceptable levels of behaviour and legal compliance, although it is observed that mere adherence to process seldom generates high-performance outcomes. The latter describes what is needed to do

6.1 THEORY TASTER

HERZBERG'S TWO-FACTOR THEORY OF MOTIVATION

Developed in the middle of the last century, Herzberg's theory of motivation remains influential amongst those seeking explanations of workers' behaviour, and is one example of the *content* theories of motivation (see Activity 7.4).

His original work was based on interviews with accountants and engineers, and sought to discover what incidents made them feel particularly good or bad about the jobs they had held. From these results, Herzberg identified two sets of factors. The first, which he termed 'hygiene' or 'maintenance' factors, were related to the job's context – for example, pay and working conditions. If these factors are given proper attention by management, then this will prevent dissatisfaction; they do not, however, motivate workers. The second group Herzberg termed 'motivators' or 'growth' factors, and were related to the person's job content – for example, challenge, achievement and recognition. The presence of such factors at work will motivate employees.

While both factors have equal importance they serve different functions. Well-developed hygiene factors will not lead to satisfaction, but will only prevent dissatisfaction: that is, a state of no dissatisfaction. In order to motivate staff managers must ensure that they give full attention to the growth factors.

While some subsequent studies have tended to confirm Herzberg's argument, others have been more critical. The two most common criticisms of his work are first, that it is based on interviews with professional workers, and that it is less applicable to low-skilled, possibly repetitive, work; second, that in asking people about their work, they are more likely to relate satisfying aspects to their own performance, and dissatisfying parts, the hygiene factors, to those aspects outside their control.

the right things (effectiveness) and, the proponents claim, deliver 'genuine' people involvement, commitment, engagement and added-value contribution. There are connotations of Herzberg's two-factor theory of motivation, which we discuss in Chapter 7, here: 'infrastructure' linking with hygiene factors and 'differentiators' involving motivators. The 11 policy areas (Purcell *et al*, 2003) are seen as the performance infrastructure requirements, while the ways in which front-line managers deliver the policies – implementing, enacting, leading and controlling – are seen as the differentiators. It is claimed that these are 'directly related to the levels of commitment, motivation and satisfaction that employees report, and this, in turn, is linked to the vital area of discretionary behaviour' (Hutchinson and Purcell, 2003, p.3).

FLEXIBILITY

Flexibility has been frequently identified as a key human resource policy goal, along with strategic intention, quality, and employee commitment, in order to ensure an adaptable organisation structure (Guest, 2001). These HR goals generate '... a range of positive organizational outcomes, such as high job performance, high-quality problem-solving, successful change, lower turnover, absenteeism and grievance levels and high cost-effectiveness' (Iles *et al*, 1996, p.18). On the one hand employers, encouraged by governments and non-governmental bodies, such as the International Monetary Fund and the World Bank, press the case for workforce flexibility in the hunt for efficiency, and on the other hand it is claimed that individual employees look for flexibility in working hours as they attempt to juggle the demands of home and work lives. It seems that the two agendas might meet in a unitary, though stressful, work–life balance (CIPD, 2008b; Taylor, 2002; Pollitt, 2003) where employers' flexibility requirements can coincide well with the wants and needs of a great many employees. An outcome, it is claimed, is that 'flexible working has a positive impact on employee performance and helps to reduce stress ... [and] that flexible workers [are] found to have higher levels of commitment and job satisfaction than other employees' (CIPD, 2008b).

Four main types of flexibility can be identified (after Blyton and Morris, 1992):

- task or functional flexibility, where employees may be multi-skilled
- numerical flexibility, using different types of employment contracts and sub-contracting, as in Atkinson's (1984) core–periphery concept
- temporal flexibility, where the number and pattern of hours worked varies – for example, zero hours, and annual hours
- wage flexibility, where wages are individualised, and may be performance-related.

Atkinson's (1984) 'flexible firm' model described a heroic picture with committed core employees being highly regarded, well paid, and with improved career prospects, and who offer in return functional flexibility, often through multi-skilling. On the periphery are the distanced externals: the 'atypical', 'non-standard' or 'non-core' workers (described in negative terms) with low security to ease the organisation's needs for adjustments to market demand.

Current observations are that organisational forms are changing, with bureaucracies being dismantled and replaced by looser, networked organisational forms and processes, featuring partnerships and contracting-out of activities. 'In the name of right-sizing, de-layering and concentrating upon core competencies, the outsourcing of services continues to expand' (Marchington *et al*, 2005, p.2) as organisations move from vertical towards horizontal integration. With this come changes in the employment relationship. Marchington *et al* (2005, p.18) present an additional dimension to the understanding of employment flexibility – namely, the extent to which the employment contract is under the influence of a single employing organisation or subject to control or influence by multiple employers, as might be the case with agency workers (Figure 6.2). This axis is added to the previously accepted continuum depicting variations in the internalisation or standardisation of the employment contract (as in the core–periphery concept).

Figure 6.2 The twin dimensions of employment flexibility

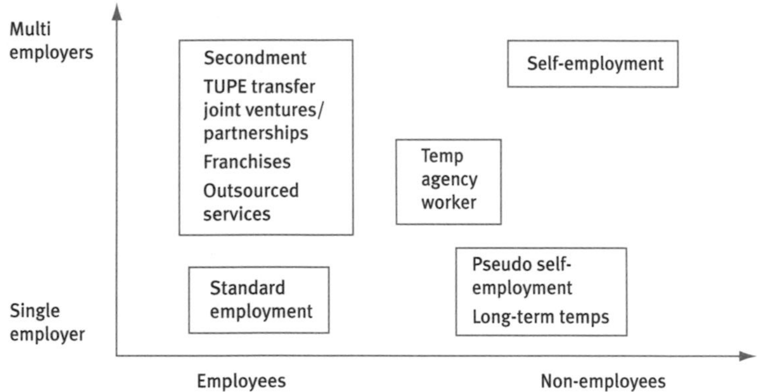

Source: The introduction of *Fragmenting Work* (2005) edited by M. Marchington *et al.* By permission of Oxford University Press

As the authors describe, the internalised, standard employment relationship is seen in the bottom left-hand corner. In the top right-hand corner is self-employment, 'where there is no contract of employment and where the self-employed individual sells his or her skills to a range of organizations and is, therefore, not dependent on a particular organization for income' (*ibid*, p.18).

The horizontal axis, from employees to non-employees, depicts the shift away from internalised full-time employees to a diversification of contracts including part-time, casual, temporary, and self-employed workers. 'Part-time work might be considered to be close to the standard contract as there is nothing in principle stopping part-time work being organized on the same basis as internalized, full-time work with the same social rights and same regularity of employment' (*ibid*, p.18). At the extreme of where the guarantees of employment and income are, at best, short-term, are the so-called pseudo self-employed workers, who often work at a distance from the employer – such as homeworkers and freelancers – 'but who may be highly dependent upon one employer, even if there is no formal contractual guarantee of continuous employment or minimum income' (*ibid*, p.19).

In the centre of the field we find temporary agency workers, in ambiguous circumstances: self-employed yet employed, where the agency is commonly regarded as the legal employer, even though it is the client who exercises control. 'The employing organization, which acts as host to the temporary agency workers, directs their work activities side-by-side with those of direct employees on similar tasks … This employment relationship … (involves) both deviations from the status of direct employees, and control from more than one employing organization' (*ibid*, p.19).

The top left-hand side '… covers an area where employment is internalised but where there is more than one employing organization that can be considered party to the relationship.' Here 'there is a direct employment relationship but other employers – acting as agents or suppliers – may be involved in the employment experience, and even in controlling the employment relationship' (*ibid*, pp18–19).

Lying at the heart of the wage–work bargain, flexibility means different things to the different parties to the deal. While conventional definitions are expressed from the point of view of the employer or organisation, descriptions of the consequences for the worker are required in the interests of balance. Attention is drawn to the dark side of flexible employment by Toynbee (2008) in Case study 6.2.

THE DARK SIDE OF FLEXIBLE EMPLOYMENT

6.2 CASE STUDY

Labour MPs representing the poorest places see how appalling conditions under bad employers can be. They see where agency workers are brought in to undercut existing wages – remember Gate Gourmet. Or where workers who want to be taken on permanently are fired and rehired to avoid them acquiring rights. They see outsourced NHS cleaners, and workers throughout the public sector, are denied a chance they once had to work their way up. Agencies don't train people to fill higher-level jobs for which they are not contracted.

Source: Toynbee, P. (2008) MPs must fulfil Labour's pledge to low paid and temporary workers. *The Guardian*, 23 February 2008 p.33

And an alternative to the conventional wisdom regarding the economic necessity of flexibility, at both global and individual levels, is provided by Elliott (2004) in Case study 6.3.

6.3 CASE STUDY

FLEXIBILITY – AND INEQUALITY

It is an unshakeable article of faith – from the International Monetary Fund in Washington to the Organisation for Economic Cooperation and Development (OECD) in Paris and taking in just about every finance minister and central banker across the seven seas – that flexibility is the key to lower unemployment. Countries with flexible labour markets (ie lower rates of trade union membership, low non-wage costs, tough benefit rules) price marginal workers back into jobs. Countries with inflexible ones have high levels of youth unemployment and joblessness among those with low skills. Take a look at the UK or US for how it should be done, or any country in Europe for how it shouldn't. It may be hard and painful, but that, sadly, is the way it has to be.

Just because one view becomes the orthodoxy does not, of course, make it right. Unemployment rates in the UK and the US were low in 2000 after two decades of structural reform, but not spectacularly so in comparison to other OECD countries. The Netherlands, Switzerland, Norway and Austria all had lower jobless rates, and none had signed up to 'flexibility'. An alternative explanation is that unemployment in the UK and the US has fallen due to higher levels of aggregate demand while staying high in some of the continental economies because of a demand deficiency.

It may be that the flexibility of labour markets has little real bearing on unemployment but a much greater impact on inequality, with the removal of job protection and lower levels of trade union membership leading to poverty wages for those at the bottom of the pile

Elliot, L. (2004) 'Job flexibility can tie you up in knots', *Guardian Weekly*, 25–31 March, p.16

BEHAVIOURAL FLEXIBILITY

Most attention has been given to organisational and labour market flexibility rather than personal flexibility. For firms to be flexible they depend on the flexibility of the workforce – an orientation, attitude, or style among employees, including team-oriented, lateral and autonomous perspectives (Iles *et al*, 1996, p.21). Anell and Wilson (2000, p.168) suggest the following qualities might be required in employees:

> a desire to seek feedback on performance, a desire to improve, an ability to see multiple perspectives, a broad vision, an ability to visualize relationships, a readiness to accept responsibility for decisions, self-confidence, proactivity, a liking for change and a desire for co-operative independence.

Among senior managers, personal and strategic flexibility and internal characteristics such as problem-solving or creative thinking are desirable. These authors describe elements of 'behavioural flexibility' in managers in terms of the ability to manage complexity and uncertainty, adaptability, tolerance of ambiguity, openness, empathy, non-judgementalism, interest in others, and willingness to acquire new behaviours and attitudes. Sennett refers to 'a particular strength of character – that of someone who has the confidence to dwell in disorder … who flourishes in the midst of dislocation' (1998, p.62).

THE PSYCHOLOGICAL CONTRACT

6.4 CASE STUDY

'PRICEWATERHOUSECOOPERS INCREASES EMPLOYEE FLEXIBILITY'

Professional-services firm PricewaterhouseCoopers (PWC) is described as a knowledge-driven organisation. When its employees leave, the firm not only loses the training and knowledge they have built up, but also the client relationships they have developed.

PWC now has a strategy based around choice for its employees, whose average age is only 27. There is a generous scheme of maternity and paternity leave, childcare vouchers for returning mothers and other benefits. Moreover, most employees are equipped to be able to work from home, and almost all of them choose to do this at least once a month.

The company has launched an in-house concierge service. Employees are offered a wide range of domestic services at discount price. They include activities [such] as waiting in for plumbers, builders and electricians. Take-up appears to be greatest among company consultants, who often work offsite for months.

PWC has also introduced the notion of 'paid time off', rather than the more restrictive 'annual leave'. Employees can use their paid time off allocation for short-term illness, childcare and jury service, as well as holiday.

According to the author, the strategy appears to be successful. Despite skill shortages in the consultancy sector, staff retention at PWC has improved by between 4 and 5% over the last year.

Source: Perry, M. (2001) 'Flexibility pays', *Accountancy Age*, 6 December, pp15–18, in (2002) *Human Resource Management International Digest*, Vol.10, No.4, pp13–15

To think about ...

1 What does this case show us about the benefits of flexibility to organisations and staff?

2 Is this type of flexibility restricted to the type of professional worker employed by PWC, or does it have wider application?

Although questions have been raised about its meaning and value (Guest, 1998) the concept of psychological contract has become a central theme of people management. It describes the employment relationship in terms of mutual expectations or obligations, in order to make sense of the range and degrees of commitment that flow in both directions. It is here that organisational policy and procedures mix with individual managerial and employee attitudes and behaviours, with complex outcomes.

There are two main definitions of the psychological contract (Marks, 2001). The first is derived from the work of Argyris (1960) and Schein (1978) and refers to the perceptions of mutual obligations held by the two parties in the employment relationship, the organisation and the employee. The second definition, which is based on the work of Rousseau (1995, p.9), asserts that the psychological contract is formulated only in the mind of the employee and is therefore about 'individual beliefs, shaped by the organization, regarding terms of an exchange between individuals and their organization'.

6.5 CASE STUDY

'SHIFT PATTERN SWITCH IMPROVES STAFF TURNOVER AND RECRUITMENT AT SEEBOARD: HIGH-RISK INITIATIVE BRINGS RICH REWARDS'

Seeboard Energy Ltd is a utility company with around 1.8 million customers, mainly in south-east England. Its customer-contact centre operates from 8.00am–10.00pm (Saturday 8.00am–6.00pm). Staff answer around 3,000,000 calls a year and respond to around 800,000 letters or emails from customers.

Three-week rolling shifts

In 1999, the company introduced three-week rolling shifts to cover the contact centre's main hours of operation. The shifts were:

* early: 7.30am–3.30pm or 8am–4pm
* core: 8.30am–4.30pm, 9am–5pm or 9.30am–5.30pm
* late: 10am–6pm, noon–8pm or 2pm–10pm.

The change led to a significant rise in employee turnover, particularly among women. The company also experienced increasing difficulty attracting potential employees – again, particularly women. Commercially, at an average cost of £3,000 to recruit and train an employee, it was proving an ineffective use of the company's resources.

Staff focus groups were set up in July 2000, and team leaders and managers asked employees to give their views. In addition, questionnaires were sent out to staff. Findings indicated one major issue: the three-week rolling shift pattern did not provide staff with enough stability with which to balance their home and work commitments. In particular, this was an issue for women with childcare responsibilities, as it made arrangements for childcare much more complex.

Fixed shift pattern

The company's solution was to introduce fixed shift patterns. It piloted the approach in an area of the organisation that had the highest number of vacancies (150).

Measuring the impact

Under the three-week rotational shift system, staff turnover was 20%, with more than 65% of this figure being women. By April 2001, under the fixed shift system, this had halved to 10%, with 50% of this figure made up of women. In addition, over a one-year period, the response rate to recruitment advertisements improved significantly, and many of the applicants were women.

Source: Pollitt, D. (2003), pp12–14

According to Rousseau (1995, p.1) the ideal contract details expectations of both the employee and the employer, but these contracts are incomplete and so become 'self-organising'. A contractual continuum is commonly offered, from transactional (covering incentive pay and well-specified performance levels) to relational (including loyalty and concern for employee well-being). Transactional terms are exemplified by 'a fair day's work for a fair day's pay' and focus on short-term (and usually monetary) exchanges. The relational contract 'focuses on open-ended relationships involving considerable investments by both employees (company-specific skills, long-term development) and employers (extensive training)' (*ibid*, p.91).

A useful typology is offered by Rousseau (Table 6.1), using the dimensions of time-frame and performance requirements, who (1995, p.98) says that four types of contract emerge 'with distinct behavioural implications for workers':

- transactional contracts – of limited duration with well-specified performance terms
- transitional or 'no-guarantees' condition – essentially a breakdown in contracts, reflecting the absence of commitments regarding future employment as well as little or no explicit performance demands or contingent incentives
- relational contracts – open-ended membership but with incomplete or ambiguous performance requirements attached to continued membership
- balanced contracts – open-ended and relationship-oriented employment with well-specified performance terms subject to change over time.

Table 6.1 Types of psychological contracts

	Performance terms	
Duration	**Specified**	**Not specified**
Short-term	*Transactional* (eg retail checkout operators employed during the Christmas season) • low ambiguity • easy exit/high turnover • low member commitment • freedom to enter new contracts • little learning • weak integration/identification	*Transitional* (eg employee experiences during organisational retrenchment or following merger or acquisition) • ambiguity/uncertainty • high turnover/termination • instability
Long-term	*Balanced* (eg high-involvement team) • high member commitment • high integration/identification • on-going development • mutual support • dynamic	*Relational* (eg family business members) • high member commitment • high affective commitment • high integration/identification • stability

Source: Rousseau, D. (1995) *Psychological Contracts in Organizations: Understanding written and unwritten agreements.* London: Sage, p.98

In other words, the 'psychological contract' is a term for describing what is implicit in terms of reciprocity and exchange within the employment relationship.

It is suggested (CIPD, 2005, p.3) that employers have been encouraged to take the psychological contract seriously due to changes ranging from the need for externalised workers to display functional flexibility, to the survivors of down-sizing carrying 'more weight', and 'human capital' becoming more critical to business performance.

IMPLICATIONS FOR HUMAN RESOURCE MANAGEMENT

The CIPD (2005, p.6) describes 'getting' commitment from employees by drawing on the motivators contained within Herzberg's two-factor theory, outlines what organisations 'need' to do, and draws attention to the importance of the line manager role, in these terms:

> Research suggests that in order to feel committed employees must feel satisfied with their work. Job satisfaction is more likely to be achieved where the employer offers employees what they want. Surveys consistently show that employees generally want interesting work, opportunities to develop, fair treatment and competent management. The line manager has a key role to play in maintaining commitment. Employers need to focus on tapping in to what employees are looking for and how they feel about their work. They need to involve and engage them. And they need to train line managers in how to manage people.

We might consider to what extent employers can indeed offer what employees want in many sectors of the economy. A flavour of the confidence to be found in some HR literature is provided by Hiltrop's (1996) reassurances, lack of doubt and claims for what employers must, need, and should do (Case study 6.6).

6.6 CASE STUDY

MANAGING THE CHANGING PSYCHOLOGICAL CONTRACT THROUGH REWARD

There is no doubt that increasing competition and changing expectations among employees have prompted a growing disillusionment with the traditional psychological contract based on lifetime employment and steady promotion from within. Consequently, companies must develop new ways to increase the loyalty and commitment of employees.

For instance, given the pressure to do things better, faster and cheaper, reward systems should recognise contribution rather than position or status. Reward strategies may also be used to rebuild commitment for survivors in downsizing organisations.

In addition, considering the shift towards decentralisation and empowerment, it is essential that individuals and groups are given more responsibility over salary decisions. Furthermore, rewards should be based on continuous performance and continuous improvement, rather than single events or past achievements.

Hiltrop, J.-M. (1996, pp36–49)

THE FLEXIBLE FIRM AND CONTINGENT WORKERS

Theories of the psychological contract have been built around full-time permanent employment and there is discussion about the extension of the concept to incorporate the experience of contingent workers. As Marchington *et al* (2005, p.78) point out:

> temporary agency workers attempt … to satisfy their obligations simultaneously to two employers – the agency and the client. This simultaneity raises questions about organisational commitment and loyalty.

Since commitment within the psychological contract is assumed to be based on 'volition', then lack of volition, and conflicts of loyalty, will have an effect on psychological contracting among contingent workers. We might expect non-permanent staff to show a more transactional approach, and show less commitment, than permanent staff. However, this is not necessarily the case according to McDonald and Makin (2000, p.89) who suggest that 'the observance and commitment to the norms, symbols, and rituals of desirable groups is often higher among those just outside, but wishing to join, the group than it is among established members'.

To what extent can we come to understand the concept of the psychological contract through examining its being breached or violated? Coyle-Shapiro and Kessler (2000) describe the situation in which the majority of employees have experienced contract breach, in a large local authority directly responsible and accountable for a range of public services including education, environmental health and social care to the local population. This view was also supported by managers, as representatives of the employer, who further indicated that the organisation, given its external pressures, was not fulfilling its obligations to employees to the extent that it could. Overall, the results indicate that employees redress the balance in the relationship through reducing their commitment and their willingness to engage in organisational citizenship behaviour when they perceive their employer has not fulfilled its part in the exchange process. See also the banking survey reviewed in Case study 6.10.

OLD AND NEW PSYCHOLOGICAL CONTRACTS

The terms of the new contract are still unclear, but Maguire (2002) – drawing from Kissler (1994) – presents a number of distinctions between the old and new psychological contract which are shown in Table 6.2.

As Maguire (2002, p.8) puts it:

> The key differences between the 'traditional' and the 'new' psychological contract relate to the decreased expectation of paternalistic human resource practices, the replacement of the concept of organisational worth with 'self-worth', the substitution of personal accomplishment for promotion as the route to growth, and the decreased importance of tenure.

6.7 ACTIVITY

Thinking about the organisation you work for or one with which you are familiar, to what extent is employment characterised by 'old' or new contracts?

Table 6.2 The distinction between 'old' and 'new' characteristics of psychological contracts

Old contract	New contract
Organisation is 'parent' to employee 'child'	Organisation and employee enter into 'adult' contracts focused on mutually beneficial work
Employees' identity and worth are defined by the organisation	Employees' identity and worth are defined by the employee
Those who stay are good and loyal; others are bad and disloyal	The regular flow of people in and out is healthy and should be celebrated
Employees who do what they are told will work until retirement	Long-term employment is unlikely; expect – and prepare for – multiple relationships
The primary route for growth is through promotion	The primary route for growth is a sense of personal accomplishment

The CIPD suggests (2005, p.4) that the 'old' psychological contract is 'in fact' still alive, and that surveys show the majority of employees feeling satisfied with, and not worried about losing, their jobs. However, these surveys also show there are concerns about long hours and work intensity, and levels of trust in the organisation have fallen, particularly in the public sector.

It is commonly heard that the 'old' psychological contract, with its emphasis on employment security, has been held to have been violated because of extensive downsizing among white-collar employees from the late 1980s and early 1990s (Mumford, 1995). This proposition has been examined by Beaumont and Harris (2002), using data from UK manufacturing industries for the years 1978 to

6.8 CASE STUDY

LOYALTY OF YOUNG WORKERS – EVIDENCE OF THE NEW PSYCHOLOGICAL CONTRACT?

Simon Caulkin reports on research by the Work Foundation on the motivation of the newest generation of workers, the 18- to 24-year-olds.

Employers need to understand better how Generation Y – as the Work Foundation researchers term them – differs from previous cohorts of workers, and what that means for employment policies. For young workers, the new implicit contract of employability, rather than a job for life, is the only one they have known. And they have learned its lessons fast. Accordingly, they have developed a much more instrumental approach to employment than their predecessors. They have high expectations of careers development and gaining early responsibility, and attach substantial importance to the employer's 'brand' – not just out of desire to work for a company that matches their own values but also with an eye to improving their CV.

The Work Foundation terms this 'gold-dusting' – buffing their record to attract other employers. Loyalty to the organisation lasts only as long as they are achieving personal goals.

Source: Caulkin, S. (2003) 'How to catch a rising star', *The Observer* Business pages, 9 November, p15; Guardian Newspapers Ltd

1995. The authors call into question the view that historically high and sustained downsizing among white-collar employees was a leading cause.

Examining the psychological contract in terms of the parties' fulfilment of their obligations to each other highlights gaps in what employees expect and receive from their employer as well as discrepancies in what employees feel they owe the employer and actually give. This is illustrated in the study reported in Case study 6.8.

6.9 ACTIVITY

In a study of a restructuring of the employment relationship in a home counties local authority, Kessler and Coyle-Shapiro report that employees saw the employer falling short in terms of pay and support for training, for example. And, from the other side of the bargain, they saw themselves 'over-giving' their working time (work having become more intense), delivering fairly in terms of in-job flexibility, and under-delivering in relation to movement between jobs (inter-job flexibility).

The study describes how the authority has sought to address these concerns through a 'new deal' with employees. In the area of pay, for example, there is a commitment to reach a new negotiated local agreement on pay and consideration and to get rid of PRP. In the area of training and development, there is an undertaking to introduce a corporate training and development strategy. Reviews on the causes of long-hours working and the workings of the internal market are promised. Finally, in relation to involvement, the authority pledges to introduce team briefing, a suggestion scheme and produce a corporate staff bulletin to replace different corporate information sheets (Kessler and Coyle-Shapiro 1998).

- Is it possible for organisations to repair a fractured psychological contract?
- How might it be done?

We can conclude that contextual factors are key to understanding the psychological contract. If the employer is felt to have breached the contract, then should we automatically assume that employee behaviour will necessarily be affected negatively? It seems that in times of high job insecurity, employees may be less inclined to display negative behavioural outcomes due to the power disparity between the employer and employee, or to fear of redundancy, although attitudes towards the employer will be changed, if not translated into action.

EMPOWERMENT

Downsized, de-layered, and lean organisational structures have led to more intensive workloads. Coupled with this trend is a hunt for more acceptable alternatives to close control and supervision in order to ensure the efficient running of the organisation – and so the individually empowered worker, self-regulating and self-motivated, is the focus of attention. And the persuasive concept of the customer-facing organisation also leads to the goal of empowerment, where committed employees demonstrate 'devolved

6.10 CASE STUDY

THE PSYCHOLOGICAL CONTRACT AND RETENTION

Roger Eglin, writing in the Sunday Times, *suggests that emotional ties – rather than just money – are vital in getting good managers to stay with their employers.*

A group of 476 Henley alumni were questioned about their relationship with their employers. Of the replies, 11% were couched in what are described as transactional terms, while a compelling 52% came down in favour of a relationship contract. 'They want a more effective relationship with issues such as aspiration, equity and community remaining important ... for those who have the talent and can make a choice this is what counts.'

With some jobs set to move to India, Barclays Bank has struck a deal with the Unity trade union to help those affected. But rather than losing people through redundancy, Barclays is offering them training-and-development opportunities to make them more 'marketable' within the Bank.

Source: Eglin, R. (2004) 'Cash is not king in holding on to staff', *Sunday Times* (London) appointments, 15 February, p7; Times Newspapers Ltd

decision-making' and 'self-management', contributing to a framework for 'high-performance working' (CIPD, 2004b). The concept of empowerment has been identified as a recent and advanced manifestation of employee involvement (see Chapter 3), with its advocates arguing that it is the answer to gaining improved organisational performance. The universal core to accounts of empowerment is that it confers greater responsibility and accountability to low-level employees (Block, 1987; Klagge, 1998). In turn, employees are to experience enhanced job satisfaction and commitment, in an environment characterised by trust and greater tolerance of well-intentioned errors, teamwork and enhanced training.

Empowerment can be seen as a flexible and even elastic term: 'a poorly defined concept' (Greasley *et al*, 2008, p.40). According to Lashley (1995), there is a tendency in the existing literature to lump together all the various forms of empowerment, identified by Wilkinson (1998) as: information-sharing, upward problem-solving, task autonomy, attitudinal shaping, and self-management.

Greasley *et al* (2008, pp41–2) distinguish psychological and structural dimensions of empowerment:

> Structural empowerment refers to organisational policies, practices and structures that grant employees greater latitude to make decisions and exert influence regarding their work ... [and] the psychological empowerment perspective ... instead emphasises employees' perceptions and cognitions.

These authors refer to definitions of empowerment as 'increased intrinsic task motivation' and outline four cognitions that are claimed to be the basis of worker empowerment:

- meaningfulness (of a task goal or purpose judged in relation to an individual's own ideals or standards)

- competence (individual belief in the capability to perform task activities skilfully)
- self-determination or choice (autonomy in the initiation and continuation of work behaviours and processes)
- impact (the perception of the degree to which an individual can influence certain outcomes at work).

Turning to the espoused benefits of empowerment, Greasley *et al* (2008, p.43) suggest that:

> despite the strong support for empowerment in theory, in practice empowerment may exist in rhetoric only and control is reality for employees ... [Thus] the benefits of empowerment should not be assumed to automatically occur, nor should the rhetoric of empowerment be confused with the reality.

Elsewhere, the concept can be seen in terms of 'cocktails of control' (Collins,

6.11 CASE STUDY

NHS TRUST HOSPITALS

In recent years, empowerment of National Health Service (NHS) Trust employees has been given substantial political and managerial support. Cunningham and Hyman's (1996) study examined the extent to which the commitment and morale of staff in two NHS Trust hospitals had altered following the introduction of a raft of techniques under the empowerment label, designed to secure employee commitment.

Empowerment policies included:

- improved communications
- the development of effective management training programmes
- the phasing in of Trust-wide appraisal systems
- customer care initiatives such as the 'named nurse' scheme
- training in customer awareness for all staff.

Management and non-management employees were to:

- undergo significant changes in responsibilities and accountability.

Line managers were to receive devolved responsibility for:

- day-to-day management of human resources
- the control of costs.

Line managers also needed to:

- alter skill mix and reduce demarcations among staff that would make it possible to call on their commitment to achieve improvements in standards of care.

This was to be achieved through:

- delegating responsibilities down the line to staff, who, in turn, were expected to take more responsibility in their everyday work and rely less on management instruction.

Human resource/personnel departments were to:

- provide a support mechanism for line managers
- devise and implement the employee relations policies (described above).

Results were:

- the work of both managers and staff became more intensive
- over 70% of line management respondents in each Trust indicated that their workloads had increased substantially in three years
- a similar proportion of managers indicated that they had acquired significantly more responsibility over the same period
- managers reported that their workloads had particularly increased in the areas of employee relations and control of budgets
- managers claimed that their commitment had risen
- for non-managerial employees, severe problems of commitment to the organisation, declining morale, and high stress were exposed
- the overwhelming experience of non-management employees was of work intensification.

Reasons identified:

- the impact of budgetary and operational priorities
- lack of training
- resistance to the implementation of empowerment
- recognition that little real authority was being devolved to employees.

Conclusions

The limited effects attributable to empowerment could be explained by its association with harder-edged manpower policies introduced to meet financial and competitive pressures. The authors add their view, that under favourable contextual conditions, empowerment may exert more positive effects.

Source: Cunningham, I. and Hyman, J. (1996) 'Empowerment: the right medicine for improving employee commitment and morale in the NHS?', *Health Manpower Management*, Vol.22, No.6, pp14–24

1996, p.29). As we see in Case study 6.11, empowerment can be associated with increased intensification of work.

The significant role of managers in the implementation of HR policies has been identified previously (Hutchinson and Purcell, 2003), and here the success of empowerment initiatives similarly can rest upon managers' responses. The consequences of empowerment initiatives on the real lives of middle managers have been seen in the language of 'acted compliance' (Denham *et al*, 1997), reminding us of Sennett's (1998) 'superficial co-operativeness'. In contrast, views of concord and harmony in middle management are to be found elsewhere, and where discord occurs it can be explained away in terms of 'missed leadership' (Klagge, 1998).

CONCLUSION

Organisations concentrate upon meeting the needs of their stakeholders:

shareholders and customers in the private sector; government and service users – now increasingly 'customerised' – in the public sector. Responsiveness to the 'whip' of the market, previously a private sector concern, is now increasingly required in the public sector as it becomes 'marketised'. The organisation and its workers, internal or external, core or contingent, are required to focus on performing.

Agile response is the order of the day as time-frames are shortened, and so flexibility is sought, from collective and structural flexibility to individual and behavioural. As organisations are re-engineered, and downsized, and spans of control are increased, management attention is devoted to 'empowering' the worker, without losing control. To better understand the discretionary element of employment relationships, the psychological contract, and its management, has become a focus of attention.

6.12 THEORY TASTER

SENNETT AND THE NEW ECONOMY

In his book, *The Corrosion of Character* (1998), Richard Sennett examines the consequences for workers of the need for organisations to operate in highly competitive markets. He suggests that the flexibility they need to display, the willingness to accept change, and the loss of security that results can have damaging effects on personal character.

Character, he argues, is an emotional experience that involves loyalty, mutual commitment and the pursuit of long-term goals. As society pursues immediate needs and businesses seek to respond to the consequent short-term goals, organisations find themselves regularly needing to restructure and redesign. In such a new economy he suggests that character traits are damaged with negative effects on workers' morale and motivation. People thus co-operate but without any underlying commitment: 'superficial co-operativeness'.

It seems that the air is filled with managerial information and messages, suggesting what might or should be done. There are confident, sometimes strident, assertions and claims, based on research findings and examples of what appears to be best practice, and some of these might remind us of Pollert's (1991) 'desperate search for panaceas'. Amongst this traffic it is possible to detect weaker signals, describing increasing intensification of work and workers feeling pressurised. Where there

6.13 DISCUSSION QUESTIONS

1 Critically assess the respective advantages and disadvantages to organisations and to employees of the different forms of workplace flexibility.

2 Identify and evaluate the specific actions that managers can take that will improve employees' psychological contract with the organisation.

3 Is empowerment anything more than just another management fad that will soon be replaced by something new? Give reasons for your view.

EXPLORE FURTHER

A good description of the various forms of flexibility is provided in Pilbeam, S. and Corbridge, M. (2006) *People Resourcing: Contemporary HRM in practice*, 3rd edition. Harlow: FT/ Prentice Hall.

Sennett's account of the social consequences of flexibility is recommended to all readers: Sennett, R. (1998) *The Corrosion of Character: The personal consequences of work in the new capitalism*. London: Norton.

For a comprehensive account of the psychological contract, readers are referred to the seminal work of Rousseau, D. (1995) *Psychological Contracts in Organizations: Understanding written and unwritten agreements*. London: Sage. Rousseau laid the foundations for much study. Her more recent articles and books are well worth reading for those interested in examining the development of this topic.

A flavour of the empowerment material can be obtained from Block, P. (1987) *The Empowered Manager: Positive political skills at work*. San Francisco: Jossey-Bass. This is an old text, but undertaking a 'cited reference' search will allow you to track the development of this field to the present day.

CHAPTER 7

Performance Management, Motivation and Reward

Gary Rees and Mark Lowman

LEARNING OUTCOMES

After reading this chapter, you should be able to:

- understand the assumptions that underpin the application of performance management (PM)
- identify the different ways that PM can be defined and interpreted by organisations
- recognise the contribution of organisational theory, industrial engineering and behavioural science systems to the development of PM
- understand the relationship between performance, motivation and reward
- evaluate the extent to which PM can assist in improving organisational effectiveness and efficiency.

INTRODUCTION TO PERFORMANCE MANAGEMENT

The changing environment for organisations requires new products and services, new organisational structures and systems, and hence new competencies and working practices for employees. Increasing competition and ever-greater demands from customers, investors and government mean that 'high performance' has become a requirement for organisational success (Boxall and Purcell, 2003). Against this background of increasing change and higher performance requirements, how can organisations ensure that employees understand the part they play in achieving organisational objectives, and have the required skills, knowledge and attitudes to do so? How can performance be optimised and the required business outcomes achieved? This is the challenge of PM. Chapter 6 examined a number of key practices that are claimed to enhance organisational effectiveness. In this chapter we build on these and consider the concept of PM and its implications for managing and leading employees.

Performance management can be defined within an organisational context (Institute of Personnel Management [now the CIPD], 1992, p.1) as:

> A strategy which relates to every activity of the organisation set in the context of its human resources policies, culture, style and communications systems. The nature of the strategy depends on the organisational context and can vary from organisation to organisation.

The above definition highlights the fact that all activities within an organisation are contributing in some way – either positively or negatively – to performance and so PM can be viewed holistically, as 'running the business' (Mohrman and Mohrman, 1995). Performance management is a shared responsibility of all employees and a core management activity rather than just a personnel system. However, there is no one 'best practice' for managing performance and the overall approach adopted must be contingent upon the particular organisational setting and the individuals involved. It is about maximising organisational effectiveness within the current and changing context (Jones, 1995). Having said this, there are a number of overlapping HR management policies and practices that together form the basis for a PM process. These might be formal or informal.

The PM process includes the alignment of objectives and performance through measurement, assessment and monitoring. Where there is a gap between objectives and performance, appropriate HR supporting mechanisms are required (Figure 7.1).

Figure 7.1 Human resource supporting mechanisms

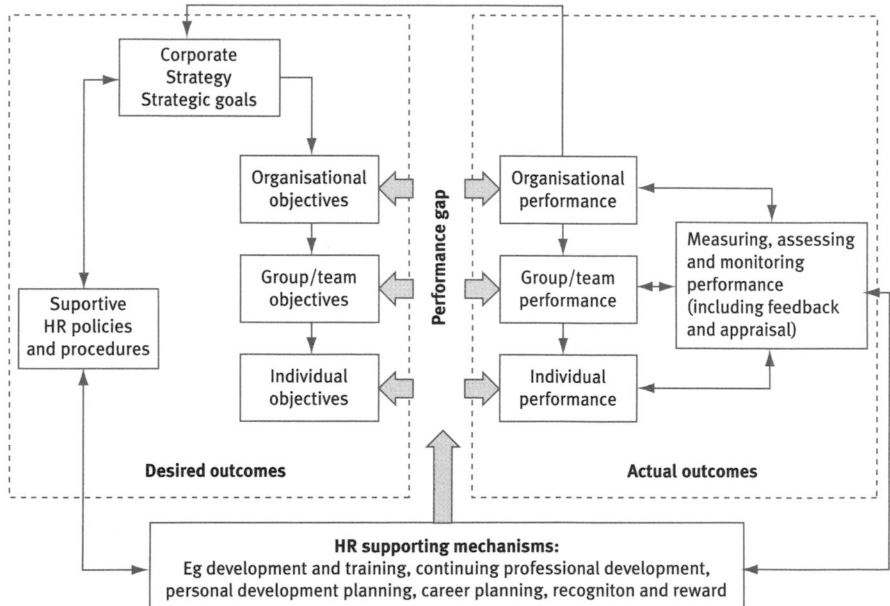

Some form of performance appraisal is central to PM (Fletcher, 2004), whether it be self-appraisal, appraisal by line or project management, appraisal by peers, or even appraisal by subordinates. This appraisal can be very simple and informal as part of 'a natural process of management' (Fowler, 1990) or a more structured, formal framework.

Performance appraisal is most often undertaken with the aim of improving performance, motivating employees and/or allocating rewards. An honest and accurate assessment of current performance can be a strong driver for further learning, development and performance improvement. The process of performance feedback and the setting of improvement targets can itself be a strong motivator (Locke and Latham, 1990), and for there to be equitable distribution of rewards some fair method of comparing contributions between individuals is required. Otherwise, unfair systems will fall into what Herzberg termed 'hygiene factors' and be demotivators (Mullins, 2007).

Appraisal methods can be divided into two main approaches: those oriented towards results (outputs), and those oriented towards competencies (inputs). Results-oriented appraisal is based on the setting of quantifiable, achievable and time-bounded objectives, most often in a participative process between manager and subordinate, and geared to achieving organisational objectives. Competency-oriented appraisal takes a different approach, with assessment based on the demonstration of certain key skills and behaviours thought to be associated with high performance. The trend is towards combining both results- and competency-based approaches in an attempt to deliver the dual benefits of achieving immediate performance targets and supporting longer-term development of key skills and capabilities.

In addition, PM systems differ in the emphasis they give to rewards or development. The trend is for increasing emphasis on development rather than reward, and de-emphasising the link between PM and pay in particular (Armstrong and Baron, 2005). There is also a move away from purely performance-related or competence-related pay and towards 'contribution-related' pay, which takes into account all aspects of an individual's contribution, including both performance (results) and competence (Brown and Armstrong, 1999). This mirrors the similar trend seen in appraisal methods, as described above.

Performance management and development are overlapping and interdependent processes. Performance reviews, whether they are periodic appraisals or continuous, day-to-day interactions between managers and employees, provide encouragement and substance for learning and development. This might be as informal training, self-managed learning by the individual employee, coaching by the manager, or more structured training and development interventions. Whatever the form, development is intended to have a direct impact on performance capabilities and can also have a powerful motivational effect (Tamkin *et al*, 1995).

Reconciling PM as a developmental process and as a pay decision-making process is not straightforward. That closely linking performance appraisal to pay reduces the focus on development and performance improvement is well understood (Kessler and Purcell, 1992). A perhaps more fundamental issue is whether extrinsic rewards such as pay and other recognition schemes may actually decrease long-term intrinsic motivation and so have a detrimental affect on performance. It has been argued that any competitive reward scheme creates many more 'losers' than 'winners' (Kohn, 1993), and there is some evidence for the potential negative performance impacts of contingent pay schemes in practice (Marsden and French, 1998).

Effective PM is not only dependent upon what is done but also upon how it is done. Purcell *et al* (2003) provide research evidence to support the proposition that no one particular HR practice is critical to organisational success, but good management by line managers, applying various approaches effectively and appropriately according to the context, is the key factor. Committed and capable line managers are, therefore, essential to successful PM (Hutchinson and Purcell, 2003). Again, the emphasis is on PM as a shared, organisation-wide activity.

It has been proposed that four ethical principles should be applied to PM: respect for the individual, mutual respect, procedural fairness, and transparency of decision-making (Winstanley and Stuart-Smith, 1996). Here, too, there is an emphasis on how things are done and not just what is done. Procedural fairness (or fair process) is important because it builds trust and commitment. Trust and commitment lead to 'voluntary co-operation' with individuals going the extra mile in sharing knowledge and ideas (Kim and Mauborgne, 1997), or demonstrating 'discretionary behaviour' beyond the formal requirements of the job (Purcell *et al*, 2003).

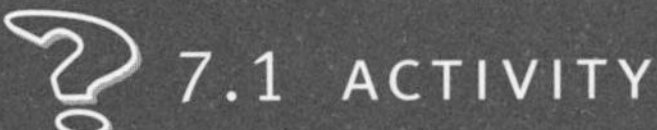

Provide illustrations of the practical application of the four ethical principles that underpin PM.

There is increasing evidence that PM can have a positive impact on employee commitment and organisational performance (Fletcher and Williams, 1996; Guest, 1997). However, evidence is not universally positive, and some studies suggest performance appraisal and pay to be the least effective HR policies, as perceived by the employees (Hutchinson and Purcell, 2003). This mixed picture probably reflects the spectrum of different PM approaches adopted across organisations. Rather than adopting mechanistic off-the-shelf approaches, organisations must fit whatever they do to their current and future context. For example, organisations must consider how appropriate reward strategies fit within their context. The CIPD reward management survey (CIPD, 2003d) showed that organisations seem to be moving more towards flexible benefit packages, thereby allowing staff to make some choices that suit their personal circumstances and preferences. The same argument applies to appraisal, with organisations moving away from top-down descriptive systems to more participative, self-evaluative and developmental approaches.

PERSPECTIVES ON PERFORMANCE MANAGEMENT

Performance management can be viewed as a technique or tool to enhance performance, but tends to go well beyond that in practice. The range of factors that could be attributed to PM depend upon the perspective adopted.

'CONTROLLING' PERFORMANCE

From a managerial perspective, in which a manager has to ensure the most effective and efficient use of resources (including people) in achieving business objectives, PM can be seen as an issue of control and manipulation.

The assumption underlying this perspective of PM is that the organisation, in the form of a manager, can make a positive impact upon an individual's work performance. Within this assumption, managers are expected to demonstrate both general management skills as well as skills directly related to the PM process. The latter could include task skills such as objective-setting, understanding technical aspects of the job, monitoring progress and measuring results. General management skills, in contrast, could include leadership, mentoring, coaching, and interpersonal relationships. Managers may demonstrate strong task skills but are often lacking confidence in the softer interpersonal and social skills (Bowles and Coates, 1993).

The managerial perspective also assumes a hierarchy of control, with a direct relationship between manager and subordinate. This is more difficult to achieve in complex organisational structures, such as multi-dimensional matrix structures. For example, a subordinate may report to several different line managers, who are all based in different locations. The control aspect of PM is legitimised through the perceived objectivity of the process. This objectivity then becomes the driving force for achieving performance outputs (Levinson, 1970; 1976).

THE ETERNAL TRIANGLE

Herzberg (1968) presents the eternal triangle perspective, whereby there are three general philosophies of personnel (or HR) management – namely, organisational theory, industrial engineering and behavioural science.

The organisational theorists (Weber, 1947) believe that human needs are either so irrational or so varied and adjustable that personnel management has to be as pragmatic as the occasion demands. Herzberg cites the example of job design, where, if jobs are organised in a proper manner, the result will be the most efficient job structure, and the most favourable attitudes will follow. Whereas, within the eternal triangle theory, the industrial engineers (Taylor, 1911) believe that humankind is mechanistically oriented and economically motivated, and we must therefore attune the individual to the most efficient working process. Here we need to design the most appropriate incentive system and design the most appropriate working system for the human machine. Behavioural scientists (Schein, 1984) focus on group sentiments, attitudes of individual employees and the organisation's social and psychological climate, with the emphasis on instilling healthy employee attitudes and appropriate organisational climate. This model illustrates a useful analogy for the use and possible misuse of PM as means to improve performance in organisations.

ALIGNING INDIVIDUAL AND ORGANISATIONAL NEEDS

We need to consider the fundamental framework of fitting the person to the job or the job to the person, because the outcome of this may affect the type of factors that impact upon PM. Traditionally, PM concerns itself with the cascading of jobs (tasks) through the organisation, marrying the person to the job.

The question then arises as to how much attention is given to the individual in the process. Levinson (1970) argues that the key factor in PM's success will be whether it manages to align the individual and organisation's requirements. This means establishing the individual's psychological needs, rather than merely assuming them. Mismatches of the psychological contract may result in individuals leaving a particular job or the organisation altogether at considerable cost to the organisation. The benefits of matching individual and organisational needs may be in the form of greater commitment, more harmonious working relationships, more successful development of the individual and greater performance outputs.

STAKEHOLDER BENEFIT

Other stakeholders, such as shareholders, customers and employees, will have their own views on performance achievements and these different views may be contradictory. The different parties involved have different perspectives, expectations and experience of performance. For example, shareholders are interested in long-term value of stocks and assets. Management have an interest in protecting and advancing their own position, power and rewards. Customers are increasingly demanding high-quality customised products and services. Employees may have a variety of expectations, including job security, fair remuneration, recognition, status, personal training and development opportunities.

In addition, all of these stakeholders may adopt different roles at different times or have multiple, simultaneous roles. Therefore, far from being objective and commonly agreed, performance and how it should be managed is primarily value-judgemental and subject to potentially competing interests.

7.2 ACTIVITY

Thinking about any organisation with which you are familiar, identify those aspects of staff management which seem to be consistent with performance management. Which of the four perspectives do they reflect?

THE NATURE OF PERFORMANCE

HOW CAN WE DEFINE PERFORMANCE?

There is no single, universal definition of performance. The definition of performance depends very much on the particular perspective adopted. For example, some definitions of performance relate to the organisation and various expectations in terms of outputs (Bernadin *et al*, 1995):

> Performance should be defined as the outcomes of work because they provide the strongest linkage to the strategic goals of the organisation, customer satisfaction, and economic contributions.

Other definitions emphasise behavioural aspects, in addition to outputs or results (Brumbach, 1988, p.389):

> Performance means both behaviours and results. Behaviours emanate from the performer and transform performance from abstraction to action. Not just the instruments for results, behaviours are also outcomes in their own right – the product of mental and physical effort applied to tasks – and can be judged apart from results.

There are also psychological and employee-centred views, such as that of Appelbaum *et al* (2000), where 'performance' is a function of employee ability, motivation and opportunity.

WHO DEFINES PERFORMANCE?

It is not only a question of how performance is defined but also of who within the organisation is, or are, responsible for defining performance standards. Often, it is the organisation itself that determines performance and how it will be measured. Performance requirements are part of a strategic planning process, cascading top-down through the organisation from senior management (Humble, 1972). However, this does not have to be the case. Semler (1993) describes a bottom-up approach, where employees at Semco were allowed to set their own performance targets and define appropriate rewards. There is also the possibility of a combined top-down and bottom-up approach, with mutual adjustment of goals and objectives (Nonaka and Takeuchi, 1995). Alternative approaches to the traditional superior–subordinate appraisal are available, including 360-degree appraisal, peer appraisal, self-appraisal and team-based appraisal (Fletcher, 2004). There is a tendency towards more multi-level and multi-source feedback systems. This more integrated approach may help to overcome some of the problems inherent in defining performance and performance standards, as described above.

Fundamentally, though, for the organisation to succeed, someone, somewhere has to combine the targets to ensure that the organisational objectives are indeed being met. This is a line management responsibility, but HR might have to ensure and empower that process taking place. If it is not achieved, then the organisation's future may be at risk.

WHAT ASPECTS OF PERFORMANCE CAN BE MEASURED?

It is impossible to measure all aspects of an employee's performance. Similarly, there are areas that will prove difficult to measure in themselves. For example, how does an organisation measure knowledge creation and use, or creativity and innovation? What an organisation chooses to measure depends on the PM framework adopted within the organisational context. This depends on what the organisation values in its employees. To what extent is learning valued as part of the PM process, for example? However, one must be sure that if something is valued, it should also be measured (Johnson and Scholes, 2002), because measuring is a mechanism for communicating that a particular activity is valued.

Performance management systems typically rely on setting of goals and targets, which are themselves definable, and can be measured through primarily quantitative means (Levinson, 1970; 1976). This could be an objective to increase sales by 7% on last year's figures, for example. The question of objectivity relates to qualitative measures as well as these 'quantitative' measures. Similarly, PM assumes explicit performance measures and cannot always incorporate tacit inputs, throughputs and outputs at individual, group and organisational levels. The temporal argument relating to PM has to be considered in order to make an accurate assessment of performance. Performance targets are typically set in time and the time-scale might in itself affect accurate measurement. How does one allow for long-term performance improvements and outcomes within an annual appraisal cycle, for example? The critical issue then becomes when we measure and record performance.

Armstrong and Baron (2007) argue that performance management data can be derived from the outcomes of performance reviews and 360-degree assessments. Examples of the usefulness of the data can relate to levels of capability, readiness for promotion or job expansion, the match between required and actual behaviour and competence levels. Armstrong and Baron (2007, p.111) argue that performance management data can be used to:

- demonstrate an organisation's ability to raise competence levels
- assess how long it takes for a new employee to reach optimum performance
- provide feedback on development programmes, including induction, coaching and mentoring in terms of increased performance or capacity to take on new roles
- demonstrate the success of internal recruitment programmes
- indicate how successful an organisation is at achieving its objectives at the individual, team and department level
- track skills levels and movement in any skills gap in the organisation
- match actual behaviour against desired behaviour
- assess commitment to values and mission
- assess understanding of strategy and contribution.

Although PM may emphasise the individual, the increasingly interdependent nature of work, and the consequent emphasis on team and groups, makes measurement more challenging. It is not just individual performance that is important but also the contribution that the individual makes towards group effort, and the combined output of the group as a whole.

MEASUREMENT AT WHAT COST?

Performance measurement is not without potentially significant costs in terms of staff time and administration. Not only are implementation costs to be considered but also the long-term maintenance costs of any PM system once established. To what extent do organisations consider the total costs of the PM system versus the impacts, both positive and negative, on performance outcomes? An example would be the internal focus of systems within the automotive manufacturing industry, where the needs of customers were ignored to the long-term harm of the organisation. Organisations may assume that a PM system will have a positive impact, but any improvement must be offset against the – often substantial – costs of running the system itself.

7.3 CASE STUDY

ROYAL BANK OF SCOTLAND

The Royal Bank of Scotland has recently launched an online toolkit for its HR staff. Providing resources such as surveys, measurement, research and benchmarking against other organisations on people management issues, it is designed to measure the effectiveness of the Bank's HR strategy and its influence on business performance.

To complement this initiative the company has established a Human Capital Board, comprised of business and HR directors. Its role will be to prioritise people management policies and practices.

In recognition of the key role of line managers in enhancing employee performance, the Bank intends to provide line managers with a concise version of the toolkit.

Source: Czerny, A. (2005, p.9)

To think about ...

What are the benefits and drawbacks of providing HR staff *but not line managers* with performance management data?

FACTORS AFFECTING PERFORMANCE

If the industrial engineering approach presented by Herzberg is adopted, we simply have to define performance and performance standards. Following this, performance gaps are analysed and performance measured against the standards. A pragmatic approach may simply ask whether an individual has carried out their job and role to the appropriate level, and whether they can continue to do so. In order to understand the effectiveness of how the individual carries out their role (the expected set of behaviours associated with the job), behavioural and psychological factors must be assessed as well. In other words, we need to incorporate elements of the behavioural scientists' approach, as described above.

There are inexhaustible reasons why people do not perform to standard, some of which are outlined in Figure 7.2.

The critical issue is determining not just which of these factors (and others perhaps) affect performance, but the combination or prioritisation of these factors.

To take understanding further we need to attempt to answer the question not just what affects performance, but how and why people's performance is affected.

Figure 7.2 A summary of factors affecting performance

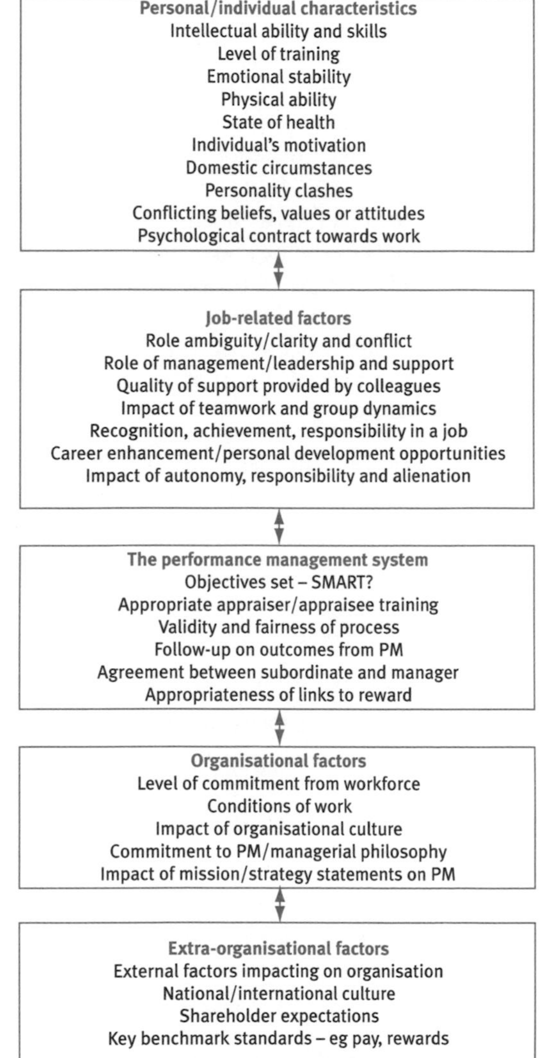

The CIPD Performance Management Survey Report (2005, p.2) found that 75% of those companies surveyed agreed that performance management motivates individuals, with 22% disagreeing.

HOW DOES MOTIVATION AFFECT PERFORMANCE?

Traditional motivation theories from both the content and process perspectives suggest that there is a strong link between motivation and performance (Herzberg, 1968; Maslow, 1943; Porter and Lawler, 1968). In order to explore this link, we need to understand the nature of motivation. From a selfish perspective the individual employee may simply ask 'What is in it for me?' 'Why should I perform differently or harder?'

What concrete evidence is there that motivation is linked to performance? Taking another perspective, does a lack of motivation affect performance? When considering the content theories of motivation, there are clear hygiene factors, such as working conditions, salary and security, which, if not fulfilled, may lead to performance being adversely affected. Although people strive to achieve goals, this may not represent the entirety of their motivations. Factors such as inequity are demonstrated with expectancy models of motivation, such as Porter and Lawler (1968), but how motivational forces are affected by the intervention of inequities or realignment of goals has to be considered. Assuming the industrial engineering model of goals and needs, then people will strive to achieve the desired goal consciously and in a planned way. However, it is difficult to establish to what extent employee behaviour typically follows this planned route, and to what extent an annual appraisal might ensure that employees consciously address organisational goals on a daily basis.

It could be argued that much of motivational theory is outdated and needs to be adapted to meet modern organisational contexts. Nohria, Groysberg and Lee (2008) argue that employee motivation is linked to drives that employees have. Their research suggests that four basic emotional needs or drives shape motivation. The four drives are:

- to acquire – by obtaining scarce goods or intangibles such as social status
- to bond – by forming connections with individuals and groups
- to comprehend – by satisfying our curiosity and mastering the world around us
- to defend – by protecting against external threats and promoting justice.

Nohria *et al* (2008) argues that these drives underlie everything that we do.

The question that is then raised is how managers can take action to satisfy these four drives and thereby increase employees' overall motivation.

Figure 7.3 How to fulfil the drives that motivate employees

Source: Nohria, N., Groysberg, B. and Lee, L.-E. (2008) 'Employee motivation: a powerful new model', *Harvard Business Review*, July–August, p.82. Reproduced with permission.

Nohria *et al* (2008, p.80) argue that in previous research studies,

> an organisation's ability to meet the four fundamental drives explains, on average, about 60% of employees' variance on motivational indicators (previous models have explained about 30%).

Each of the four drives is considered independent, and cannot be ordered hierarchically or substituted for one another. Nohria *et al* (2008) argue that each drive is best met by an organisational lever, as shown in Figure 7.3.

HOW SUSTAINABLE IS PERFORMANCE MANAGEMENT?

One of the dangers of a PM system is that it creates movement (Herzberg, 1968), but not motivation.The carrot can be offered as a means of making the donkey move, and due to the nature of the reward itself (the carrot), the donkey will move. However, the primary means of making the donkey move again may mean offering another carrot (or an equivalent stimulus). Organisations may have difficulty offering continued rewards, often increasing in 'value' in order to move the employee. During times of economic hardship this may prove particularly difficult. The critical question for employers is how to recruit, select and retain employees who are self-motivated to achieve organisational goals. Organisations need to create an environment conducive to meeting employees' needs and expectations, as defined by a healthy psychological contract. These themes are examined in more detail in Chapter 9 and Chapter 6 respectively.

WHAT HAPPENS AFTER PERFORMANCE MANAGEMENT?

If a standard formal appraisal interview occurs with the appraisee, a range of actions or options is available to superiors and subordinates alike. As we have suggested already, there may be a portfolio of approaches that interact within the PM process, such as 360-degree feedback, self-appraisal, upward appraisal, coaching and mentoring interventions, etc.

Companies may operate a system of forced ranking, or forced distribution, whereby groups of employees are compared against each other and ranked from best to worst, instead of being judged against independent performance standards. Although this approach is more common with appraising managers, it can be applied to any area of work. Employees who are placed in the lowest category (for example, the lowest 5%) may be dismissed from the organisation or given a fixed time to improve their current performance to the expected organisational standards. Conversely, the top-performing employees may be provided with significant learning opportunities, career growth and perhaps significant financial and personal rewards (Boyle, 2001).

As we indicated earlier, perhaps one of the more contentious areas for debate lies within the issue of whether to link pay and performance. Heneman (1992, p.258) argues that 'the results to date on the relationship between merit pay and subsequent motivation and performance are not encouraging', and this view is supported by Williams (1998, p.172) who reports that 'there is negligible evidence of a rigorous kind which supports the positive benefits commonly claimed for merit pay.'

As both performance and motivation are affected by many factors, performance-related pay (PRP) (or any other intervention) cannot be linked in a causal manner. Williams (1998, p.173) argues that managers' and employees' views have to be considered in order to analyse the effect of PRP on motivation and performance. While the debate of PRP or not PRP goes on, it is worth considering some of the operational difficulties that have been associated with reward practice. The following set of questions has been raised by Williams (1998, p.176) and adapted to fit the categories provided:

With regard to organisational culture, teams and individual attitudes to PRP:

- Is PRP appropriate to all organisations?
- Is there a climate of trust (particularly in line manager–subordinate relations)?
- What effect does PRP have on team and co-operative building?
- Does a focus on individual performance lead employees to place self-interest ahead of those of the organisation generally?
- Does PRP create divisiveness?
- Does PRP encourage short-termism?

He similarly raises questions about the PM process itself:

- What criteria should be used for measuring performance? Outputs? Inputs? Both?
- Can individual performance be measured objectively and fairly?
- Can performance be defined comprehensively?
- Do line managers have the willingness and ability required to operate PRP?
- How much of performance is within the individual's control?
- How should average performers be treated?
- Can PRP give rise to unlawful discrimination?

Questions related to the value of rewards must also be addressed:

- What amount of pay constitutes a significant increase in the eyes of employees?
- Will PRP diminish the value of intrinsic rewards?

It may be relatively simple to provide an answer to each of these individual questions. However, when considered together, the complexity of linking PRP to performance becomes much more evident. Thus simple, prescriptive solutions cannot be found.

HOW IS PERFORMANCE IMPROVED?

Dependent upon the source(s) of the performance problem outlined in the previous section, the organisation must decide on the type and scope of problem intervention. There may have to be consideration of the macro-level issues affecting the broader organisational context, or attention given to micro-level individual issues.

Some of the techniques available include:

- learning
- development
- training
- coaching, mentoring
- team-building
- culture change programmes
- reward schemes
- structure, process, systems, job redesign, etc
- management approach.

According to the CIPD viewpoint (CIPD, 2004d, p.1), the keys to successful introduction and application of PM are:

- being clear about what is meant by performance
- understanding what the organisation is and needs to be in its performance culture
- being very focused on how individual employees will benefit and play their part in the process
- understanding that it is a tool for line managers and its success will depend on their ability to use it effectively.

THE FUTURE OF PERFORMANCE MANAGEMENT

Perhaps the 'expiry date' of the philosophy of fitting people to jobs, expecting them to do their jobs and be compliant with organisation needs, is close. If organisations expect employees to act as business partners and business performers, then perhaps they need to have more involvement in the running of the business. If employers expect employees to think for themselves, then by definition, they have to delegate, trust, nurture and develop (all) employees.

The question of equal treatment for all employees also has to be taken into account. Harrison and Kessels (2004) discuss the notion of the 'knowledge worker' and the 'non-knowledge worker', a point further emphasised by Drucker (1993), who differentiates between knowledge workers who contribute to the core of the economic activity in a knowledge-intensive organisation, and service workers who facilitate that contribution. Implicit in these descriptions is the understanding that some employees contribute more than others to the success of the organisation, and they should be managed and rewarded accordingly, receiving a proportionately higher amount of management time, resources, recognition and reward.

Apart from the employer perspective, employee expectations continue to change. Arnold (1996) argues that the traditional working relationship has changed, with a movement away from the old to new deals, as illustrated in Theory Taster 7.4.

7.4 THEORY TASTER

CONTENT AND PROCESS THEORIES OF MOTIVATION

Understanding what motivates workers is a key aspect of management that can assist in the development of high-performance work organisations. The many theories associated with the concept are typically divided into two approaches: content theories and process theories.

Content theories seek to identify people's needs at work and how they seek to achieve them. Managers have to understand the variety of needs that workers have, and seek to design work in ways that will help satisfy them.

Herzberg's two-factor theory is one example of a content theory – see Theory Taster 6.1.

Process theories on the other hand, seek to understand the – often complex – relationship between the many variables that go to make up motivation. Managers need to understand what initiates behaviour, and how it is directed and sustained. Such theories are often, therefore, more complex than content theories. Adams's equity theory (see Theory Taster 3.5) is an example of a process theory.

Under the new deal, what are the implications for PM, and does the archetypal individual match the 'knowledge worker' analogy described above? Although there may not be a universally accepted definition of a knowledge worker, they need to generate knowledge that adds value to the organisation. Harrison and Kessels (2004) further argue that 'knowledge workers form a vital part of the knowledge economy, and it is logical to predict that they will pay increasing attention to their own employability and economic attractiveness as they become more aware of their market value'. From a human resource development perspective, the emphasis should be on developing people rather than on the job itself. However, the challenge for employers may be in retaining employees for the duration of their most productive work (while they add value) and no longer.

CONCLUSION

The HR strategy has to encompass all aspects affecting performance, at contextual, organisational, team and individual level. To do this, it has to be part of the main business strategy, closely aligned to organisational culture and supported by appropriate mechanisms such as organisational structure, HR policies and procedures, and be strongly aligned to the HRD strategy.

More flexible and fluid arrangements are necessary, within which there is a greater appreciation of the subjective, tacit, multi-stakeholder aspects of performance. From a more strategic perspective, the resource-based view of HR (Boxall, 1996; Boxall and Purcell, 2003) suggests ways in which organisations can build upon unique clusters or 'bundles' of human and technical resources in order to improve levels of performance and thereby achieve competitive advantage in the marketplace. The agility highlighted by Dyer and Shafer (1999) and adapted by Boxall and Purcell (2003, p.202) may provide an insight as to how organisations can use PM within a bundle of HR activities, as shown in Figure 7.4.

Figure 7.4 Dyer and Shafer's model of HR strategy in agile organisations

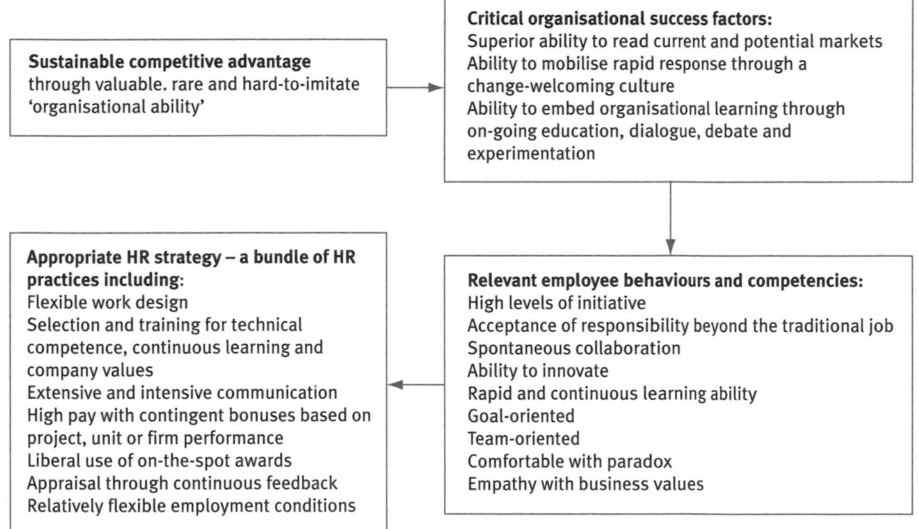

Source: As summarised by Boxall P. and Purcell J. (2003) *Strategy and Human Resource Management*. Basingstoke: Palgrave Macmillan, p.202. Used with permission of the publisher

The significance of maintaining competitive advantage is further highlighted in a CIPD Report (CIPD, 2003e), where it is argued that organisations need to strive to be knowledge-intensive firms. The report's findings stated that, among other factors, PM is central to the success of knowledge-intensive firms.

Performance management may contribute to the success of the firm, but the vital issue is how the talents of employees can be retained, developed and utilised so as to add value to the organisation. Although we may concentrate on the output measurement from PM and deal with its consequences, the question to be answered is 'How do we increase performance?' The answer may take us back to developing and nurturing the organisation's greatest asset – employees: a theme developed in Chapter 10.

7.5 DISCUSSION QUESTIONS

1 Is PM anything more than good management?

2 Identify the main components of a PM system and assess their relative importance.

3 Can PM work if it is distanced from the payment system of an organisation?

EXPLORE FURTHER

Armstrong, M. and Baron, A. (2005) *Managing Performance: Performance management in action*. London: CIPD. A comprehensive overview of PM, building on the findings from a series of CIPD surveys of PM in action, including the most recent from 2004.

Baron, A. and Armstrong, M. (2007) *Human Capital Management: Achieving added value through people*. London: Kogan Page. Provides a guide on how to measure performance and link to business strategy.

CIPD (2007) *Human Capital Evaluation: Developing performance measures*. Human Capital Panel Report. London: CIPD. The report discusses a performance measurement framework that incorporates key performance indicators.

Fletcher, C. (2007) *Appraisal, Feedback and Development: Making performance review work*, 4th edition. London: Taylor & Francis. Provides a detailed account of the many issues affecting performance appraisal, balancing theory and practical application in a concise and informative style.

Nohria, N., Groysberg, B. and Lee, L.-E. (2008) 'Employee motivation: a powerful new model', *Harvard Business Review*, July–August.

CHAPTER 8

Job Design

Ray French

LEARNING OUTCOMES

After reading this chapter, you should be able to:

- understand the concepts of job design and job redesign
- assess the potential importance of job design as part of the process of managing and leading people
- recognise the contribution this concept can make to the development of employees as 'thinking performers'
- identify the possible negative impacts and/or unintended consequences of job design and redesign
- evaluate the relative role of rhetoric and reality in these topic areas.

INTRODUCTION

The idea that a person's job characteristics have a significant impact on their attitudes and behaviour, and that these in turn link to job and organisational performance, is not new. As we shall see in this chapter, a preoccupation with job design can be traced back to the early 1900s. It is possible to suggest that the notion of management itself began to gain ground at the point when the owners of organisations perceived that workers' jobs could be rigorously designed, structured and supervised in order to control and predict performance. The premise that tasks and responsibilities should be arranged to ensure high levels of performance and psychological well-being has enjoyed a broad acceptance, certainly amongst academics studying this area, since the 1950s. A major claim, put forward in this chapter, is that effective job design continues to be highly relevant to all organisations and a necessary element in meeting an organisation's goals and objectives. The actual work that people do has always, of course, also had a fundamentally important impact upon their experience of work. If job design can be shown to have significance in terms of enhancing both performance and employee satisfaction, then it will – and should – form a key part of the work of those involved in managing people.

As we have seen in previous chapters, much of the extensive literature on the topic of motivation has focused on workers' psychological characteristics in the form of needs, expectations or orientations. However, it is also true to claim that motivation is linked to the nature of jobs. In this way, managers could motivate other employees through design and management of tasks as much as or even more than via interpersonal interventions, such as providing feedback. Many writers emphasise the need to match workers to the jobs they carry out, thereby highlighting positive aspects of this topic area. Others, however, point to what they perceive as the alienating nature of the types of jobs filled by large sections of the workforce.

While traditional job design has often emphasised job simplification or, as referred to by some writers, de-skilling, more recent contributions to the subject area have typically recommended expanding jobs in order both to increase employee job satisfaction, or at least to reduce boredom, and to engender greater flexibility in a workforce. It is often proposed that such flexibility is desirable in view of changes in the wider business environment. In the UK context, Hutton (2004, p.1) presents this argument as follows:

> Britain's fundamental economic structures are changing; industries and services built around knowledge are growing, while those built around mass industrial production and raw muscle power are declining. Work is becoming more intelligent and an intelligent workforce is going to be one that wants to be intelligent about how it organises itself. The more autonomy and control it can have, the more content it will be.

One should be wary of assuming that there is, or will shortly be, a proliferation of 'intelligent' work. On the contrary, the emergence of increasing numbers of such workplaces as fast-food outlets and call centres have mainly been associated with standardised repetitive 'Taylorist'-style jobs. Beyond such work, with its associated routine tasks, one also finds what Clegg *et al* (2008) refer to as 'grunge jobs', comprising both work carried out in the lower reaches of the supply chain supporting global business, and that performed by an underclass of sometimes illegal workers operating in very poor conditions outside the formally recognised and regulated job market.

Nonetheless there is also evidence that increasingly many workers will be required to act as thinking performers – and this segment of the workforce will form the main focus in this chapter. In such an environment it is posited that organisations seeking distinctive high performance should be involved in job design which contributes towards a positive psychological contract between employer and worker. This, it is suggested, can also aid and reinforce successful organisational performance. We have discussed both the issue of flexibility and the psychological contract in more detail in Chapter 6.

It is also necessary for all organisations to engage in job design as an 'infrastructure' task, to ensure that work is allocated into suitably sized role descriptions capable of being carried out effectively. At the same time, it is essential to ensure suitable demarcation of roles both vertically (in terms of skill, knowledge and hierarchical level) as well as horizontally (in functional terms). This aspect of basic job design is a prerequisite for minimal threshold standards of performance by organisations and is needed to avoid fundamental problems relating to the nature of work and roles.

8.1 ACTIVITY

Read the statement below which appears on Tesco's corporate website and answer the question which follows.

A great place to work

Our staff have told us what is important to them – to be treated with respect, having a manager who helps them, having an interesting job and an opportunity to get on. Helping to achieve what is important to our staff will help us deliver an Every Little Helps Shopping Trip for our customers.

Tesco (2008)

- It might be thought that the aim of securing interesting jobs in the supermarket context is the most challenging of the four aims set out above. At the start of your study of this topic and without referring to material set out later in this chapter, suggest ways that Tesco's managers could provide interesting jobs for store workers.

Answer from your knowledge of large supermarkets, or as a shopper if you have no personal experience of store-working.

DEFINITIONS AND FRAMEWORKS

Job design, as defined by French *et al* (2008, p.207), is 'the planning and specification of job tasks and the work setting in which they are to be accomplished'. These authors, in drawing our attention to the general area under scrutiny (the interface between workers, organisations and jobs) go on to suggest that processes of job design operate within a context in which both structural and social elements are taken into consideration. The authors elaborate on their definition by proposing that the objective of job design is to facilitate meaningful, interesting and challenging jobs, and that, within this field, a manager's responsibility is to design jobs that will motivate an individual employee. This finding underpins much academic research in this area which often posits a link between aspects of jobs and employees' psychological well-being. We will examine several examples of work within this tradition in this chapter.

Watson (2006) draws a distinction between the terms job design and work design. He notes that job design refers to task patterns that could occur in any part of a work organisation, while work design is underpinned by more broadly defined principles which could reflect that organisation's culture and structure. This refining of terminology is useful in that it highlights the role of managerial choice in devising principles for organising work. Thus job design and, beyond this, work design can form part of a more strategic approach to managing people. Watson (2006) makes the distinction in this context between *direct* and *indirect* control principles. In the former case there is a stress on prescribed task procedures with only a minimal level of commitment required from employees. In contrast, indirect control principles emphasise far greater discretion for employees in the way they perform tasks; this is in turn dependent on their higher levels of commitment, leading to mutual trust between members of the organisation in question.

It would be true to say that for much of its history job design, and the broader concept of work design, has been associated with principles of direct control. In reading earlier work on this subject, one finds particular resonance of these ideas in the work of Frederick Taylor and his model of *scientific management* often subsequently referred to as Taylorism. As we will see, Taylor's work, together with principles associated with Henry Ford, contain assumptions that jobs can be designed on a rational basis in order to maximise workers' efforts with a view to quicken production, radically reduce costs and increase output to a very significant extent. It can be argued that mass production and consumption patterns have been predicated on these principles. At the time of the millennium several commentators promoted the case for Ford as one of the key influential figures of the twentieth century, in part because of his impact on social trends due to the production of affordable cars, but also because many millions of people worked in jobs that bore the stamp of his (and Taylor's) vision. This tradition within job design has either minimised the issue of workers' motivation or put forward a model of needs at work which centre on maximising income – for example, the concept of rational economic man. Leach and Wall (2004) link different views of job design with specific epochs, making the distinction between traditional job design – which emphasises the design of jobs in order to minimise skill requirements and training times – with more contemporary *job redesign* which, contrastingly, recommends increasing the number of tasks carried out by an individual worker such as through job rotation and 'enlarging' and/or 'enriching ' individual jobs. We will explore these concepts in greater detail later in the chapter.

It has already been noted that the extent of variety, discretion and feedback has historically varied enormously between jobs, and this continues to be the case in the early twenty-first century. For example McDonald's and other fast-food restaurant chains have frequently been depicted as operating according to principles of calculability and predictability resulting in standardised work processes which largely eliminate workers' autonomy and creativity. With the advent of globalised organisations, such standardisation takes on a new dimension as the working patterns of such a system are, it is claimed, transferable across the world resulting in the diminution of local cultures' influence. So the pattern of job design principles can be seen to comprise both standardisation and job enrichment at any one point in time. After all, McDonald's has been typically characterised as a quintessential contemporary business success story, at least up until the early twenty-first century.

In view of the complex picture outlined here job design may usefully and better be defined as:

> Principles underlying the organisation of jobs, in particular the relative number and variety of required tasks and the extent of worker discretion in performing the job(s).

It is possible to locate key developments in the approach to job design, although while these have been developed in particular epochs, each can still be applied to current work situations. It is now time to look at these approaches in more detail.

SCIENTIFIC MANAGEMENT

As indicated earlier, for its most famous proponent Frederick Taylor, scientific management involved organising tasks into highly specialised jobs. Managers take on responsibility for planning, co-ordinating and monitoring work, with the task worker restricted to the level of operative. Recruitment and training are simplified and workers are grouped together in large units such as factories or call centres, enabling a high volume of chiefly standardised goods or services. One example is the Fordist production line system, which, in addition to demarcating jobs, also controlled the speed of work. It is difficult to over-emphasise the significance of this model of job design. Henry Ford, in laying the conditions for mass production of cars, was able to reduce costs very substantially, which in turn led to greatly increased levels of car ownership in the USA. As we have already stated, this led to his being considered one of the pivotal figures of the twentieth century in the industrialised world.

Scientific management as a driver for job design has attracted considerable controversy and a good deal of criticism in the areas set out below:

- it can lead to product inflexibility
- it has been criticised as dehumanising and for failing to recognise 'higher-order' human needs such as self-actualisation
- it may foster compliance and an instrumental view of work as a means to an end, as opposed to engendering commitment and loyalty
- monotony and boredom can result in reduced performance outcomes.

More generally, scientific management is perceived by some commentators as a particular direct form of control of work and workers by management. Braverman (1974) is prominent among writers who go on to assert that this concept of job design is fundamentally associated with an attempt to 'de-skill' workers. One need not accept Braverman's class-based analysis to recognise that managers as a group are, in the nature of their role, concerned to control and regularise jobs and work. Nonetheless, not all jobs have been subject to this version of job and work design and the ability of particular groups of workers to retain or even enhance skill levels remains an important factor in job design.

8.2 THEORY TASTER

BRAVERMAN AND THE DE-SKILLING THESIS

Writing in 1974, Harry Braverman took issue with the view that organisations had supplanted Taylorist methods of work organisation with more enlightened approaches to job design which took account of workers' human needs. Rather, he suggests, even craft or skilled workers have seen technology used as a substitute for their acquired skill. Further, where these traditional skills and abilities are still held by workers, the need to exercise them in modern work organisations has declined. Thus such workers can be more easily replaced by technological processes. The consequence is that levels of job satisfaction that such workers enjoy as a result of their experience and training are reduced, as are their feelings of job security.

Adler (1999) has put forward an interesting restatement of the impact of simplified 'Taylorist' jobs on employees' attitudes to their work situation. His research indicated that under conditions of scientific management, employees could still be motivated by a sense of a 'job well done'. For example, they were found to respond positively to managers' encouraging them to compete with co-workers, both in terms of quality and output. When they were respected and trusted by managers, the workers under study reciprocated with commitment and loyalty.

JOB REDESIGN

Job redesign emerged in part as a reaction to the perceived negative effects of scientific management. Its academic roots lie in the so-called 'human relations' school which emphasised people's social needs which, it was claimed, could and should be met in the workplace. Herzberg's two-factor theory of motivation proposed that pure motivation derived from the content of work as opposed to 'hygiene' factors such as pay, physical working conditions and quality of supervision. Hygiene factors, for Herzberg, were sources of dissatisfaction which could be lessened if, for example, pay was improved. However, workers would only be truly motivated if their job or work met their needs for recognition, autonomy and achievement. Herzberg's view was that virtually all human beings would respond to work which was rich in motivating factors, if they had the ability to do the job and the opportunity to carry out meaningful work. We will question this near-universal perspective later in this chapter.

In a highly significant contribution to this topic area, Hackman and Oldham (1980) proposed, on the basis of research, that five key characteristics could be used to identify the extent to which a job would, in reality, be motivating:

- skill variety – if different and diverse activities demanded the exercise of a range of skills and abilities
- task identity – the extent to which a job involves a whole and identifiable piece of work with a tangible end result

- task significance – the perceived value and effect of a job on other people
- autonomy – where a worker is free to schedule the pace of his or her work, has some choice in how the work is carried out, and is relatively independent of supervision
- feedback – the degree to which a worker gets information about the effectiveness of his or her performance. This feedback could be obtained through observation of work outcomes.

It is argued that each key characteristic is linked to a positive psychological state which, in turn, leads to desirable work outcomes. For example, task significance could result in a feeling of satisfaction in the meaningfulness of work undertaken, with positive outcomes of work motivation and effectiveness following on from this psychological state. In summary, Hackman and Oldham stated that intrinsic motivation is dependent on an individual's experiencing *three* critical psychological states: experienced meaningfulness (as noted above), experienced responsibility for work and knowledge of the results of work activities.

Hackman and Oldham recognise that individuals can respond to the characteristics differently; they are after all a function of the individual's perception, so the motivating potential of a job may vary between people. Several factors will influence the manner in which any one individual will respond to changes in their job design:

- growth-need strength – It is suggested that people vary in the extent to which they desire accomplishment and autonomy at work. People high in this category will therefore respond positively to enriched jobs; contrastingly, other workers might find newly enriched jobs a source of anxiety
- knowledge and skill – People who perceive they can perform adequately (known as a sense of self-efficacy) respond more positively to enriched jobs. This highlights the importance of individuals' perceptions and also the development of knowledge and skills at work
- context satisfaction – Hackman and Oldham found that employees who were more satisfied with contextual factors such as pay and working conditions would be more likely to respond positively to job enrichment than fellow workers dissatisfied on these measures.

8.3 ACTIVITY

How can Hackman and Oldham's model be applied to the following jobs?

- dentist
- railway ticket collector
- university lecturer
- tiler
- your current or previous job (assuming this is not one of the above)

However, despite recognising potential differences in the ways particular workers might respond to job enrichment, in overall terms Hackman and Oldham's model sets out a clear agenda for managers and others to devise meaningful and varied jobs.

The job redesign approach attempted to put forward a model which, through increasing the scope of jobs, could result both in greater efficiency and output (however defined) while also increasing the motivation of a workforce. Hackman and Oldham, while stressing the importance of 'moderating factors' which depress levels of motivation – for example, lack of knowledge or skill, 'low growth-need strength' and other negative factors in the work context – clearly advocate the design of jobs which can lead to psychological well-being among the people who perform them.

We have noted that Hackman and Oldham question whether, and to what extent, jobholders are likely to respond positively to jobs that are 'redesigned' in this way. Their approach in addressing this issue is essentially a psychological one focusing on presumed needs and other psychological characteristics of human beings (which as we have noted could vary). It may be, however, that individual workers can also *choose* work that although comparatively meaningless, may offer the prospect of other desired rewards including pay, for wider reasons based on their calculation of costs and benefits. Goldthorpe, Lockwood *et al* (1968) identified a category of workers who took an instrumental attitude or *orientation to work*. Formed outside the workplace and influenced by, among others, family and peers,

8.4 THEORY TASTER

MASLOW'S HIERARCHY OF NEEDS

Abraham Maslow's Hierarchy of Needs Theory is an example of the content theory of motivation – see Theory Taster 7.4.

According to this theory, each of us has levels of needs:

- physiological – the need for food, shelter and sleep
- safety – security and protection from danger
- love (or social needs) – a sense of belonging, friendship and affection
- esteem – self-respect and recognition from others
- self-actualisation – the achievement of our full potential.

In essence, the theory suggests that lower-order needs must be satisfied first. However, once they are, they no longer motivate: rather, higher-level needs become the key to motivation.

Based on this view, managers must be conscious of the extent to which lower-level needs have been met, and strive to offer opportunities for the meeting of higher-level ones. However, as suggested in this chapter, workers may be content to meet such needs outside of work. Managers must not assume, therefore, that providing work targeted at higher-level needs will necessarily motivate workers.

the instrumental orientation regards work as a means to an end, and workers within this category often make a conscious decision to enter psychologically unfulfilling but highly-paid work. These workers may meet their higher-order needs away from the job. With 168 hours in every week, work rarely consumes more than a third of this time for most people. There is ample opportunity for individuals with strong growth needs to find satisfaction beyond their place of work

This is not to say that decision-makers should make no attempt to design satisfying work for jobholders; there may be considerable practical benefits in so doing. It is useful however to adopt a contingency perspective in this area – that is, to understand that the nature of job design may depend on a variety of factors including the work itself and the chosen orientations to work as well as the psychological needs of the workforce. It may also be that work and the place

8.5 CASE STUDY

CALL CENTRE IS 'MY DREAM JOB'

At 22, Snehal Sampat has landed her dream job.

She works as a customer adviser in Norwich Union's call centre in Bangalore, southern India.

In Britain such a job would be considered very ordinary. But in India it is a sought-after position.

Ms Sampat said that one of the attractions is the salary.

'The pay is absolutely fantastic,' she said. 'In India, call centres are one of the fastest-growing industries. If you perform, you stand to earn a lot of money.'

A lot of money by Indian standards, that is. Ms Sampat earns £40 a week. Her equivalent at a British call centre would be on £250.

But in India, £40 is twice what a teacher earns and about the same as a newly qualified doctor.

Prestige

Ms Sampat and her call centre colleagues, all of whom are graduates, are able to enjoy the fruits of the consumer society – mobile phones, DVDs, Western clothes and smart rented flats.

By the end of the year Norwich Union will employ 3,500 people in Bangalore, Delhi and Pune.

'About 2 million people a year come out of Indian universities and technical colleges,' said John Hodgson, the firm's offshoring director. 'Their basic English is at a high level. They seek employment with Western companies because it's seen as a high-prestige job, an important stepping-stone in their lives.'

Expansion

Indian call centres are 40% cheaper to run than British ones, and the number of outsourcing staff is expected to grow tenfold in five years.

It is good news for India, where a third of the population lives in absolute poverty.

Source: Bond (2004)

To think about ...

- How can one account for Snehal Sampat's orientation to work as indicated in this case study?
- Should Norwich Union be concerned to examine ways of 'enriching' the job of customer adviser in its Indian call centre operation? Give reasons for your answer.

of work within an individual's life may vary between cultures. Schwartz (1999) found that the extent to which any one society accepts an individual's right to psychologically fulfilling work (this he said was true of Germany, for example) could contrast with other societies which viewed work more as a duty or even obligation to society. This second view – for example, held in Japan – plays down the extent to which work has to be seen as meaningful for the individual.

It should finally be noted that enriched work with its hoped-for concomitant high commitment, can itself be regarded as a form of subjugation due to the demands it imposes on employees working within its precepts. Grey (2005, p.80) notes that:

> what now appears quite normal and natural is that managers will work long hours, do whatever needs to be done to get the job done, and are motivated to do so by the intrinsic interest of their work, the payment they receive and, in general, a sense of responsibility and professionalism.

Grey goes on to paint a picture of managers stressed out by endless demands and locked into a particular set of corporate imperatives which, while in many respects preferable to that endured by workers in less enriched and self-managed jobs, themselves involve considerable sacrifices in many respects.

LESSONS FROM JAPAN

Any overview examining how job design has developed as a concept would not be complete without acknowledging the influence of ideas originating in, and imported from, Japan. The purpose here is not to provide an account of how Japanese techniques came to be commended to UK organisations from the 1980s onwards. Neither will we undertake a detailed analysis of what is a highly complex concept of management underpinned by deep assumptions within Japanese society. Rather, we will concentrate on how Japanese management principles have impacted on the specific area of job design, where it is claimed the following factors are particularly relevant:

- teamwork
  Japanese management techniques have often advocated the grouping of workers into teams, even in areas of work which would otherwise be organised on an individual basis. This concept can be extended to encompass task decision-making – for example, through quality circles.
- multiskilling
  The physical grouping of workers can also be extended to enable more similar job descriptions – that is, setting a context of work in which employees are required to have generalised job skills. It follows that these jobs are minimally demarcated. We see here an early embodiment of the principle of flexibility.
- Total Quality Management (TQM)
  For our purposes the key element of TQM is the principle that quality control should be the concern of all workers and therefore form part of every employee's job role. This could be seen as one manifestation of job enlargement, building both additional duties and responsibilities into their jobs.

8.6 THEORY TASTER

TOTAL QUALITY MANAGEMENT (TQM)

Derived from Japanese management methods, and in contrast to other methods of monitoring the quality of a business's output, such as inspection and quality control, TQM is said to be a means of ensuring customer satisfaction through a process of continuous improvement of all work operations. Importantly for the study and leadership of people, to be successful its advocates point to the need for all employees to be involved in TQM. It requires creative thinking, and the use of teamwork to solve problems and meet customers' needs. From this standpoint, competitive advantage and differentiation can be achieved through recognising the – often untapped – resource that organisations have in their workforces.

Japanese work design principles have been incorporated within a wider philosophy including 'single-status' employment conditions and lifetime – or at least long-term – tenure of employment. Some elements are not unique to the Japanese context – for example, Swedish car-makers had also (quite independently) introduced small-group working into their production processes along with aspects of job enlargement. Nonetheless, the Japanese system, as described, can be said to be a distinctive and coherent view on job design, and the latter might be seen as a differentiating factor. There have been well-publicised instances of Japanese practices being introduced to the UK – for example, in the Nissan and Toyota car production facilities. Some of the principles outlined here have been widely adopted. While the economic difficulties experienced by Japan have cast some doubt on the extent to which they can be regarded as a panacea, many employers now assume that quality issues should be the concern of all workers and that this should be operationalised through job design.

One should, of course, take a realistic view of the extent of improvements emanating from such approaches to job design. These, it is claimed, centre on the twin benefits of greater productivity and more positive attitudes among job-holders. Important and commendable as they are, these benefits will not outweigh other factors affecting the organisation. One example is provided by figures indicating the comparatively strong productivity of Japanese-owned car plants in the UK. Rhys (Murray-West, 2002), in acknowledging their excellent productivity, noted nonetheless that measuring performance by productivity was

> using only a Soviet Union measure of performance. Productivity is a necessary condition of performance, but it is in no way sufficient to guarantee profitability. It hasn't stopped Nissan slipping into loss-making, which indicates the pressure they are under from the strength of sterling.

He also referred to the crucial importance of the desirability of the product itself!

BUSINESS PROCESS RE-ENGINEERING (BPR)

This concept, we will argue, should also be examined when considering approaches to, and influences on, job design. BPR emerged in the 1990s and is associated with Hammer and Champy (1993) and Davenport (1993). These writers advocate a radical approach to organisational development. In effect they recommend ignoring past and current practice when considering how to both structure an organisation and design work. They place a strong emphasis on processes, and attention to these at the same hierarchical level. Such chains of process are thus horizontal and often cross traditionally functional boundaries.

The focus on an absolute need to serve the customer can result in very dramatic changes to work processes and jobs. Buchanan and Wilson (1996) conducted a 'patient trail' in a British hospital. They found that that a hospital patient might routinely have dealings with between 50 and 150 different members of the hospital's staff, becoming at different times the responsibility of most of the hospital's departments in the course of diagnosis, on-site treatment and aftercare. Problems that arose from this complex process were attributed to hospital staff being quite naturally concerned primarily with what happens at their own stage of the patient's journey. Staff working within such a fragmented environment were not always aware either of what had gone on before or what would subsequently happen to the patient.

There is a clear suggestion that organisations should re-structure away from vertical or functionally based departmental structures if there is to be a true focus on the customer (this ignoring the debate whether patients can be truly thought of as customers). But in addition to organisational re-structuring, BPR also implies that jobs themselves should also be reorganised around principles of customer care and that employees should increasingly be empowered to make the decisions affecting a customer's relationship with the organisation.

GOAL-SETTING AND JOB DESIGN

Mullins (2007) notes that seemingly diverse methods of job design can in reality be interconnected with some extent of overlap between them. He also brings the concept of goal-setting into view as another approach to job design. This conclusion is also drawn by French *et al* (2008), who suggest that goal-setting involves developing, negotiating and formalising employees' targets and objectives. Locke's (1990) work on goal-setting suggested that specific and difficult goals supported by task feedback are more likely to lead to higher performance, although they should not be seen as too difficult or impossible and they would in any case only be effective if the worker had feelings of self-efficacy.

8.7 CASE STUDY

CALL CENTRES NEED NOT BE SUCH A NIGHTMARE

Companies that treat staff like battery hens and keep customers on the line for ages do themselves no favours, writes Roger Eglin.

When Bernard Marr, a research fellow at Cranfield School of Management, was approached by DHL, the parcels giant, to measure performance at its call centres, he was shocked by the conditions he found.

Marr began by interviewing people to identify what made for best practice, and he has just produced a study on call-centre management. He says:

> You wouldn't believe what it was like in some of the call centres I visited. The conditions were little different from what a chicken must experience at a factory farm. There was almost an army-like atmosphere. There were huge queues of customer calls and managers were running about shouting at staff to reduce the queues. It was very scary.

He had personal experience of the abysmal service that has given call centres such a bad name with consumers.

> I wanted to change my broadband supplier. There was no direct line to the cancellation department, so I had to find the best way in. I waited in the queue for 45 minutes to get through. Then when they put me through, I had to wait another 30 minutes. It was clear they had no idea of what customers were experiencing.

Marr said that the problem with call centres was that they were run as separate business units, with managers spending all their time trying to control the time and cost per call. They were not seen as part of the company, although they had become the primary point of contact for customers.

> One centre wanted to produce better customer satisfaction. Staff were given a target of settling a call within two minutes, but customer satisfaction still went down because after two minutes staff would just pull the plug or pass calls to other departments. This was producing the wrong sort of behaviour and they didn't achieve any of their strategic objectives.

Marr said companies ended up monitoring the number and length of calls because it was easy to do, but they failed to realise it was a pointless exercise because it focused on measuring efficiency without understanding what the business was about. Marr went on:

> A successful centre is one that really talks to the customer, yet only a few companies understand this. They just want to reduce the numbers. The staff do not like it. If you interview front-line staff who are given time to talk to the callers, they will tell you they work harder. If someone has a bad experience with the call centre, it shapes his or her perception of the company. If things are really bad, they will never go back to that company.
>
> Doing something about it is commonsense – but it doesn't filter through to top executives. They don't understand the importance of call centres or that they are a company's public face.

But Marr had a surprise at Fujitsu, the Japanese IT company. There he found happy staff at call centres in Crewe and Stevenage that contributed greatly to the company's success. 'The atmosphere was so different,' he said. 'People were enthusiastic, trying to understand what customers wanted.'

Fujitsu started developing its call centres in 1999 when Stephen Parry joined the company. It now employs 4,000 staff in call centres worldwide.

Much of Fujitsu's success stems from the close relationships it develops with clients. Instead of focusing on the time it takes to deal with a call, Fujitsu explores whether the call was necessary in the first place. It aims to cut down the number of calls and create more time to answer the ones that matter.

Sometimes it can be difficult to establish the customers' problems because they are reluctant to discuss the details of their business with an outsider. It took time to overcome the reluctance of a fast-food company to let Fujitsu explore why it was making so many calls. Eventually a team from Fujitsu spent an afternoon there and discovered that the restaurants were having trouble accessing the company's system because of inadequate server capacity.

'They should have learned sooner,' said Marr. 'It was costing them a lot of money.'

Source: Eglin (2004)

To think about ...

1 How did a preoccupation with customer relationships impact on the jobs of Fujitsu call centre workers?

2 To what extent do you think the call centre staff at Fujitsu are truly 'empowered'?

3 Identify the difficulties managers could face in attempting to change the ethos of a call centre towards the Fujitsu model as set out in the case study.

CONCLUSION

The argument for linking principles of job design to contemporary high-performance workplaces can be summarised as follows:

- A constantly changing and ever more competitive business environment means that work organisations in all sectors require multi-skilled, proactive and customer-focused staff in order to be successful. These staff can be characterised as thinking performers.
- An increasingly educated workforce, used to exercising discretion and choice in other areas of their lives will, in any case, demand jobs which are psychologically fulfilling.
- High-performance work organisations will therefore increasingly need to design (or enable their workers to design) jobs that provide variety, scope for initiative and autonomy and that empower job-holders.

Noon and Blyton (2002) group these arguments under the heading of the 'upskilling thesis'. These writers go on, however, to question the extent to which this thesis is borne out in practice, proposing that there remain very wide differences in terms of both the range of tasks undertaken by workers and the degree of autonomy experienced across the labour market.

A contingency approach to the area, while recognising the value of 'humanising' jobs, would suggest that different models of job design are appropriate in different situations. For example, we should critically address the proposition that work has largely become more 'intelligent'.
A large-scale research project carried out by Professor Peter Nolan into work patterns in the
UK identified a more complex and subtle picture. Nolan (quoted in Wignall, 2004) records
that

> we still have 10.5 million manual workers in this country. That's 40% of the workforce. They're in warehouses, filling envelopes, filling shelves. Stacking shelves is something like the eighth quickest-growing occupation. ... People think we now have a service economy where everyone sits at a computer, and that's just not true. Jobs are being created by new technologies, but those jobs are the same kind of jobs that people were doing before.

It is not the intention here to dismiss the possibility that all jobs can be enriched or made more customer-focused. This is certainly true to an extent, and managers should continue ways in which this may be achieved. However, one should recognise the role of rhetoric – or even hyperbole – in some literature in this subject area, and the relatively unchanging nature of many people's work.

One can also put forward a view that organisational effectiveness can be achieved through different models and indeed conceptions of job design. The fast-food sector provides a notable example of continuing simplification of tasks, albeit within a teamworking framework. Here we have classical contingency principles operating – that is, it all depends on the level of predictability required (both product and service) and the expectations of a workforce, many of whom in this case may have only short-term plans regarding their work and employment. In contrast, work in other sectors may lend itself far more easily to encouraging greater initiative and autonomy on the part of job-holders.

As we saw in Chapter 6, it has been argued that organisations should seek to implement and maintain functional flexibility, this concept encompassing job rotation, multi-skilling and, where appropriate, teamworking as part of an overall strategy of flexibility or adaptability. Other aspects of flexibility included numerical flexibility, the precursor of many instances of downsizing, and financial flexibility which, in an attempt to control salary costs, has seen numerous examples of subcontracting work, zero hours contracts and even the wholesale movement of jobs to other parts of the world. However, even this seemingly inexorable logic may be contingent on particular circumstances. Clark (1993) suggests that there might be instances where workers' specialist knowledge is perceived as sufficiently important to justify retaining and bolstering it. The same author also notes that a worker's commitment to high-quality work can emanate from a feeling of 'ownership' of that work or job. There is, in conclusion, a range of strategic choices available to organisational decision-makers when approaching the area of job design.

8.8 DISCUSSION QUESTIONS

1. Assess the importance of job design within the overall process of managing people. Give reasons for your answer.
2. How strong is the evidence that meaningful work will motivate a workforce?
3. To what extent is it true to say that principles of job design apply equally in all societies?

EXPLORE FURTHER

Hackman, J. R. and Oldham, G. R. (1980) *Work Redesign*. New York: Addison-Wesley. Read this source text for an in-depth discussion of how job characteristics can affect workers' attitudes.

Watson, T. J. (2006) *Organising and Managing Work*. Harlow, FT/Prentice Hall. Chapter 8 provides an interesting wide-ranging summary of issues relevant to job and work design, illuminated by cases and conversations deriving from the author's own research.

Grey, C. (2005) *A Very Short, Fairly Interesting and Reasonably Cheap Book About Studying Organizations*. London: Sage. This book provides a thought-provoking and entertaining account of the development and application of many of the principles dealt with in this chapter.

CHAPTER 9

Recruitment and Selection

Ray French and Sally Rumbles

LEARNING OUTCOMES

After reading this chapter, you should be able to:

- comprehend the potential importance of recruitment and selection in successful people management and leadership
- identify aspects of recruitment and selection that are needed to avoid critical failure factors
- understand recruitment and selection policies and procedures that are said to characterise the high-performance organisation
- evaluate selection methods according to criteria of reliability, validity and fairness
- recognise the role of rhetoric in recruitment and selection literature.

INTRODUCTION

The recruitment and selection of an organisation's workforce can play a pivotally important role in shaping its effectiveness and performance. We are frequently told that work organisations of all types are able to acquire, with a high degree of accuracy, workers who already possess, or have the potential to develop, relevant knowledge, skills and aptitudes. If we accept this claim (which will be questioned to some extent in this chapter), then recruiting and selecting staff in an effective manner can both avoid undesirable costs – for example, those associated with high staff turnover, poor performance and dissatisfied customers – and engender a mutually beneficial employment relationship characterised, wherever possible, by high commitment on both sides.

Recruitment and selection as an activity manifestly has the capacity to form a key part of the process of managing and leading people. In itself a routine part of organisational life, it is suggested that recruitment and selection has become ever more important as organisations increasingly regard their workforce as a source of competitive advantage. Of course, not all employers engage with this proposition even at the rhetorical level. However, there is evidence of increased interest in the utilisation of employee selection methods which are valid, reliable and fair. For example, it has been noted that 'over several decades, work psychology has had a significant influence on the way people are recruited into jobs, through rigorous development and evaluation of personnel selection procedures' (Arnold *et al*, 2005, p.135).

This aspect of employee resourcing is characterised, however, by potential difficulties. Many widely used selection methods – for example, interviewing – are generally perceived to be unreliable as a predictor of job-holders' performance in reality (eg Garcia, Posthuma and Colella, 2008). Thus it is critically important to obtain a *realistic* evaluation of the process from all concerned, including both successful and unsuccessful candidates. There are ethical issues around selecting 'appropriate', and by implication rejecting 'inappropriate', candidates for employment. We put forward the view in this chapter that notwithstanding the difficulties outlined here, recruitment and selection is one area where it is possible to distinguish policies and practices associated with critical success factors and performance differentiators which, in turn, impact on organisational effectiveness in significant ways.

9.1 CASE STUDY

WHY WORK AT IKEA?

The following extracts are taken from the IKEA Group corporate website 'Why work at IKEA?' section.

Because of our values, our culture and the endless opportunities, we believe that it's important to attract, develop and inspire our people. We are continuously investing in our co-workers and give them sufficient opportunities and responsibility to develop.

What would it be like to work at IKEA?

- You'd be working for a growing global company that shares a well-defined and well-communicated vision and business idea.
- You'd be able to develop your skills in many different ways, becoming an expert at your daily work, by taking new directions in other parts of the company, or by taking on greater responsibility, perhaps even in another country.
- Human values and team spirit are part of the work environment. You'd not only have fun at work, you'd be able to contribute to the development of others.
- At IKEA you'd be rewarded for making positive contributions.
- You'd have the chance to grow and develop together with the company.

Values at the heart of our culture

The people and the values of IKEA create a culture of informality, respect, diversity and real opportunities for growth. These values include

- Togetherness and enthusiasm
  This means we respect our colleagues and help each other in difficult times. We look for people who are supportive, work well in teams and are open with each other in the way they talk, interact and connect. IKEA supports this attitude with open-plan offices and by laying out clear goals that co-workers can stand behind.
- Humbleness
  More than anything this means respect. We are humble towards our competitors, respecting their proficiency, and realising that we constantly have to be better than they are to keep our market share. It also

means that we respect our co-workers and their views, and have respect for the task we have set ourselves.

- Willpower
  Willpower means first agreeing on mutual objectives and then not letting anything actually stand in the way of actually achieving them. In other words, it means we know exactly what we want, and our desire to get it should be irrepressible.
- Simplicity
  Behind this value are ideas like efficiency, common sense and avoiding complicated solutions. Simple habits, simple actions and a healthy aversion to status symbols are part of IKEA.

Source: www.ikea.com. Used with the kind permission of IKEA

To think about ...

1 In what ways could an employer seek to assess qualities of supportiveness, humility, willpower and simplicity among candidates in the course of a recruitment and selection process? How accurate do you think judgements made on these measures are likely to be?

2 What selection methods could IKEA employ to assess whether potential workers can 'develop skills' and 'take on new directions and responsibilities'?

DEFINITIONS

Recruitment and selection are often presented as comprising linked stages in a process of employee resourcing, which itself may be located within a wider HR management strategy. Bratton and Gold (2007, p.239) establish a clear link between the two terms in the following way:

> Recruitment is the process of generating a pool of capable people to apply for employment ot an organisation. Selection is the process by which managers and others use specific instruments to choose from a pool of applicants a person or persons more likely to succeed in the job(s), given management goals and legal requirements.

In setting out a similar distinction in which recruitment activities provide a pool of people eligible for selection, Foot and Hook (2005, p.63) suggest that:

> although the two functions are closely connected, each requires a separate range of skills and expertise, and may in practice be fulfilled by different staff members. The recruitment activity, but not normally the selection decision, may be outsourced to an agency. It makes sense, therefore, to treat each activity separately.

The systematic model of recruitment and selection set out by these and other authors should not necessarily imply that this process is underpinned by scientific reasoning and method. Thompson and McHugh (2002, p.235) are among writers who take a critical view on the general use and, in particular, the validity of employee selection methods. In commenting on the use of personality tests in selection, these authors state that 'in utilising tests employers are essentially clutching at straws and on this basis will probably use anything that will help them make some kind of systematic decision'. They identify now discredited selection methods, such as the use of polygraphs to detect lying, and other methods, such as astrology, which are deemed more appropriate in some cultures than in others. It is indeed important to keep in mind that today's received wisdom in the area of recruitment and selection, just as in the management canon more generally, may be criticised and even widely rejected in the future.

The process of recruitment and selection continues nonetheless to be viewed as best carried out via sequential but linked stages of first gathering a pool of applicants, a screening-out process, followed by the positive step of actual selection. This apparently logical ordering of the activities is largely viewed as essential to achieve minimum thresholds of effectiveness.

APPROACHES TO RECRUITMENT AND SELECTION

Typically, decisions on selecting a potential worker are made primarily with a view to taking on the most appropriate person to do a particular job in terms of their current or, more commonly, potential competencies. In recent years this concept has been extended to search for workers who are 'flexible' and able to contribute to additional and/or changing job roles (eg Sheth and Sharma, 2008). This approach contrasts with a more traditional model which involves first compiling a wide-ranging job description for the post in question, followed by the use of a person specification, which in effect forms a checklist along which candidates can be evaluated on criteria such as knowledge, skills and personal qualities. This traditional approach, in essence, involves matching characteristics of an 'ideal' person to fill a defined job. There is a seductive logic in this apparently rational approach. However, there are in-built problems in its application if judgements of an individual's personality are inherently subjective and open to error and, furthermore, if these personal characteristics are suited to present rather than changing circumstances.

The competencies model, in contrast, seeks to identify abilities needed to perform a job well rather than focusing on personal characteristics such as politeness or assertiveness. Torrington *et al* (2008, p.170) identify potentially important advantages of referring to competencies in this area, noting that:

> they can be used in an integrated way for selection, development, appraisal and reward activities; and also that from them behavioural indicators can be derived against which assessment can take place.

Competency-based models are becoming increasingly popular in graduate recruitment where organisations are making decisions on future potential. Farnham and Stevens (2000) found that managers in the public sector increasingly viewed traditional job descriptions and person specifications as archaic, rigid and rarely an accurate reflection of the requirements of the job. There is increasing evidence that this popularity is more widespread. A CIPD report (2007) found that 86% of organisations surveyed were now using competency-based interviews in some way; and in another, over half of employers polled had started using them in the past year (Williams, 2008). It is suggested that the competence-based model may be a more meaningful way of underpinning recruitment and selection in the current fast-moving world of work and can accordingly contribute more effectively to securing high performance.

9.2 THEORY TASTER

PERSONALITY: THE BASICS

Personality is a notion that we all understand at a general level, and one which is essential to people management and the management of teams. However, classifying personality in ways that are useful for analysis has been problematic. Very large-scale studies (often initiated in the USA) have identified a set of traits that can be used to describe people. These 'Big Five' descriptors are the underlying structure for many personality tests. Statistical analyses have shown these traits to be sufficiently different from one another, and that together they provide a 'whole' picture of a person. The traits are extraversion/introversion, emotional stability/neuroticism, openness/closed-mindedness, conscientiousness/heedlessness, agreeableness/hostility. Typically, a test would locate an individual at a certain point on these five scales. These parameters have been used in many subsequent studies to discover their relationship to specific questions such as the relationship of certain profiles to job success, learning ability, cross-cultural differences, etc.

Many theorists conceive of personality as reflecting a developmental process (for example, Freud and Erikson). The Myers-Briggs Type Indicator, a popular tool amongst occupational psychologists, builds on Jung's approach to personality, adapted for use in assessing the strengths of individuals within a workplace context. The parameters produce a 4 x 4 matrix of preferences: extraversion/introversion; thinking/feeling; sensing (using facts)/intuiting (using ideas); and judging (planned/organised)/perception (flexible). Once again, considerable further research has revealed a picture of how these parameters might be useful in management.

Personality is a large and mature area of conceptual and applied study. Consequently, anyone wishing to pursue an interest in this field must take a balanced approach.

Many commentators refer to significant changes in the world of work and the implications these have for the recruitment and selection of a workforce. Searle (2003, p.276) notes that:

> Increasingly, employees are working in self-organised teams in which it is difficult to determine the boundaries between different job-holders' responsibilities. The team undertakes the task and members co-operate and work together to achieve it. Recruitment and selection practices focus on identifying a suitable person for the job, but … isolating a job's roles and responsibilities may be difficult to do in fast-changing and team-based situations.

There is here an implication both that teamworking skills could usefully be made part of employee selection and also that an individual's job specification should increasingly be designed and interpreted flexibly. Linstead *et al* (2004, p.594) posit a world of work in which 'unforeseen problems are thrown up constantly and there is rarely time to respond to them in a considered way'. In this type of business environment, decisions made can be 'rational' in terms of past practice and events but may in fact be revealed to be flawed or even obsolete when they are made in the new context.

In both the traditional and competencies approaches there is an implication that organisations aiming for high performance may need to use selection methods which assess qualities of flexibility and creative thinking. Of course, many jobs may still require task-holders to work in a predictable and standardised way so one should exercise caution when examining this rhetoric. Interestingly, however, recruitment and selection practices should themselves be kept under constant review if we accept the reality of a business world characterised by discontinuous, rather than incremental, change.

THE RESOURCING CYCLE

The resourcing cycle begins with the identification of a vacancy and ends when the successful candidate is performing the job to an acceptable standard. It is a two-way process. Organisations are evaluating candidates for a vacancy, but also these candidates are viewing the organisation as a prospective employer. Conducting the process in a professional and timely manner is necessary for normal effectiveness in helping to ensure that not only is the 'best' candidate attracted to apply and subsequently accepts the post, but also that unsuccessful candidates can respect the decision made and possibly apply for future vacancies, along with other suitable candidates.

The first step in the recruitment process is to decide that there is a vacancy to be filled. Increasingly, a more strategic and questioning approach may be taken. If, for example, the vacancy arises because an employee has left, managers may take the opportunity to review the work itself and consider whether it could be processed in an alternative way. For example, could the work be done on a part-time, job-share or flexi-time basis? Alternatively, the job could be automated. The financial services sector in the UK provides one example of where technological developments have resulted in both significant job losses and changed patterns of work since 1990. On the assumption that a post needs to be filled, it will be necessary to devise specifications. Whether a competency-based approach or the more traditional method of formal job descriptions and person specifications is chosen, a CIPD report (2007) notes that specifications need to reflect the duties and requirements of the job along with the skills, aptitudes, knowledge, experience, qualifications and personal qualities that are necessary to perform the job effectively. Consideration should also be given to how the recruiter intends to measure and elicit information regarding those skills. Are they essential to job performance or merely desirable, and can they be objectively measured?

ATTRACTING APPLICANTS

The objective of a recruitment method is to attract an appropriate number of suitable candidates within reasonable cost constraints. Pilbeam and Corbridge (2006, p.151) note that 'There is no ideal number of applications and no intrinsic value in attracting a high volume of candidates.' Neither is there a single best way to recruit applicants; rather, the chosen recruitment medium must ensure that there are a sufficient number of suitably qualified candidates from which to make a selection without being overwhelmed with large numbers of unsuitable applications. Using a recruitment agency to find a small number of suitable candidates, particularly for senior or specialised posts, may prove a significantly more cost-effective and efficient method than a major advertising campaign which generates a large response from unsuitable candidates. The choice of method will also be influenced by the availability of candidates – that is, is there likely to be a shortage or surplus of candidates? For example, in 2005 there was a large pool of Polish migrant workers wanting to work in Britain, but within a couple of years this had significantly diminished as the euro/pound exchange rate dropped. Also, British employers found applicants needed more careful screening such as for depth of technical English.

9.3 ACTIVITY

Look at the recruitment section of your local newspaper. What sort of vacancies are typically advertised here? Compare and contrast these with the types of vacancies advertised in broadsheet newspapers such as *The Times*, *The Guardian* or the *Daily Telegraph*. What indicators are there in the wording of advertisements as to whether there is a surplus or shortage of candidates?

Which method of recruitment should be adopted? There is no single best way, and a contingency approach involving an analysis of what might be effective in particular circumstances is advocated. Some organisations – for example, in the local government sector – will always advertise all vacancies to ensure equality of opportunity, whereas manufacturing organisations tend to rely on recruitment agencies (CIPD, 2007). Human resources professionals should carefully consider and review which methods have been most effective in the past and which method or methods would be most appropriate for the current vacancy. They should also, critically, keep new methods under review, including, for example, the growing trends towards Internet-based recruitment (eg Ngai, Law, Chan and Wat, 2008).

RECRUITING IN THE VIRTUAL WORLD

The rise in the use of the Internet is probably the most significant development in the recruitment field in the early twenty-first century. Various surveys (CIPD, 2007; IRS (Murphy, 2008)) now suggest that this is fast becoming employers' preferred way of attracting applicants – for example, 75% of companies are now using their corporate website as their most common method (along with local newspaper advertising) of attracting candidates (CIPD, 2007). There is, however, little evidence that the Internet produces better-quality candidiates, but it does deliver more of them and more employers report that online recruitment made it easier to find the right candidate (Crail, 2007). Candidates themselves are increasingly choosing this medium to search for jobs, with 89% of graduates only searching online for jobs (Reed Employment, reported in *People Management*, 20 March 2008).

9.4 CASE STUDY

AN ALTERNATIVE APPROACH: 'TALENT PUDDLES' AT NESTLÉ

Many organisations are faced with the problem of how to create a pool of talent from which to select candidates. Jobs requiring specialist skills and knowledge can often take several months and considerable costs to fill, yet just as often suitable candidates slip through an organisation's net because there wasn't a vacancy at that particular time. Creating 'talent pools' or databases of good applicants is one way organisations have tried to keep potential candidates interested, but many cases this has been no more than keeping CVs on file which are never referred to or seen again. Nestlé, the global food and beverage manufacturer, has taken a more radical approach to managing talent by creating 'talent puddles'. Although these are similar to talent pools, Nestlé's approach has focused on creating a talent bank in specific areas of the business where there is a shortage of skilled applicants. Talent puddles focus on 'talent gaps' – specific jobs and difficult-to-fill roles – by creating a small puddle of talent that can be readily brought into the business thus reducing the costs and speeding up the recruitment process.

The initiative began with the supply-chain function which now contains 120 shortlisted candidates and has placed eight people but has since been extended to other areas of the busines. This approach to resourcing has also changed the recruiters' role. A significant portion of their time is now spent calling people and sifting through CVs from the talent puddle. When people apply, recruiters look at the quality of the applications and assess what level/grade they are operating at, ranking and recording them accordingly. Candidates are met and interviewed by the recruitment team and line managers before being placed in the talent puddle. One could argue that in effect the organisation has created its own internal recruitment agency and there is no doubt that this approach has significantly reduced the company's reliance on recruitment agencies over the past five years. However, just like recruitment agencies, one could also question how you keep 120 highly skilled potential candidates interested if you don't have an actual vacancy.

Source: adapted from the CIPD Recruitment, Retention and Turnover Annual Survey Report 2007, p.10. London: CIPD

The benefits of online recruitment to employers include the speed, reduced administrative burden and costs and no geographical limits. The benefits to applicants are that it is easier, faster and more convenient to post a CV or search a job site online than to read a selection of printed media (Whitford, 2003). However, if employers post vacancies on their own websites, candidates still have to trawl the web in order to find them. Applicants may be deterred by the perceived impersonal nature of online recruitment. Some people either are not comfortable using the Internet or do not have ready access to a computer, and there is thus still a role for conventional advertising (IDS, 2006).

Online recruitment continues to expand and employers are now combining more traditional methods with online recruitment by using printed adverts to refer jobseekers to the Internet vacancy (Murphy, 2008). Other employers – such as Microsoft – are enhancing brand visibility and credibility by having a wider Internet recruitment presence. They reach a broader audience and thus create a diverse workplace with varied skills and talents. One initiative is the introduction of 'corporate recruitment blogs'. The idea is that potential job candidates may be attracted to the company through what they see on the blog and make contact through the specific blogger who will initiate the recruitment process on behalf of the company (Hasson, 2007). See also the Cadbury-Schweppes case study (9.5) below.

9.5 CASE STUDY

IS ONLINE CHAT THE WAY FORWARD WITH RECRUITMENT?

Graduates today have a higher expectation of being able to use social networking as a primary source of information and communication. In response to this, Cadbury-Schweppes launched its 2008 UK graduate recruitment campaign with a new online chatroom to give potential applicants the chance to interact with the company's current graduates. The confectionery giant has created an easy-to-use site that allows potential graduates the opportunity to chat online and put questions to its graduate recruitment team. The site builds on the success the company had with its graduate blogs in 2005 and MP3 downloads in 2006. Chatroom sessions are advertised on the firm's graduate recruitment calendar and the team have about 8 hours of online dedicated chat to interested graduates (Berry, 2007).

- Would you use an employer's chat room?

FAIRNESS IN RECRUITMENT AND SELECTION

One factor shared by both traditional and competence models of recruitment and selection is that both are framed by an imperative to take on the most appropriate person in terms of their contribution to organisational performance. This is, of course, unsurprising given the preoccupation of organisations in all sectors with meeting objectives and targets. However, when we consider what is meant by making appropriate selection decisions, other factors, including fairness, can also be seen to be important.

Decisions made in the course of a recruitment and selection process should be perceived as essentially fair and admissible to all parties, including people who have been rejected. There is evidence to support the view that applicants are concerned with both procedural justice – that is, how far they felt that selection methods were related to a job and the extent to which procedures were explained to them – and distributive justice, where their concern shifts to how equitably they felt they were treated and whether the outcome of selection was perceived to be fair (see Gilliland, 1993).

Fairness in this regard can be linked to the actual selection methods used. Anderson *et al* (2001) found that interviews, résumés and work samples were well-regarded methods, while handwriting tests (graphology) were held in low regard. Personality and ability tests received an 'intermediate' evaluation. This is linked to the concept of face validity: how plausible and valid does the method used appear to the candidate under scrutiny? It is reasonable to suggest that employers should take care in choosing selection methods in order to maintain credibility among applicants as well, of course, as assessing the predictive value of the methods.

Fairness in selection also extends to the area of discrimination and equal opportunities, as we saw in Chapter 5. In the UK, for example, current legislation is intended to make unlawful discrimination on the grounds of age, race, nationality or ethnic origin, disability, sex, marital status and sexual orientation. The law identifies both direct discrimination, where an individual is treated less favourably on the sole grounds of their membership of a group covered in the relevant legislation, and indirect discrimination, which occurs when a provision applied to both groups disproportionately affects one in reality. The Equality and Human Rights Commission highlights headhunting as one area in which indirect discrimination may occur. Headhunters may, in approaching individuals already in jobs, contravene this aspect of the law if existing jobs are dominated by one sex or ethnic group, for example. Compliance with equal opportunities legislation provides one example of performance infrastructure and would, it is surmised, reap business benefits – ie recruiting from the truly qualified labour pool and avoiding negative outcomes such as costly and reputation-damaging legal processes.

High-performance organisations may seek to go beyond the compliance approach and work towards a policy or even strategy of *managing diversity* (see also Chapter 5). As defined by the CIPD (2006), a managing diversity approach:

> is about ensuring that all employees have an opportunity to maximise their potential and enhance their self-development and their contribution to the organisation. It recognises that people from different backgrounds can bring fresh ideas and perceptions, which can make the way work is done more efficient and make products and services better. Managing diversity successfully will help organisations to nurture creativity and innovation and thereby to tap hidden capacity for growth and improved competitiveness.

It is thus important to ensure that such a policy is operationalised in the field of recruitment and selection, as staff involved in this activity can be said to act as 'gatekeepers' of an organisation.

9.6 CASE STUDY

'OPPORTUNITIES FOR ALL AT ASDA'

The following statement is an extract from the 'Opportunities for all' section of Asda's corporate website [accessed September 2004].

At Asda we endeavour to discriminate only on ability and we recognise that our organisation can be effective if we have a diverse colleague base, representing every section of society.

We want to recruit colleagues and managers who represent the communities in which we operate and the customers we serve.

Ethnic minorities

We have been working at all levels to make sure that ethnic minorities are represented across all levels of our business and we operate a policy of Religious Festival Leave so that any colleague can apply to take up to two days' unpaid leave to attend their Religious Festival.

Women

We recognise that there are mutual benefits in making sure we employ women in our workplace. Besides our equal opportunities recruitment policy, we have a number of other initiatives which support our commitment, particularly our flexible working practices which include job shares and part-time working at all levels, parental leave, shift swaps and career breaks.

Disability

It is our aim to make sure that our stores are accessible for disabled people to both work and shop in. As a company we have been awarded the Two Tick symbol and we have a good working partnership with Remploy and we work together to help disabled people get back into the workplace. We offer people with disabilities a working environment which is supportive and we operate an equal opportunities policy on promotion.

If due to your disability you need some help, whether completing your application form or during the interview process, please contact the people manager in your local store or depot who will be pleased to help.

Age

The proportion of older people in the population is steadily increasing and we're seeing this reflected in the age profile of our workforce. We want to encourage the recruitment and retention of older, experienced colleagues many of whom welcome the opportunity to work beyond the traditional retirement age, to work flexibly and enjoy a phased retirement.

We've been encouraging stores and depots to recruit more mature colleagues or 'Goldies' and in one new store in Broadstairs we opened with over 40% of our colleagues aged 50 or over. And we have seen a reduction in both labour turnover and absence well below average in the store.

To further reinforce our commitment we also offer a number of flexible working schemes such as Benidorm Leave where older colleagues can take three months' unpaid leave between January and March, or grandparents' leave where colleagues who are grandparents take up to a week off unpaid to look after a new arrival.

Source: used with the kind permission of ASDA Ltd

To think about ...

1 To what extent does this statement from Asda's website indicate that this organisation has a strategy for diversity management? What has led you to your conclusion?

2 How do Asda seek to safeguard their 'Opportunities for all' policy in the area of recruitment and selection?

3 Produce a statement for use by companies setting out employment policy in the area of age discrimination and indicate how this could take effect in the recruitment and selection of workers.

VALIDITY IN RECRUITMENT AND SELECTION

It may appear self-evident that organisational decision-makers will wish to ensure that their recruitment and selection methods are effective. We have already suggested, however, that making judgements on an individual's personal characteristics and suitability for future employment is inherently problematic and that many 'normal' selection methods contain significant flaws. There is also the question of what is meant by the terms 'reliability' and 'validity' when applied to recruitment and selection.

Reliability in the context of workforce selection can refer to the following issues:

- Temporal or 're-test' stability where the effectiveness of a selection tool is assessed by consistency of results obtained over time. An individual could, for example, complete a personality inventory or intelligence test at different times over a period of several years, although in the latter case it would be important to isolate the impact of repeated practice on results.
- Consistency – that is, can the test measure what it sets out to? Some elements of IQ tests have for example been criticised for emphasising a person's vocabulary which might in turn be influenced more by their education and general background than by their innate intelligence.

Validity in this area is typically subdivided into the following aspects:

- Face validity has an emphasis on the acceptability of the selection measure, including acceptability to the candidate himself/herself. For example, it is possible (although extremely unlikely) that there is a correlation between a person's hat size and their job competence. However, you would be reluctant to measure candidates' heads as part of their selection due to their probable scepticism at the use of this measure.
- Content validity refers to the nature of the measure and in particular its adequacy as a tool. For example, the UK driving test could be criticised for not assessing ability in either night driving or travelling on motorways.
- Predictive validity centres on links between results or scores on a selection measure and subsequent outcome – most commonly job performance at a future point. Here it is important to identify when the comparison will be made – ie immediately in the case of a simple job requiring little training, or more commonly at an intermediate point, possibly after a suitable probationary period.

We argue here that validity, along with fairness, should be the overriding indicator of a selection method for high-performance organisations and that it is important to obtain sophisticated data on validity in all its forms. Pilbeam and Corbridge (2006, p.173) provide a summary of the predictive validity of selection methods based on the findings of various research studies.

1.0 Certain prediction
0.9
0.8

0.7 Assessment centres for development
0.6 Skilful and structured interviews
0.5 Work sampling
Ability tests
0.4 Assessment centres for job performance
Biodata
Personality assessment
0.3 Unstructured interviews
0.2
0.1 References
0.0 Graphology
Astrology

However, they suggest that these validity measures should be treated with caution because they can be affected by the performance indicators used, and also by the way the tools were applied. They indicate nonetheless both variability between measures and some overall degree of uncertainty when predicting future work performance during the selection process.

While it is recommended that validity should be the prime factor in choosing selection tools, it would be naïve not to recognise that other factors such as cost and applicability may be relevant. How practical, therefore, is it to conduct any particular measure? As indicated earlier, an organisation aiming for high performance is recommended to adopt valid measures as opposed to merely practical or less costly ones. Again, one should recognise that recruitment and selection is contingent upon other factors such as the work itself. A 'high performance' organisation in the fast-food industry may legitimately decide not to adopt some relatively valid but expensive methods when selecting fast-food operatives. It should be noted that the oft-derided method of interviewing can in reality be a relatively valid method if conducted skilfully and structured.

9.7 ACTIVITY

What do you understand by the term 'psychometric testing'? Assess the validity of psychometric testing as an employee selection tool. Provide two examples of when you would and would not use psychometric tests as part of a selection process, and give reasons for your decisions.

AND SO, WHAT ABOUT INTERVIEWING?

It would be prudent to argue that selection decisions should be based on a range of selection tools because some have poor predictive job ability. While it is almost inconceivable that employment would be offered or accepted without a face-to-face encounter, many organisations still rely almost exclusively on the outcome of interviews to make selection decisions.

To have any value, interviews should be conducted or supervised by trained individuals, be structured to follow a previously agreed set of questions mirroring the person specification or job profile, and allow candidates the opportunity to ask questions. The interview is more than a selection device. It is a mechanism that is capable of communicating information about the job and the organisation to the candidate, with the aim of giving a realistic job preview, providing information about the process, and thus can minimise the risk that job offers will be rejected. Organisations seeking high performance in their selection processes should therefore give considerable attention to maximising the uses of the interview and, ideally, combine this method with other psychometric measures where appropriate.

RECRUITMENT COSTS

APPARENT COSTS

These centre on the direct costs of recruitment procedures, but one might also consider the so-called opportunity costs of engaging in repeated recruitment and selection when workers leave an organisation. It is also useful to consider the 'investment', including training resources, lost to the employer when a worker leaves prematurely. The CIPD Survey report on Recruitment, Retention and Turnover (2007) estimates the average direct cost of recruitment per individual in the UK in 2007 as £4,333 – this figure rising to £5,000 for workers in the managerial and professional category – while the estimated average cost of labour turnover per leaver in 2007 was estimated as £7,750, rising to £11,000 for the managerial/professional group.

IMPLICIT COSTS

These are less quantifiable and include the following categories:

- poor performance
- reduced productivity
- low-quality products or services
- dissatisfied customers or other stakeholders
- low employee morale.

The implicit costs mentioned here are, in themselves, clearly undesirable outcomes in all organisations. In high-performing organisations 'average' or 'adequate' performance may also be insufficient, and recruitment and selection may be deemed to have failed unless workers have become 'thinking performers'.

9.8 CASE STUDY

GETTING IT WRONG

In an attempt to check the robustness of security procedures at British airports, Anthony France – a reporter for *The Sun* newspaper – obtained a job as a baggage-handler with a contractor subsequently named by the newspaper. In the course of his selection, France gave bogus references and provided a fake home address and bank details. Throughout the selection process he lied about his past while details of his work as an undercover journalist were available on the Internet.

France then proceeded to take fake explosive material onto a holiday jet airliner at Birmingham International Airport.

This case provides a good, albeit extreme, example of the possible consequences of flawed selection procedures, or as happened here, when agreed practices, such as checking personal details, are not put into effect. Such consequences are potentially wide-ranging and veer from the trivial and comic to possibly tragic outcomes.

RHETORIC AND REALITY: THE CASE OF SMALL AND MEDIUM-SIZED ENTERPRISES

There is evidence to suggest that many human resources management (HRM) practices often prescribed in the academic literature are more common in some sectors of business than in others, and that the small and medium-sized enterprises (SME) group, in particular, are less likely to have 'in-house' HR expertise and 'sophisticated' systems in place (see Cully *et al*, 1999). A study carried out by Cassell *et al* (2002) in SMEs in the North of England focused on both the use and perceived value (by employers) of a range of HRM procedures. In the area of recruitment and selection, only 31% of firms in the sample used wide-ranging employee development and recruitment and selection procedures. Interestingly, 38% of the sample questioned said that they did not use recruitment and selection procedures at all. In the companies that did make use of them, 50% found that the procedures helped 'entirely' or 'a lot' in over half of the instances in which they were used. This is some way from the picture of widespread usage and the assumed universal benefits conveyed in some sources.

The reality of the context faced by managers of SMEs will frame their responses in an entirely understandable way, and prescriptive 'textbook style' approaches may be viewed as inappropriate. It would, of course, be as damaging for SMEs as for any other organisation if a lack of 'high-quality' practices in recruitment and selection were seen to inhibit performance and, indeed, SMEs have often been criticised for a lack of a proactive and integrated approach to managing people. However, any assumption that universally applicable approaches to recruitment and selection are needed may ignore the distinctive processes and practices faced by particular organisations.

A CONTINGENCY APPROACH

The underlying principle that organisational policies and practices need to be shaped within a particular context is often referred to as the contingency approach. The argument put forward within this viewpoint is that successful policies and strategies are those which apply principles within the particular context faced by the unique organisation.

One example of a 'contingent factor' which can impact upon recruitment and selection is national culture. French (2007) draws attention to important cross-cultural differences in the area. For example, different cultures emphasise different attributes when approaching the recruitment and selection of employees. It is also the case that particular selection methods are used more or less frequently in different societies – see also Perkins and Shortland (2006). So in individualistic cultures such as the USA and UK, there is a preoccupation with selection methods that emphasise individual differences. Many psychometric tests do indeed originate from the USA. Furthermore, in a society which emphasises individual achievement as opposed to ascribed status (eg through age or gender), one might expect a raft of legislation prohibiting discrimination against particular groups. Here the expectation is that selection should be on the basis of individual personal characteristics or qualifications. This may contrast with more collectivist societies – for example, China, where personal connections may assume a more prominent role. Bjorkman and Yuan (1999) conducted one of several studies which reached this overall conclusion. It may also be true that selection methods are given varying degrees of face validity in different societies. A CIPD survey (2004f) on graphology discovered that although relatively few companies in the UK used graphology as a trusted method of selecting employees, its adoption was far more widespread, common and therefore accepted in other countries, including France.

In summary, the contingency approach with the underlying message that managing people successfully depends on contextual factors – 'it all depends' – can readily be applied to the area of recruitment and selection. The increasingly large number of organisations operating across national boundaries, or who employ workers from different cultural backgrounds, can benefit from formulating policies within an awareness of cultural difference.

ORGANISATIONAL CULTURE

It is unsurprising that the culture of a particular work organisation will influence selection decisions, with recruiters both consciously and unconsciously selecting those individuals who will 'best fit' that culture. In some organisations recruitment policy and practice is derived from their overall strategy which disseminates values into the recruitment and selection process. Mullins (2007, p.727) provides the example of Garden Festival Wales, an organisation created to run for a designated and short time-period. This organisation's managers were particularly concerned to create a culture via recruitment of suitable employees. This is an interesting example because this organisation had no prior history and it indicates the power of recruitment and selection in inculcating particular cultural norms.

Other research has demonstrated that individuals as well as organisations seek this 'best fit', providing evidence that many individuals prefer to work in organisations that reflect their personal values. Judge and Cable (1997) and Backhaus (2003) found that job-seekers may actively seek a good 'person–organisation fit' when considering prospective employers. This, of course, provides further support for the processual two-way model of recruitment and selection. However, justifying selection decisions on the basis of 'cultural fit' means that there are ethical issues to consider in terms of reasons for rejection: are organisations justified in determining who does and does not 'fit'? It may be that practical concerns also emerge – for example, in the danger of maintaining organisations in the image of current role models – which may be inappropriate in the future. Psychologists have also long recognised the threat posed by 'groupthink' where innovation is suppressed by a dominant group and an 'emperor's new clothes' syndrome develops, with individuals reluctant to voice objections to bad group decisions.

9.9 ACTIVITY

Return to the IKEA case study (9.1) at the start of this chapter.

IKEA put great stress upon recruiting employees who will complement their organisational culture.

- What are the potential benefits of selecting a workforce in terms of an organisation's culture?
- What are the philosophical and practical arguments against selection based on values and work culture?

CONCLUSION

This chapter indicates the key importance of recruitment and selection in successful people management and leadership. A recognition of the importance of this aspect of people management is not new and 'success' in this field has often been linked with the avoidance of critical failure factors including undesirable levels of staff turnover and claims of discrimination from unsuccessful job applicants.

It has been argued here that it is also possible to identify aspects of recruitment and selection which link with critical success factors, differentiating organisational performance and going some way to delivering employees who can act as 'thinking performers'. It is proposed, for example, that a *competencies* approach focusing on abilities needed to perform a job well may be preferable to the use of a more traditional matching of job and person specifications. In addition, many organisations may increasingly wish to identify qualities of flexibility and creative thinking among potential employees although this may not always be the case; many contemporary jobs do not require such competencies on the part of job-holders. It is also the case that organisations should be preoccupied with the question of *validity* of selection methods, ideally combining methods which are strong on practicality and cost, such as interviewing, with other measures which are more effective predictors of performance. It is proposed finally that a *managing diversity* approach, welcoming individual difference, may enhance organisational performance and create a climate in which thinking performers can emerge and flourish.

However, it is proposed that a *contingency approach* to recruitment and selection, recognising that organisational policies and practices are shaped by contextual factors, remains valid and that 'effectiveness' in recruitment and selection may vary according to particular situational factors. In this regard it is noted that cultural differences could be an important factor in predicting the relative success of recruitment and selection measures.

9.10 DISCUSSION QUESTIONS

1. Indicate with examples three ways in which recruitment and selection policies and practices can be used by an organisation aiming to develop staff as 'thinking performers'.
2. Evaluate the evidence regarding the potential validity of biodata and personality assessment as tools for selecting employees.
3. What do you understand by the contingency approach to recruitment and selection? Provide two examples, from academic sources or your own experience, to illustrate this approach.

EXPLORE FURTHER

Arnold, J., Silvester, J., Patterson, F., Robertson, I., Cooper, C. and Burnes, B. (2005) *Work Psychology: Understanding human behaviour in the workplace*, 4th edition. Harlow: FT/Prentice Hall. Chapter 5 provides a clear and interesting discussion of different selection techniques and their validity.

Redman, T. and Wilkinson, A.(2006) *Contemporary Human Resource Management: Texts and cases*, 2nd edition. Harlow: FT/Prentice Hall. Chapter 3 takes a decision-making perspective on the topic of employee selection.

Thompson, P. and McHugh, D. (2002) *Work Organisations: A critical introduction*, 3rd edition. Basingstoke: Palgrave Macmillan. In Chapter 15 entitled 'Masks for tasks', the authors take a critical perspective on the topics of how we assess others' attributes and how such perceptions are used in employee selection.

CHAPTER 10

Learning, Training and Development: Creating the Future?

Sarah Gilmore and Gary Rees

LEARNING OUTCOMES

After reading this chapter, you should be able to:

- understand the organisational and economic need for skills – what they consist of, and how they affect the HRD function and its activities
- identify where responsibility for HRD lies, and outline why that is contested
- understand the systematic training cycle, and evaluate its contribution and its shortcomings
- consider historical and contemporary approaches to the evaluation of learning within the context of the training cycle and the concerns about the value-added of training and development activity.

INTRODUCTION: RESPONDING TO CHANGE AND CREATING THE FUTURE

As previous chapters have outlined, changes within the wider business environment have been accompanied by 'new' agendas for reconfiguring organisational structure, culture, work arrangements and the psychological contract that underpins them. This period of change has also seen a shift occurring in the occupational structure of the UK. It has involved a change from production-oriented manual labour to more services-based non-manual work and has implied an alteration in skills demand from manual skills to generic cognitive skills such as communication, problem-solving and the ability to use IT. The human resource development (HRD) function and allied practices arguably play a strategically crucial role in facilitating many of the changes witnessed during this period. It also faces the same imperatives as the human resources management (HRM) function – to operate strategically as a change agent and business partner, working in conjunction with a variety of organisational stakeholders. This seems to require a balance between maintaining the present organisational focus through a sound skills and knowledge base of the workforce while simultaneously seeking to identify and install the abilities needed to compete successfully in the future. Many commentators argue that these new skills will revolve around the creation of 'knowledge-creating practices' where learning from workplace experiences facilitates the swift creation and development of new products and services which allows companies to compete more efficiently and effectively in increasingly dynamic consumer-oriented markets.

Meeting these imperatives means that the HRD function does not operate in an organisational vacuum. Indeed, HRD practices at organisational level are often influenced by three interconnected pressures. The first pertains to government education and training policy because this will determine the skills and knowledge quotient possessed by the UK workforce and also provide learning, training and development frameworks and opportunties for organisations and their employees to access in order to upskill. The second relates to the national and organisational need for a skilled workforce (outlined further below), and the last imperative concerns current organisational and other related theories influencing organisations and HRD itself. The ways in which these forces and interests interact and engage will influence the location of HRD at both national and organisational levels. However, the status of the function will ultimately depend upon the ways in which it can demonstrate how its activities add value to the economy and to the organisation through providing a clear line of sight from its interventions and the attainment of organisational objectives. This is not as easy as it might appear, but it is an activity that the function has to engage with if it is to attract and sustain investment in its work.

10.1 ACTIVITY

Consider your own organisation or one you are familiar with. Is there a department or function devoted to training? If not, who takes responsibility for the training and development of staff? If a functional unit does exist, how do they engage in their work with key organisational stakeholders who have an interest in training and development? What kinds of interventions are designed and delivered by this function – or do other people outside the function deliver training? If so, who are they? How is training evaluated? How will companies without a dedicated function be able to meet future performance challenges without it?

What this chapter seeks to do is to outline the national and organisational need for skilled labour before moving on to an investigation into how HRD activities and interventions have been structured. This depiction and analysis of the systematic training cycle will incorporate a different starting-point to HRD activity: placing learning transfer at centre stage rather than the process itself before investigating approaches towards training evaluation and the relationship between training and high-performance outcomes.

THE NEED FOR SKILLS AND DEVELOPMENT

As previously indicated, HRD does not operate in a vacuum. Factors such as globalisation, the industrial restructuring occurring in the UK and in many other Western countries during the 1990s, the continuing challenges set by technology, as well as the emergence of the 'knowledge economy', are continuing to have a profound impact on the need for skills in order to ensure that companies and national economies can compete within competitive markets. Whereas skills were once *a* key lever for prosperity, they are increasingly *the* key lever – pivotal in the ability for an economy or organisation to compete internationally (Leitch, 2006). But although the UK economy is generally in a strong position, having had 14 years of unbroken growth with the highest employment rate in the G7, there has been a long-standing concern with the less than world-class nature of our workforce skills. This was outlined in the Leitch Report (2006). As he noted, more than one third of adults do not hold the equivalent of a basic school-leaving qualification. Almost one half of adults (17 million) have difficulty with numbers, and one seventh (5 million) are not functionally literate. This is worse than the UK's principal global competitors who are advancing rapidly. China and India are creating 4 million graduates a year as set against the 250,000 produced in the UK. But continuing to improve the performance of UK skills will not be sufficient to catch up or to overcome some of the problems outlined above because over 70% of the 2020 workforce have already completed their compulsory education. Leitch's review asserted that even if the UK were to meet current skills targets, there would still be a shortfall in skills beside those of our competitors in 2020. We are currently running just to stand still.

10.2 ACTIVITY

Investigate three of the main government approaches towards training: NVQs, the New Deal and Modern Apprenticeships. What are the main features of each programme, and what assessment can you make of their success in terms of meeting the skills shortages and gaps identified in the Leitch Report?

Does your own organisation utilise these schemes in any way? If so, where does it make use of them, and why? What is your company's experience of them and the value they add?

In addition to concerns regarding national and organisational competitiveness, the New Labour Government has continued to make a direct link between the attainment and consistent development of skills, lifelong employment and social inclusion. Should the UK be able to build on educational reforms at schools, colleges and universities, it might be able to make the country's skills base one of its strengths and thus heighten business competitiveness. However, should the skills agenda fail to be met, the UK not only risks poor economic performance but increasing inequality, deprivation and child poverty with the possibility of a generation being cut off permanently from employment. The best form of welfare, according to this mantra, is to ensure that people can adapt to change. In this way, the government skills agenda is not only concerned with organisational or economic competitiveness but is directly focused on the need to maintain and strengthen social cohesion in the UK through sustained employment for its citizens. Skills shortages and skills gaps therefore signify more than the need for suitably qualified employees to sustain organisational competitiveness.

SKILLS SHORTAGES AND SKILLS GAPS

So what are skills shortages and where are the skills gaps? In answering that question, it is important to see the labour market as being composed of several smaller markets, each being defined by the skill types and levels demanded by employers and being supplied by employees, rather than seeing it as a homogeneous mass. Thus 'skills' can be described as the capabilities and expertise required in a particular occupation or activity, and are often equated with the ability to perform a task to a predefined level of competence (Frogner, 2002). Basic skills such as literacy and numeracy are required in most jobs. But other skills such as teamworking and communication are often referred to as 'transferable' or 'generic' skills because they can also be used across a large number of different occupations. Specific, vocational skills refer to those particular skills needed to work within an occupation or occupational group and tend to be less transferable between occupations (Gibb and Megginson, 2001).

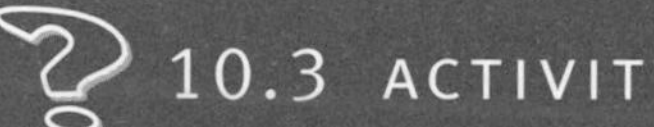

10.3 ACTIVITY

Where do skills gaps and skills shortages exist in your organisation and sector, and why do they occur, do you think? How might they be overcome, and what approaches would be most useful – the use of governmental vocational education and training schemes, a scheme that was focused on the skills needs of your specific sector, or interventions aimed at the organisational level? Or would a combination of all three be more appropriate?

Skills shortages arise when there are more vacancies requiring certain skills than there are people available in the external labour market with those skills. In relation to employment, the 2001 and 2004 National Employers Skills Surveys found that skills shortages are particularly common for skilled trades positions such as skilled construction, metal and electrical trades as well as personal service occupations such as nursery nurses, teaching assistants, nursing auxiliaries and air travel assistants. For those employers recruiting for jobs, the main skills areas in which shortages are found are technical and practical skills, communication skills, customer-handling, teamworking and problem-solving skills, indicating a relatively high incidence where generic skills are lacking. In addition to skills shortages, skill gaps can also occur. These are deficiencies in the skills of an employer's *existing* workforce, both at the individual level and overall, which prevent the firm from achieving its business objectives. The 2004 NESS indicated that one in five establishments (20%) reported skills gaps in its workforce, and some 1.5 million workers were described by employers as not being fully proficient. This represents 7% of the total workforce in England.

Both numerically and in density terms (ie the number of staff with skills gaps as a proportion of employment), the majority of skills gaps lie within 'lower-level' occupations rather than in management or professional positions. Approaching a third of a million staff in sales and customer service roles and a quarter of a million elementary occupation workers (which includes such jobs as cleaners, shelf-fillers, waiters and bar staff) were described as not being fully proficient. However, the main reason employers give as to why employees are not fully proficient is that they lack experience or have recently been recruited – indeed, this was at least part of the reason explaining almost three in four of all skills gaps. It means that many of these deficiencies may be relatively short-term and capable of being bridged over time or as a result of training and development interventions.

Other causes of skills gaps are more difficult to overcome and cannot be expected to diminish in the short to medium term because the reason for their existence lies with a lack of employee motivation and inability to keep up with change. Approximately a quarter of all staff with skills gaps (27%) are not fully proficient at least in part because they are not motivated to gain necessary skills, and 24% lack proficiency at least in part because of their inability to adapt to change. But employee culpability needs to be set against a scenario where organisations also lack the ability to train staff appropriately – even when companies engage in training and have training plans.

SO WHERE DOES RESPONSIBILITY FOR SKILLS AND DEVELOPMENT LIE?

At this point it is important to raise the question as to where responsibility and accountability for skills lies as well as who pays for upskilling and who decides the content of skills interventions at national and local level. Traditionally, responsibility and accountability for the provision of training and employee and development has been left to employers. However, the experience of relative economic decline witnessed in the 1980s raised a number of questions regarding the role played by education and training policies in reversing that trend. It has become increasingly evident that employers cannot achieve the major investment needed by the national economy in training. This is not due to employers not being trusted to engage in training with anything other than a focus on self-interest, but because until relatively recently the framework for vocational education and training was poorly integrated with a plethora of different awards being available from a variety of different award bodies (Coopers and Lybrand, 1986; Leitch, 2006). However, whether such an approach (often termed 'voluntarism') should be abandoned entirely is still a subject for debate, as the Leitch Report and its recommendations illustrated. The review of skills conducted by Leitch found that the supply-side in education dominates what skills get delivered, with the demand-side not being interpreted as 'what employers need'. The regionally based vocational education and training structure often misses sector needs and the complexity and bureaucracy that accompanies many of these schemes is a major deterrent to companies that might benefit from participation in such schemes and programmes.

But employers do not escape criticism. As Harrison (2005) notes, some of the main reasons employers do not train enough are often linked to a short-term focus on profit and a view of training as a cost rather than as an investment. There is also a fear by many that trained and developed employees are more likely to be poached by competitors, reinforcing the view that uncertain returns are made on an investment in training. This view also coincides with many companies' preferring to recruit for skills and development rather than to nurture it internally.

The argument as to which agency (government, employers, employees) takes responsibility for development of the UK workforce, or employees, is of no recent date and looks set to continue. At an organisational level, attitudes towards HRD may come down to managerial philosophy, culture, experiences of training and development as well as other variables. Typically, approaches will often be determined by managerial views as to whether employees need training to meet a given performance need (and therefore training is seen here as being instrumental and organisationally determined). Or, alternatively, does the company view employees as the main resource of the organisation, with training assisting in maximising employee potential in a more organic, emergent way – meeting the needs of individual and employer – with the result that the organisation will similarly learn, grow and sustain its future?

Similarly, does the organisation adopt an organisation-wide approach to all training and development in a highly systematic way, governed by regulatory policies and procedures, or perhaps put an emphasis upon the development of the team or the individual? The paradoxical question whether we fit the person to the job or fit the job to the person may be of critical importance here and will reflect organisational priorities. Does the organisation need to train its employees for specific tasks, or does it wish to invest in long-term development of employees so that they are more adaptable and prepared for change? Sometimes both approaches might operate simultaneously and task-focused training might sit alongside more developmental opportunities – as the Activity below might demonstrate with regard to your own organisation.

10.4 ACTIVITY

Consider how your organisation determines whether an activity is deemed to be 'training' or to come under the category of 'development'. Some obvious indicators may be the title of the activity – for example, 'induction training' or 'management development', which is tied into the organisation's continuing professional development (CPD) processes and policy. Consider the design of the activity – whether it is interactive (eg discussion-based) or one-way communication (instruction or lecture), whether it involves an assessment of individuals or teams, etc.

Consider whether the activity is geared towards all employees in a systematic way ('one size fits all') or whether it is geared around an individual and his or her potential. Once you have gathered data on these considerations, ask yourself whether the activity can be classified as a 'training intervention' or more of a 'developmental activity'.

DEFINITIONS OF LEARNING, TRAINING AND DEVELOPMENT

Training is a planned and systematic way of improving a person's knowledge, skills and attitudes so that he or she can perform the current job more competently (Malone, 2003, p.76).

Development is the process of preparing a person to take on more onerous responsibilities or equip him or her for future promotion within the organisation (*ibid*).

Learning is the process which brings about persistent change in behaviour. Learning gives a person increased competence to deal successfully with his or her environment as by acquiring knowledge, skills and attitudes (Malone, 2003, p.152).

Although seeking universal definitions of 'learning', 'training' and 'development' may prove more onerous than the pursuit of the Holy Grail, the interrelationships between these terms are important. It could be argued that training adopts a

10.5 THEORY TASTER

LEARNING THE BASICS

Early theories on learning were derived from studies on animals. By using rewards and punishments, Skinner demonstrated how to manipulate animal learning. As one would expect, consistent positive reinforcement led to changes in behaviour – we use praise in the same way. Negative reinforcement (admonishment for humans) also changed behaviour, but curiously, intermittent reinforcement (either rewards or punishments) had a stronger and more lasting effect. Skinner and other 'behaviourists' laid the foundations for the more complex 'cognitive' theorists who developed ideas on the *process* of learning.

Piaget's work identified a developmental process whereby the child is able to tackle increasingly more difficult problems. Most of the UK education system exhibits a similar pattern with increasing complexity experienced as one moves from schoolwork to undergraduate and postgraduate study – each is more difficult and builds on the skills and knowledge of one's previous level of experience.

Kolb developed the concept of a 'learning cycle' which is useful in vocational learning. In the cycle, perceptions of the world (the concrete experience stage) are reflected upon (observation and reflection stage) and new ideas are developed (abstract conceptualisation stage). These are then tested in reality (active experimentation stage) and registered in another 'round' of the cycle as further set of concrete experiences is reflected upon. So the cycle continues.

Honey and Mumford used Kolb's learning cycle to suggest four learning styles. The 'activist' is interested in new experiences and ideas; the 'reflector' spends time considering the situation; the 'theorist' works out connections between the concepts at hand; and the pragmatist is biased towards applying these in the real world. For effective vocational learning, one needs to engage all styles, but Honey and Mumford's work has been useful in highlighting how a 'one-size-fits-all' approach to training and education may not suit all learners.

shorter-term remedial perspective compared to development, which could adopt a longer-term nurturing perspective. But to what extent does this argument depend upon the organisational context? If a medical consultant takes 13 years to qualify, would this be considered to be 'training' or 'development', or possibly both?

WHAT DOMINATES IN YOUR ORGANISATION – TRAINING, DEVELOPMENT OR LEARNING?

These questions are useful ones to consider and to revisit over time. To what extent has a shift occurred from training to development and learning? Where does the balance lie? Whatever the balance, organisations will need to organise and structure their work in this area. For many years, the ways in which this was achieved was via the aegis of the systematic training cycle (STC).

THE SYSTEMATIC TRAINING CYCLE

Many organisational functions such as Marketing, Finance and Operations will have their own particular framework which informs the ways in which they conduct their work. This is also true for the HRD function and trainers have developed their own logical or systematic approach. The systematic training cycle has been in existence since the early 1950s and is often associated with attempts to regularise and structure training activity post-World War II.

As can be seen from Figure 10.1, a systematic training cycle consists of four interlinked processes. Usually the entry point to the cycle is the need to analyse training needs, but it is equally true that the process of evaluation can be the catalyst. Training needs can be analysed at three levels: the organisational, the occupational and the individual. Once these needs have been assessed, the cycle moves on to the design and delivery stages. At this point the practical work of the training developer becomes highly iterative as these two particular elements of the cycle are hugely intertwined. When the intervention is complete, it should be evaluated – and this process is covered later on in this chapter. Suffice to say at this juncture that it is the one element of the cycle that tends to be dropped or enacted fairly superficially, for a number of reasons. However, in an environment where

Figure 10.1 A basic model of a systematic approach to training

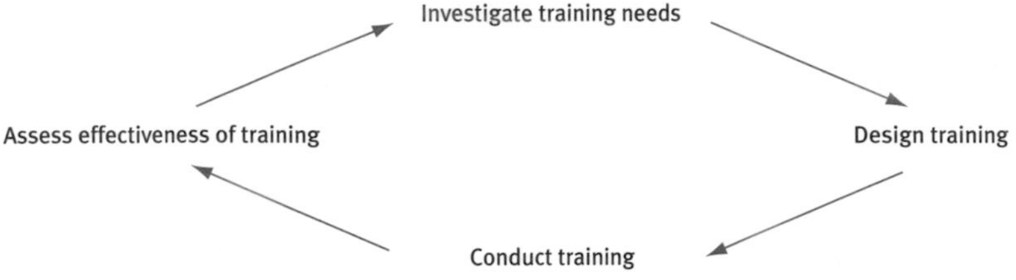

Source: Buckley, R. and Caple, C. (2004) *The Theory and Practice of Training*. London: Kogan Page, p.25

every function is now required to illustrate its contribution to the organisation – often in numerical, financial ways – failure to engage in this activity puts the function at risk of challenge.

Stringent criticism has been, and continues to be, levelled at the STC generally on the grounds that it is unresponsive to change, and is slow and costly in terms of resources, with the investment in time it demands being difficult to justify. Further criticism relates to the extent to which this ubiquitous diagram is systematic: do trainers always start with investigating training needs, and progress around the cycle? When practically engaging with this cycle, there is a great deal of interaction between each part of the process, which is not reflected in the diagram. Furthermore, the systematic approach can give the impression of being too cold and clinical, with little consideration of the human aspects of the procedure. However, as noted by Stewart (1999), its continuing influence and application seem to be established. The cycle could be envisaged as a logical relationship between the sequential stages in the process of investigating training needs, designing, delivering and validating training. As illustrated by Megginson (Boydell, 1983), it could be argued that systematic training came out of scientific management with the principles of such an approach still being influential in informing approaches to organising and managing. As Stewart notes (1999), the cycle can be mapped onto processes of individual performance review as well as strategic management, and the Investors in People Standard also has strong resonance with this model.

While its interconnected four stages aim to give structure and focus to both the work of the function and the design of training and development interventions, one crucial area that is not included concerns the need to ensure that learning is transferred from training and development activities. Another consideration is to what extent learning from workforce activity is shared and used to instigate improvements to organisational outputs – whatever they may be. Both aspects of learning transfer are important.

THE IMPORTANCE OF LEARNING AND LEARNING TRANSFER

Given the crucial importance of learning transfer, an alternative approach to the systematic training cycle could start from this perspective. It could involve a focus on workplace learning with a concern as to how learning transfer occurs from HRD interventions into the enactment of daily workplace activity. Studies of workplace learning indicate that even though formal learning interventions are planned and undertaken in order to improve organisational performance, most learning on the job is unplanned, unorganised and informal. This means that organisations will create much of their essential knowledge in the workplace via day-to-day processes embedded in normal working activities. So if everyday problem-solving and other activity generates learning as an informal and incidental side-effect, this extends beyond the boundaries of HRD and formal training and requires the function to embrace a broader range of learning activities. How does the HRD function recognise and enhance informal learning at the workplace? How is the emphasis of HRD activities to be shifted from training towards other informal methods of learning? And is such a move a correct one for all organisations and all sectors of the economy? What is the place in such a model for traditional approaches towards training and development? Would it be helpful for your own organisation?

10.6 ACTIVITY

Think about training programmes you might have attended. How was learning transfer facilitated? From your experience of work-based development and training, what methods are employed to assist in translating experiential and other learning into relevant workplace activity?

Slotte *et al* (2004, p.484) present a model (see Figure 10.2) that attempts to link learning at work and HRD – acknowledging formal and informal learning as equally important elements of learning at work but also emphasising that they entail different processes and different outcomes. Thus, informal learning occurs through daily workplace activities and produces what is termed 'implicit' or 'tacit' learning (learning that is taken for granted, and held in the minds of those who generate and use it), with formal learning taking place in the context of organised training activities. This generates explicit (ie learning that is more easily capable of explanation and thus capable of being shared with a wider audience) knowledge and skills. Because of the importance of informal learning and the tacit knowledge

Figure 10.2 Learning at work

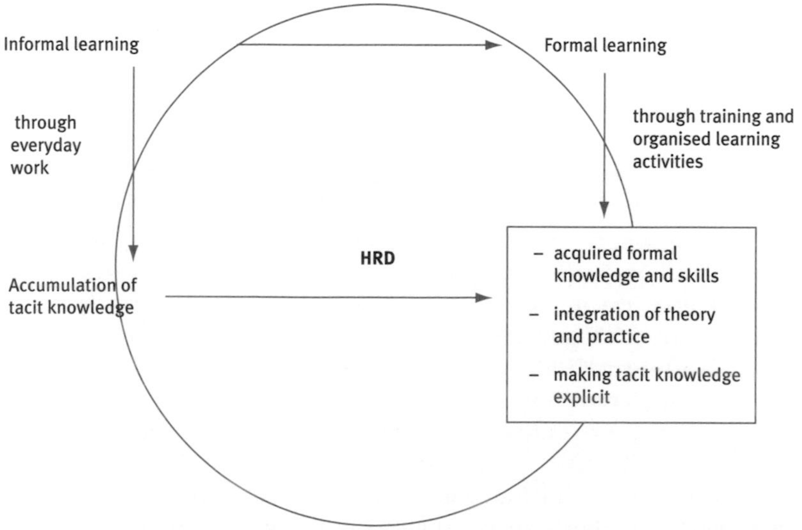

Informal learning
Formal learning
through everyday work
through training and organised learning activities
HRD
Accumulation of tacit knowledge
- acquired formal knowledge and skills
- integration of theory and practice
- making tacit knowledge explicit

Source: Slotte, V., Tynjälä, P. and Hytönen, T. (2004) 'How do HRD practitioners describe learning at work?', *Human Resource Development International*, Vo.7, No.4, p.486. Used with permission of Taylor & Francis Ltd

it produces, it must be put to use in practices intended to promote professional development. But as Slotte *et al* note, informal learning is not enough.

They give three reasons for this. First, tacit knowledge does not yield only positive outcomes but can also lead to bad habits and dysfunctional practices that do not serve the organisation well. Secondly, because new knowledge is being created so rapidly, informal learning cannot ensure that the knowledge and skills of organisation and people will keep pace with it. Finally, formal education and planned learning situations make it possible to exploit informal learning effectively, turn tacit knowledge into explicit knowledge and integrate conceptual knowledge and practical experience as a foundation for the development of expertise.

For Slotte *et al*, the HRD function plays an interesting role on the boundaries between formal and informal learning. HRD is often defined very broadly, covering functions related to career development as well as organisational development. It also has to connect with other functions such as HRM, which also have an interest in fostering learning capacity, to integrate a learning culture into overall business strategy and to promote the organisation's efforts to achieve high-quality performance. But due to this broad remit, HRD has remained a complex and nebulous entity with much of the discourse covered here being inherently challenging (hence the comfort of the systematic training cycle) using training needs analysis as part of the process of making that which is tacit explicit, while simultaneously identifying some of the potential barriers to training transfer occurring within formal programmes (Rosset, 1997). Finally, key questions for HRD specialists are: how do we ensure that learning (and learning transfer) has taken place, and how do we ensure that learning can be maximised in terms of organisational/business performance measures? Given the imperatives for the training and development function to clearly illustrate its business partner status, the area of evaluation is crucial.

THE POLITICS AND PRACTICES OF EVALUATION

Salinger and Deming (1982) suggest that the following evaluation questions must be aligned with evaluation strategies:

- To what degree does the training produce appropriate learning?
- To what degree is learning transferred to the job?
- To what degree is the knowledge or skill level maintained over time?
- Does the value of participants' improved performance meet or exceed the cost of training?

The organisation has to make some judgements about the measurement criteria to apply to these questions, and set appropriate processes in place to deal with any shortfall in the standards required. The difficulty in this approach might then link to an instrumental approach towards HRD, which may in turn remove the emphasis away from the individual and his or her aspirations towards purely organisational objectives, resulting in problems of employee motivation, job satisfaction and retention. 'The perceived difficulties associated with the evaluation of training often render the subject of much rhetoric but considerable practical neglect' (Sadler-Smith *et al*, 1999, p.369).

Table 10.1 Purposes of evaluation

Brinkerhoff (1987)	Phillips (1992)	Easterby-Smith (1986)	Bramley (1996)
1 To prove that training is aimed at worthwhile and important organisational issues	1 To determine whether a programme is accomplishing its objectives	1 For proving the worth and impact of training	1 For feedback (for control of training quality)
2 Operates smoothly and is enjoyable for participants; achieves its objectives	2 To identify the strengths and weaknesses in HRD	2 For improving future training interventions	2 For control (relating training policy and practice to organisational goals)
3 Uses the best and most cost-effective designs	3 To determine the costs and benefits	3 For learning where 'the attempt to observe something actually changes the thing one is observing' (1986: 13–17)	3 For research (adding to knowledge of training theory)
4 Is used effectively on the job	4 To decide who should participate in future programmes	4 For intervention (affecting the way the programme is viewed and engaged in by the key players – participants, managers and facilitators)	
5 Provides valuable organisational benefits	5 To identify which participants benefited most	5 For 'power games': use of evaluatory data in a political way	
6 To reinforce major learning points			
7 To assist in marketing future training			
8 To determine if the programme was appropriate			

Source: Sadler-Smith, E. *et al* (1999) 'Adding value to HRD: evaluation, Investors in People and small firm training', *Human Resource Development International*, Vol.2, No.4, p.372. Used with permission of Taylor & Francis Ltd

The extent of the issue of whether to carry out training evaluation is very much set within contextual constraints and considerations. Who, why, when, how and what is being evaluated is important. From a business perspective, what is the purpose of carrying out training evaluation? For many organisations the process is used primarily to discover whether resources are being used appropriately. But having ascertained this, what actions are taken as a consequence? Sadler-Smith *et al* (1999, p.371) refer to systematic and taxonomic approaches to evaluation whereby an attempt is made to describe systematically the whole training and development process, with evaluation traditionally thought of as the final stage of the systematic training cycle. Within this approach, the 'why' evaluate question is paramount. An outcome of Sadler-Smith *et al*'s work is the construction of a range of purposes that could be fulfilled by evaluation (see Table 10.1).

With reference to the approach described by Sadler-Smith *et al* (1999), a range of approaches could be adopted which both include and develop the classic Kirkpatrick evaluation model: see Table 10.2. Typically, training evaluation

Table 10.2 Summary of taxonomic evaluation models

Kirkpatrick (1967)	**Phillips (1992)**	**Warr *et al* (1978)**	**Hamblin (1974)**
1 *Reaction*: to gather participant reactions at the end of a training programme	1 *Reaction and planned action*: participant satisfaction and planned actions	1 *Context*: obtaining information about the situation to decide if and how training can help	Training leads to Reactions which lead to Learning which leads to Changes in behaviour which lead to Changes in the organisation which lead to Changes in the achievement of ultimate goals
2 *Learning*: to assess whether the learning objectives for the programme have been met	2 *Learning*: measures changes in knowledge, skill and attitudes	2 *Input*: identifying the interventions most likely to achieve the desired results	
3 *Behaviour*: to assess whether job performance changes as a result of training	3 *Job application*: measures changes in on-the-job behaviour	3 *Reaction*: what the trainees' opinions of the training are	
4 *Results*: to assess the impact of training on job performance	4 *Business results*: measures changes in business impact variables	4 *Outcomes*: immediate (learning); intermediate (behaviour); ultimate (results)	
	5 *Return on investment*: compares programme benefits to the costs		

Source: Sadler-Smith, E. *et al* (1999) 'Adding value to HRD: evaluation, Investors in People and small firm training', *Human Resource Development International*, Vol.2, No.4, p.372. Used with permission of Taylor & Francis Ltd

consists of two aspects – measuring results (the degree of learning that has taken place), and measuring impact (the effect on the people involved, their teams, functions and the organisation). However, a decision has to be taken as to which of these aspects – the degree of learning or its impact – is more important.

10.7 ACTIVITY

At this point you might like to consider how your own organisation evaluates training using one of the models outlined in Table 10.2. How does it evaluate at the higher levels?

To what extent is the nature and need for learning determined by these two different perspectives? Bramley and Kitson (1994, p.11) argue that

> most trainers use an individual, educational model of training process where the emphasis is on encouraging individuals to learn something which is thought to be useful and then expecting them to find uses for the learning.

These authors use the Kirkpatrick model to further differentiate between different levels of evaluation by adopting the model shown in Figure 10.3.

Figure 10.3 Models for evaluating training

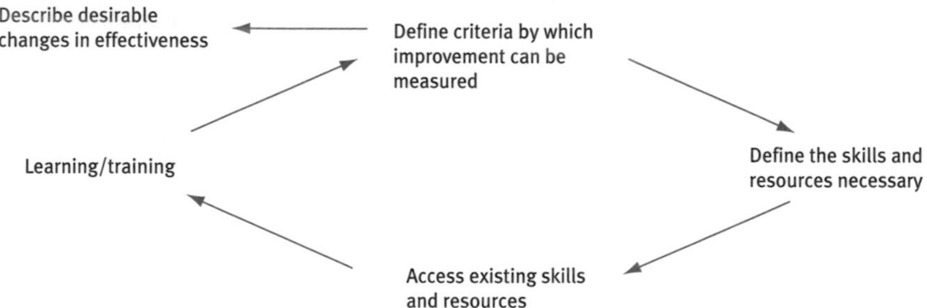

Source: Bramley, P. and Kitson, B. (1994) 'Evaluating training against business criteria', *Journal of European Industrial Training*, Vol.18, No.1, pp10–14. Reproduced with permission, Emerald Publishing

The individual training model is more appropriate for Kirkpatrick's levels 1 and 2 criteria, but may prove difficult to evaluate higher levels. However, levels 3, Reaction and Learning, and 4, Behaviour and Results, may be more suited to the increased effectiveness model cited in Figure 10.3. The question arises as to why organisations typically fail to evaluate at level 4 (seeking to determine the effect of training upon observable business performance).

CURRENT RESEARCH INTO TRAINING EVALUATION

The CIPD's Report (Anderson, 2007, p.2) on its model of learning evaluation indicates that 'a "one-size-fits-all" set of metrics to establish the value of learning is inappropriate'. In order for organisations to assess the value of learning, a broader perspective has to be adopted – one that is based on ensuring that HRD activity is in alignment with the organisation's strategic priorities: see Figure 10.4.

Figure 10.4 The value and evaluation process for strategic LTD

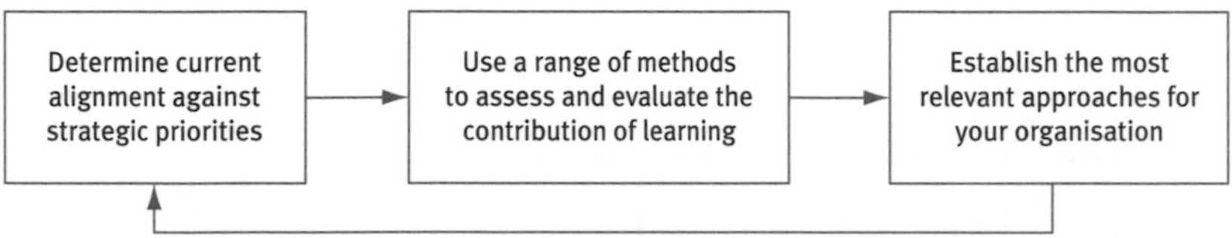

Source: Anderson, V. (2007) *The Value of Learning: From return on investment to return on expectation*. London: CIPD, p.4

The CIPD's *Value of Learning* research (Anderson, 2007) highlights four different approaches to assessing the learning value contribution that are of direct interest to managers, as shown in Figure 10.5. The four quadrants of the model help us to understand how to assess the value of learning contribution while also allowing for flexibility in respect of how the activities in each segment can be achieved.

Figure 10.5 Approaches to assessment and evaluation

Learning function measures	Return on expectation measures
Return on investment measures	Benchmark and capacity measures

Source: Anderson, V. (2007) *The Value of Learning: From return on investment to return on expectation*. London: CIPD, p.38

Learning function measures tend to focus on the efficiency and effectiveness of the learning function (or wherever the body of learning and development occurs within the organisation). How well is the learning function managed internally? Does it provide the appropriate range of training and development provision? Could the provision be more cost-effective?

Return on expectation measures consider the extent to which the anticipated benefits of the learning investment have been realised. The CIPD *Value of Learning* Report (Anderson, 2007) posits the following key questions:

- What were the original expectations of organisational stakeholders for the learning or training? Have those expectation since changed?
- What changes have occurred as a result of the learning processes?
- To what extent have stakeholder expectations been met?

Return on investment measures focus on how costs incurred compare against the benefits of learning and training interventions, and may involve an assessment of the payback period (the time it takes for the costs to be recovered) for specific learning or training investments.

Fundamental to these measures is whether learning is contributing to defined performance targets and measures.

10.8 CASE STUDY

CANON UK AND IRELAND

Canon UK forms a major part of the European operation of Canon Inc, the well-known Japanese corporation that specialises in all forms of imaging products. Canon operates in over 20 European countries and the European headcount in 2006 was over 10,000.

Caroline Price, the Strategic Business Partner, Human Resources, is a member of the executive management team and has responsibility for all aspects of human resources, including learning and development. The strategic learning contribution is to enable the organisation to 'grow skills and productivity to prepare for future business as well as to cope with current business challenges. This involves the development of flexible attitudes that continue to "fit" with the Canon philosophy as it evolves in very dynamic market situations.'

Measuring and reporting on the value of learning is a key issue for Canon UK. Key indicators that form part of the on-going assessment of the value of learning are metrics related to broad HR priorities such as recruitment and retention, employee satisfaction and pay. These form part of a wider approach to benchmarking and the use of a balanced scorecard.

Because a key contribution of learning is to equip the organisation to meet future-oriented challenges, it is also important that measures of value are future-oriented. 'Return on investment' models for assessing the value of learning are tailored accordingly to focus more on 'return on expectation' and achievement against business targets. In line with this, Canon makes sure that some measures of value are built into the learning design process for major corporate learning initiatives.

In a company like Canon, where metrics and measures are an important part of management processes, it is important that learning and development professionals are able to measure and report on the value of their activity. A challenge, however, is to ensure that inappropriate data is not 'forced' into a scorecard measure or metric for the sake of completeness. Caroline Price highlights the importance here of understanding 'what is behind the figures', taking account of the very fast pace of change within the organisation and its environment that can make comparative data go out of date very quickly. For Price, evaluating 'what is different' as a result of learning processes in the organisation is as important as completing a numerical assessment.

Canon is aware that 'soft' measures can be just as useful as hard data. Numerical and quantifiable data, therefore, is complemented by informal and often anecdotal assessments of the value that learning is adding to the business. Like many organisations Canon has come some way with the process of assessing and reporting on the value of learning, but the company is also aware that there is scope for further work in this important area.

Source: http://www.cipd.co.uk/helpingpeoplelearn/_vcnukndirl.htm)

Benchmark and capacity measures tend to focus on external or internal comparison of standards related to HR processes and performance. These comparisons can then lead to judgements as to whether there is 'good practice', 'excellence', or areas in need of development. Such a comparison could be a one-off, but the CIPD report urges that a continuous improvement process may prove more useful.

Although each approach is different, organisations may wish to consider which approach is most suited to their context and needs, and then consider an alternative approach.

CONCLUSION

In some ways this chapter has operationalised the systematic training cycle – although it was not the explicit intention of the authors to do so! The starting-point of the chapter was an identification of training needs: the need for skills and the premium being placed on their attainment in order to compete effectively. This places a requirement on government, organisations and increasingly on the individual as well to engage not only in providing training to ensure occupational effectiveness but to ensure that companies and inviduals can learn from the daily challenges of work itself. For the HRD function – where it exists – this is setting a challenge. Not only are they required to ensure that training and development provision exists to meet current business challenges, they have to engage in consistent environmental scanning to identify what the business needs for skills and knowledge will be in the (often uncertain) future. Whereas the broad parameters of short- to medium-term strategic goals might be possible to map out, acquiring precise details might not. This will mean that when engaging in the design and delivery of training and development opportunities, the function will have to be highly agile and responsive – potentially creating a future from workplace experiences as well as strategic targets. If this is picture has credibility, it means that those responsible for HRD might have to revisit and review the ways in which the function operates and how it structures its 'offerings'. To what extent is the systematic training cycle now a valid and appropriate structuring mechanism for both the work of the function and its outputs? Does it need to be replaced, or, where your company is concerned, does it simply require adjustment?

As stated earlier on in the chapter, the competitive pressures on organisations have resulted in all organisational functions facing heightened accountability for their contribution to the company. This has been seen in such initiatives as 'the balanced scorecard' (Kaplan and Norton, 1992) as well as the range of metrics used when implementing the range of quality standards. Although it is challenging to evaluate phenomena as nebulous and intangible as learning and development, the HRD function cannot escape the imperative to show how it adds value. Should it fail to do so, then it cannot expect to escape the criticism of elitism (at the very least) or the threat of outsourcing.

If the HRD function can demonstrate its added value on a continual basis, and link this closely to changing strategic objectives and goals, then it may sustain itself. The bottom line for any organisation is its people and the continued development of its people, demonstrated by its core competence, core capability or human capital, which are all vested in Human Resource Development.

10.9 DISCUSSION QUESTIONS

1. Choose one of the government's vocational education and training schemes. To what extent is it based on the systematic training cycle? Illustrate your answer with examples.
2. Some organisations have been able to develop more innovative approaches to learning and development than others, moving away from a dominant focus on job skills development. Why do you think that this movement might be occurring, and in which industries? How do these innovators facilitate creativity?
3. Using one of the models of evaluation outlined in this chapter, how would you evaluate a management development programme that has been in existence for three to five years?

EXPLORE FURTHER

For those interested in the pragmatics of workplace training and development, the combined texts/papers give an excellent overview of key areas of theory and practice.

Anderson, V. (2007) *The Value of Learning: From return on investment to return on expectation*. London: CIPD.

Blanchard, P. N. and Thacker, J. W. (2006) *Effective Training: Systems, strategies and practices*. New Jersey: Pearson/Prentice Hall.

Buckley, R. and Caple, J. (2004) *The Theory and Practice of Training*. London: Kogan Page.

Reid, M. A., Barrington, H. and Brown, M. (2004) *Human Resource Development: Beyond training interventions*. London: CIPD.

CHAPTER 11

Conclusion

Charlotte Rayner

LEARNING OUTCOMES

The purpose of this chapter is to highlight the recurrent themes within the text in order to identify the key challenges facing managers in the contemporary workplace.

After reading this chapter, you should be able to:

- summarise the relevant external environment and its effect on the public and private sectors and HR
- identify and discuss the conundrums inherent in managing and leading people both in 'knowledge working' and highly 'standardised, low-cost' occupations simultaneously in the same contexts
- understand the underlying strategic challenges within the issue of diversity
- discuss the evolving nature of the psychological contract
- understand the reasons for the increasing importance of partnering.

PRESSURE, PRESSURE . . .

All organisations need to confront the key issues produced by the external environment. Private sector organisations in Western economies, challenged by the lower cost-base of other economies such as China and India, have moved into 'knowledge working' as a means of adding value (Handy, 1984). Emerging economies, built on relatively low-cost provision, will themselves develop as the cycles of wealth creation and increased opportunity begin to take their course. Such an evolutionary trend reflects better communication and accessibility provided by the Internet, improvements in infrastructure, and decades of tough competition necessitating cost-cutting in all sectors. As these trends evolve, all organisations become challenged to achieve sustainability in their marketplaces. The resultant pressures can be dealt with more effectively by those organisations which manage and lead employees to a high level of competence.

The public sector does not escape such pressures. Since 1990, a revolution has occurred within UK local government and public service providers. Political agendas comprising reduction in taxes (local and national) together with advances in transparency and public audit have resulted in generational change in the sector. The UK Government has consistently rewarded those organisations which do well and public service providers are now used to a variety of 'league tables'. Such processes increase expectation to perform in ever-spiralling demands. Recent downturns in global and local economies may well squeeze the public sector as governments seek to balance expenditure.

Such pressures have changed the nature of leadership and management. Hospitals now attract a different type of chief executive from what they did 15 years ago. The same is true of most of the public sector and the expanding voluntary sector. Top leaders now need to 'drive' the organisation in more senses than one: steering has always been a function, but chief executives are pressing the accelerator for change and achievement as never before.

HUMAN RESOURCES SHARES THE PRESSURE

How can we think through these scenarios in relation to the HR function, and management in general? Here the twin concepts of 'infrastructure' and 'differentiator' organisations fit well. Preceding chapters have referred to Prahalad and Hamel's (1990) concept of competences. Arguably, we can think of 'infrastructure' as *threshold competencies* needed by any organisation merely to exist as a going concern. Beyond that, as the other chapters evidence, the routes to achieving excellence (distinctive competencies or 'differentiators') are many and varied. Readers will find no panacea for specific successful differentiation. Key to the notion of 'high-performance working', which has threaded through this text (eg Wood and de Menezes, 1998), is that it presents a multiplicity of routes.

Fundamentally, managing and leading people is a tough topic. If it was easy, we would have defined and implemented that checklist by now. It is hard work which requires thought, care and considerable attention to detail in every interaction and decision made. The sheer breadth of sub-topics covered by the chapters in this book is impressive, and expertise is developing in all areas.

Likewise HR is under pressure too, with changing roles emerging (Reilly *et al*, 2007). Benign, parenting and bureaucratic processes of personnel departments still exist within some organisations. Increasingly, functions have been subcontracted as specialist providers present cost savings and technological efficiencies.

Such subcontracting patterns can leave the HR function exposed, needing to add value beyond its old administrative role (Legge, 2005). The last decade has witnessed a move to 'business partnering' where the HR function behaves as an internal consultant to sub-units of the organisation (Brocklebank and Ulrich, 2005). Thus within the HR profession we are also evolving new ways of working. Helping employees to lead and manage others involves developing skills in adjunct to their key 'profession' (Rynes, Giluk and Brown, 2007). Human resources professionals assisting groups of engineers, waste disposal experts, mortgage administrators or IT professionals enable better managerial practice to cascade through the organisation and add value for the achievement of strategic objectives.

What then are the key challenges? As the structure of work and organisations change, so HR's role of working with colleagues to manage and lead people has to change. Highly significant within these current changes are the challenges provided by three different sub-groups of staff: knowledge workers, service workers and those working in subcontracted organisations.

KNOWLEDGE WORKERS

The concepts involved in recruiting, retaining and retraining knowledge workers have changed considerably in recent years. Less emphasis is placed on recruiting and training knowledge workers for specific jobs because jobs are changing so quickly. Instead, employees are recruited and developed who can contribute in a flexible way to an organisation's future. Blueprints for effectiveness, designed by people who are distant from the task or problem, do not work well. Stripping out layers of management has, in some ways, been both cost-effective and efficient as staff close to the problems are 'empowered' to work through solutions themselves to effect appropriate change.

For such developments to succeed, managers really do need to have skills in managing and leading people. The importance of focusing effort on business objectives and the need for a clear direction and purpose is crucial in order to ensure that the managing and leading of staff has a clear aim, and thus provides the basis for performance management. This presents a fundamental infrastructure task. Staff will detect any absence of a clear direction, and its lack will undermine efforts of leading (nowhere?) and managing (for what purpose?). As a proactive partner, the HR group will be able to advise senior managers when direction has been lost, and work with them to provide a coherent and well-communicated approach to engaging skills and talents in order to align them with organisational goals.

Direction enables the working through of a set of HR-related tasks. What are the qualities of these knowledge workers? How can we either recruit and select them from outside the organisation or develop them from within the organisation? Growing sophistication informs decisions about the organisation and knowledge workers in terms of both skills and attributes at ever-deeper levels of conceptualisation (eg Holden, 2002). Although we are usually recruiting individuals, we are simultaneously trying to integrate them into a team. Diversity is now a buzz-word in organisations. Knowledge teams which are diverse and properly empowered (Chapters 3 and 6) will make better decisions than groups that are homogeneous (Page, 2007), but the management of them is currently a matter of practitioner and academic debate (eg Klein and Harrison, 2007).

How organisations approach and manage diversity, introduced in Chapter 5, will be a 'differentiator' for the future. It is much easier, and tempting, to hire similar people who get on easily, thus avoiding the 'diversity issue'. It is likely that all sectors can survive (at an infrastructure level) without embracing diversity, depending on the level of supply of specific workers. Where there are staff shortages, finding homogeneous workers will require either specialised recruitment and selection (Chapter 9), selective internal promotion through learning, training and development (Chapter 10), or increasing rewards (Chapter 7). It is hard to see how an organisation can only partially adopt the changes needed to cope with a diverse organisation and still remain effective. If trends continue, the UK and other markets with high employment levels will continue to be net importers of skilled workers, with most entrants having a diverse range of backgrounds. The UK government's adoption of a 'points system' for immigration should enable focused replenishment of the overall workforce, but remains to be tested. Those organisations which learn how to take advantage of new pools of talent have potential for differentiation.

Hand-in-hand with diversity come the effort and challenge involved in managing the inevitable conflict that difference produces. The effective manager will ensure that any ensuing problems are limited to constructive and task-related conflicts (Jehn, 1994), and do not degenerate into damaging interpersonal disputes. Potentially, diverse groups will produce innovative and smart solutions that provide (differentiated) competitive advantage. To be successful such staff will need context- or contingency-based leadership styles (Chapter 4) rather than one-best-way. Managers who can cope with such demands will have to be recruited or developed.

Getting the best from knowledge workers is dependent on their having the autonomy and discretion to contribute to their maximum ability. Clearly, this can be risky for the organisation and requires a certain level of trust and more subtle (and probably informal) forms of performance management. A full system thus comprises hired, empowered and bright, well-managed knowledge workers with managers who have commensurate skills and abilities. If the whole 'system' does not work from a process point of view, however, sustainability and the high-performance working ideal is lost.

WORKERS AND MANAGERS IN 'STANDARD' JOBS

Much HR literature focuses on achieving the best from knowledge workers. As the authors of several chapters have pointed out, we can be in danger of ignoring the less glamorous, often worse-paid staff who occupy more routine functions. Some would argue, especially from a total quality view, that all jobs can be treated as holding knowledge and all staff should be seen as knowledge workers, and this is probably true. For the most part, however, our rhetoric fails to meet that reality, and in many instances standardised jobs are potentially just that. Certain tasks (such as serving at a food counter) have been through the mill of cost-cutting. Sections of employment have very often been de-skilled, to a point of alienation from their tasks (see Chapter 6). These workers experience pressures different from those of the uncertainties connected to knowledge workers, which include the pressure from high-volume repetitive work with little control and the associated dangers of work intensification.

Performance management is usually more straightforward for these roles (and upwards through their hierarchies) because the tangible outputs are measurable (Chapter 7). In reality one is often looking to neutralise or minimise the damage that can be caused by staff not bothering (consciously or unconsciously) to undertake routine tasks effectively. In such instances a person–job fit approach (Chapter 9) is appropriate in order to align expectations on both sides of the employment relationship. Clearly, this strategy has consequences for the psychological contract, which will be discussed towards the end of this chapter. Regarding leadership in such contexts (Chapter 4), it is likely that selection will depend on strength in 'management' with 'leadership' (at a high level) being less crucial.

While performance management of standardised workers might be straightforward (because their tasks are straightforward), reward is not. In Chapter 7 Lowman and Rees described wages as an important aspect of reward, up to a point. For many standardised workers, wages are of high importance. However, an organisation must ensure that it does not create an escalating cost-drain from year-on-year wage increases at high levels because these are difficult to correct at a later stage. To recruit and retain standardised staff, the 'cocktail' of benefits has to be thought through carefully to match the needs of a targeted set of available staff. Simple financial rewards can be used in an uncomplicated contract that has supervisors who are strong in 'management' using conventional performance management processes. Alternatively, one might try to cut the wage bill and offer other types of inducements, such as prospects of internal development and promotion (used commonly by media companies), a strong sense of positive-value culture (illustrated by the supermarket Asda), or promote positive aspects of the work (as for example in parts of the voluntary sector where the nature of a job-holder's contribution makes a difference to vulnerable people). The 'leadership' aspect of our text would be more important if such non-wage angles were adopted in order to provide proximal reinforcement of the offer.

OUTSOURCED WORKERS

Table 3.2 in Chapter 3 shows an interesting and contemporary view of working situations. Many chapters in this text have commented on the need to pay more attention to the non-core staffing arrangements that result from the drive for flexibility (eg Chapter 6). Christy and Brown (Chapter 5) quite rightly make the point that it is a matter of choice whether an organisation sees its responsibility extending to all the conditions of workers in subcontract situations.

Most organisations of any reasonable size do outsource. The subcontractors, offering a better price than can be generated internally, might be using legitimate means (such as economies of scale) in their cost-cutting, but they might not. How far the contracting organisation should (and does) investigate the terms and conditions of subcontracted workers is an area ripe for investigation as the structure of our economy changes. HR is likely to be at the forefront when such investigations do become routine. They will have to be well placed in terms of their investigating skills and extend their understanding of all aspects of managing and leading people beyond the legal issues into the ethical dimension.

THE CONUNDRUMS

The demands on HR are becoming increasingly complex. How do we staff both for today and for the future when we are not sure what the future holds? How do we make realistic promises to staff about their careers when we are unsure of what the future will bring to our organisation? How do we manage an organisation that has to lead and manage better-paid knowledge workers in some areas and also low-cost workers in others?

High-performance working would suggest that differences between the two should be minimised (Pfeffer, 1994). However, few organisations seem to do this, probably because they are understandably concerned to maintain the low-cost base of those doing standard jobs. Having happy employees might be pleasant but will not pass muster as a business argument. One needs to understand the effect of unhappy workers: lower morale, higher absenteeism, lower commitment, and almost certainly lower productivity (Huselid, 1995). Engagement practices, many of which are based on strong communication, are a useful tool, and can cost little. More fundamental, however, is when engagement becomes empowering and hence is seen by local managers as undermining their own jurisdiction. The HR function can help managers across the organisation understand these psychological processes and their business-related implications.

THE PSYCHOLOGICAL CONTRACT

This issue has been raised in a number of chapters. We have moved from the paternalistic and 'caring' paradigm to one where employers may demand more from staff and offer less in terms of job security. Employees have, in turn, adapted to these changing situations by amending their expectations and thinking more strategically about employers. Guest (1998) sees the psychological contract as a key element affecting the achievement of high production levels of all workers, connecting motivation, motivators and effort. A compelling argument is presented by the links between expectancy theory and the psychological contract. The challenge here is two-fold: first to understand what motivates the workers one actually wants, and then to design the reward aspects of the job to make them congruent with that understanding.

Failure to do so can be excessively costly: lower levels of engagement and low levels of trust and commitment from employees are likely to mean poor productivity via a range of reactions such as shirking, absenteeism and high turnover rates (Buchanan and Badham, 1999). These problems tend to end up at the door of the HR department.

HUMAN RESOURCES AS PARTNERS

The role of managing and leading people is wide-ranging, and understanding it is core knowledge for those working in HR. Our understanding of high-performance working is developing, but slowly. What is emerging is the need for smart practices at both the top and the bottom of the organisation. Human resources must be involved in both, and the notion of 'partnering' has been developed as a way of achieving this. The CIPD has undertaken a major review of the HR role with complex and some unexpected results (Reilly, Tamkin and Broughton, 2007) which are essential reading for those interested in the HR role generally.

At the top of the organisation HR needs continuous involvement, both in strategic planning and ensuring the clear communication of the goals of the organisation. The setting of these goals and their communication is essential to many aspects of HR: involvement, performance management and the psychological contract. In this sense the HR function has to be a strategic partner in the highest level of management decision-making.

The model of business partnering as a vehicle to enable good practice also needs to be consistent and focused on organisational goals at the lower levels of the organisation. HR staff must be 'out and about', in constant communication with the people in the area of the organisation for which they are responsible. This might mean relocating offices from behind the cosy centralised 'HR Department' door, to be with the staff for whom the HR service is being provided. It is hard to envisage another way of building teamwork without such constant physical presence. Where HR expert services have been outsourced, those fulfilling the remaining HR roles as HR leaders, strategists or employee advocate must stay in touch with their working community.

Partnering provides HR with a model to become proactive and engaged in shaping the future of the organisation, rather than acting as a legalistic fire-fighter when things go wrong.

CONCLUSION

This text is being written at a time when it is widely acknowledged that change is a constant feature of our work context and all sectors are under pressure to produce results within a negative economic environment. The resource-based view of organisations (Barney, 1995) has helped in placing 'people' at centre-stage in the achievement of competitive advantage (Prahalad and Hamel, 1990). To mobilise this potential, managing and leading people is fundamental.

Solutions are increasingly geared to process (how we do things) rather than content (what we do). This trend is reflected in all chapters, and provides a considerably more sophisticated challenge than previously. The ideas presented in this book provide the reader with a wide set of options to take into their own work environment. 'The basics' (or 'infrastructure' aspects), which make up the threshold competencies, are needed to survive, but with changes in the psychological contract and employee expectations, 'the basics' are likely to become more complex and demanding.

Clearly, some workplaces are considerably more productive and the chimera of high-performance working is worthwhile pursuing. However, requirements in this area will also change as the leading organisations develop further, setting the standard for others to follow. The scene is set for continuing pressure, continuing change, and the need for HR to be partners in leading the response to the challenge of the ever-changing business world (Reilly, Tamkin and Broughton, 2007).

EXPLORE FURTHER

Page, S. E. (2007) 'Making the difference: applying a logic of diversity', *Academy of Management Perspectives*, Vol.21, Issue 4, pp6–20.

Klein, K. J. and Harrison, D. A. (2007) 'On the diversity of diversity: tidy logic, messier realities', *Academy of Management Perspectives*, Vol.21, Issue 4, pp26–33.

Reilly, P., Tamkin, P. and Broughton, A. (2007) *The Changing HR Function: Transforming HR?* Research into Practice report. London: CIPD.

Rynes, S. L., Giluk, T. L. and Brown, K. G. (2007) 'The very separate worlds of academic and practitioner periodicals in human resource management: implications for evidence-based management', *Academy of Management Journal*, Vol.50, Issue 5, pp987–1008.

Appendix

MAP OF CIPD REQUIREMENTS

M = Major contributor

S = Secondary contributor

KI	Item	Chapter 1	2	3	4	5	6	7	8	9	10	11
1.1	The principal factors in the external environment and their impact on the deployment of people in work	M	M	S	S	S	S	S	M	S	S	M
1.2	Elements which typically prevent or determine the design installation and delivery of:											
	• strategies	S	M	S	S	S	S	S	M	S	M	S
	• leadership behaviours			M			M				S	
	• processes and practices											
	that lead to high-performing people and organisations	M	S	S	S	M	M	M	S	S	M	M
1.3	The principles behind, the logic and the practical implications of the performance infrastructure and performance differentiator framework	All chambers have high relevance to the infrastructure and differentiator framework										
2.1	The rationale:											
	• for system/process efficiencies	S	M	S	S	S	S	S	M	S	S	M
	• for legal/ethical compliance					M	S		S	S		S
	• throughout the routines that support effective people leadership and management in organisations	S	S	S	M	S	S	M	S	M	M	S
3.1	The principal research evidence concerning the factors that promote organisational success through people	M	S	S	M	S	S	M	S	M	M	S
3.2	The effectiveness of the thinking performer paradigm and related concepts						M	M	M	M	M	
3.3	People leadership:											
	• values			M		M		S		S	S	
	• behaviours	All chapters										
	• mechanisms which contribute to the development of successful organisations	M	S	S	S	S	S	M	M	M	S	M
3.4	Strategies for:											
	• encouraging			M			S	M			M	
	• rewarding							M	M	M	M	
	• recognising and celebrating employee behaviours that contribute positively to desired organisational outcomes					M			M		M	

References

Adair, J. (1983) *Effective Leadership*. London: Pan Books.

Adair, J. (2003) *The Inspirational Leader: How to motivate, encourage and achieve success*. London: Kogan Page.

Adams, J. S. (1963) 'Toward an understanding of inequity', *Journal of Abnormal Social Psychology*, Vol.67, No.4, pp422–36.

Adams, J. S. (1965) 'Inequity in social exchange', in Berkowitz, L. (ed.) *Advances in Experimental Social Psychology*. New York: Academic Press, pp267–99.

Adler, P. S. (1999) 'The emancipatory significance of Taylorism', in Cunha, M. P. F. and Marques, C. A. (eds) *Readings in Organization Science – Organisational Change in a Changing Context*. Lisbon: Instituto Superior de Psicologia Aplicada.

Alimo-Metcalfe, B. (1995) 'An investigation of female and male constructs of leadership and empowerment', *Women in Management Review*, Vol.10, No.2, pp3–8.

Allen, M. R. and Wright, P. (2007) 'Strategic management and HRM', in Boxall, P., Purcell, J. and Wright, P. (eds) *The Oxford Handbook of Human Resource Management*. Oxford: OUP.

Anderson, V. (2007) *The Value of Learning: From return on investment to return on expectation*. London: CIPD, p.4.

Anderson, N., Born, M. and Cunningham-Snell, D. (2001) 'Recruitment and selection: applicant perspectives and outcomes', in Anderson, N., Ones, D. and Sinangil, H. K. (eds) *Handbook of Industrial Work and Organizational Psychology*, Vol. 1. London/New York: Sage, pp200–18.

Anell, B. and Wilson, T. (2000) 'The flexible firm and the flexible coworker', *Journal of Workplace Learning: Employee Counselling Today*, Vol.12, No.4, pp165–70.

Appelbaum, E., Bailey, T. and Berg, P. (2000) *Manufacturing Advantage: Why high performance systems pay off*. Ithaca, NY: ILR Press.

Argyris, C. (1960) *Understanding Organizational Behaviour*. London: Tavistock Publications.

Argyris, C. (1998) 'Empowerment: the emperor's new clothes', *Harvard Business Review*, January–February.

Argyris, C. and Schon, E. (1978) *Organisational Learning: A theory of action perspective*. Reading MA: Addison-Wesley.

Arkin, A. (2005) 'Power play', *People Management*, Vol.11, No.5, pp40–2.

Armstrong M. (2006) *A Handbook of Human Resource Management Practice*, 10th edition. London: Kogan Page.

Armstrong, M. and Baron, A. (2005) *Managing Performance: Performance management in action*. London: CIPD.

Arnold, J. (1996) 'The psychological contract: a concept in need of close scrutiny?', *European Journal of Work and Organisational Psychology*, Vol.5, No.4, pp511–20.

Arnold, J., Cooper, C. L. and Robertson, I. T. (2005) *Work Psychology: Understanding human behaviour in the workplace*, 4th edition. Harlow: FT/Prentice Hall.

Arthur, J. (1994) 'Effects of human resources systems on manufacturing performance and turnover', *Academy of Management Journal*, Vol.37, pp670–87.

ASA: Advertising Standards Association, www.asa.org.uk.

Atkinson, C. (2002) 'Career management and the changing psychological contract', *Career Development International*, Vol.7, No.1, pp14–23.

Atkinson, J. (1984) 'Manpower strategies for flexible organisations', *Personnel Management*, August.

Avolio, B. J., Kahai, S. and Dodge, G. E., (2000) 'E-leadership Implications for theory, research and practice', *The Leadership Quarterly* Vol.11, Issue 4, pp615-668

Avolio, B. Walumba, F. and Weber, T. (2009) *Leadership: current theories, research and future directions for the annual review*. Forthcoming.

Backhaus, K. (2003) 'Importance of person–organisation fit to job-seekers', *Career Development International*, Vol.8, No.1, pp221–6.

Bakan, I., Suseno, Y., Pinnington, A. and Money, A. (2004) 'The influence of financial participation and participation in decision-making on employee job attitudes', *International Journal of Human Resource Management*, Vol.15, No.3, May, pp587–616.

Barney, J. (1991) 'Firm resources and sustained competitive advantage', *Journal of Management*, Vol.17: 49–61.

Barney, J. (1995) 'Looking inside for competitive advantage', *Academy of Management Executive*, Vol.17: 99–120.

Barney, J. (1997) *Gaining and Sustaining Competitive Advantage*. Reading, MA: Addison-Wesley.

Baron, A. and Armstrong, M. (2007) *Human Capital Management: Achieving added value through people*. London: Kogan Page.

BBC News, at: http://news.bbc.co.uk/1/hi/business/7176879.stm [accessed 10 August 2008].

BBC News, at: http://news.bbc.co.uk/1/hi/uk_politics/7474801.stm [accessed 10 August 2008].

BBC Radio 4 (2008) Interview with Prof Joseph Nye, *The Today Programme* broadcast on 23 April 2008.

Beardwell, I., Holden, L. and Claydon, T. (2004) *Human Resource Management: A contemporary approach*, 4th edition. Harlow: FT/Prentice Hall.

Beaumont, P. and Harris, R. (2002) 'Examining white-collar downsizing as a cause of change in the psychological contract: some UK evidence', *Employee Relations*, Vol.24, No.4, pp378–88.

Becker, B. and Gerhart, B. (1996) 'The impact of human resource management on organisational performance: progress and prospects', *Academy of Management Journal*, Vol.39, No.4, pp779–801.

Bernadin, H. K., Kane, J. S. and Ross, S. (1995) 'Performance appraisal design, development and implementation', in Ferris, G. R., Rosen, S. D. and Barnum, D. J. (eds) *Handbook of Human Resource Management*. Cambridge, MA: Blackwell.

Berry, M. (2007) 'Cadbury-Schweppes launches UK graduate recruitment campaign with a new online chatroom', *Personnel Today*, 7 November. Available online at: www.personneltoday.com [accessed 16 May 2008].

Bjorkman, I. and Yuan, L. (1999) 'The management of human resources in Chinese–Western joint ventures', *Journal of World Business*, Vol.34, No.2, pp1–19.

Blake, R. R. and McCanse, A. A. (1991) *Leadership Dilemmas - Grid Solutions*. Houston: Gulf Publishing.

Blake, R. R. and Mouton J. S. (1964) *The Managerial Grid*. London: Gulf Publications

Blanchard, P. N. and Thacker, J. W. (2004) *Effective Training: Systems, strategies and practices*. New Jersey: Pearson/Prentice Hall.

Block, P. (1987) *The Empowered Manager: Positive political skills at work*. San Francisco: Jossey-Bass.

Bloisi, W., Cook, C. and Hunsaker, P. (2003) *Management and Organisational Behaviour*. London: McGraw-Hill.

Blyton, P. and Morris, J. (1992) 'HRM and the limits of flexibility', in Blyton, P. and Morris, J. (eds) *Reassessing Human Resource Management*. London: Sage.

Boatright, J. R. (2000) *Ethics and the Conduct of Business*, 3rd edition. Harlow: Prentice Hall.

Bond, R. (2004) 'Call centre is "my dream job"', BBC News on Line website, 14 April.

Bontis, N., Dragonetti, N. C. and Jacobsen, K. (1999) 'The knowledge toolbox: a review of the tools available to measure intangible resources', *European Management Journal*, Vol.17, No.4, pp391–402.

Bowles, M. L. and Coates, G. (1993) 'Image and substance: the management of performance as rhetoric or reality?', *Personnel Review*, Vol.22, No.2, pp3–21.

Boxall, P. (1996) 'The strategic HRM debate and the resource-based view of the firm', *Human Resource Management Journal*, Vol.6, No.3, pp59–75.

Boxall, P. and Purcell, J. (2003) *Strategy and Human Resource Management*. Basingstoke: Palgrave Macmillan.

Boxall, P. and Purcell, J. (2008) *Strategy and Human Resource Management*, 2nd edition. Basingstoke: Palgrave Macmillan.

Boydell, T. H. (1983) *A Guide to the Identification of Training Needs*. London: British Association for Commercial and Industrial Education.

Boyle, M. (2001) 'Performance reviews: perilous curves ahead', *Fortune Europe*, Vol.143, Issue 11.

Bramley, P. (1996) *Evaluating Training Effectiveness*. Maidenhead: McGraw-Hill.

Bramley, P. and Kitson, B. (1994) 'Evaluating training against business criteria', *Journal of European Industrial Training*, Vol.18, No.1.

Bratton, J. and Gold, J. (2003) *Human Resource Management: Theory and Practice,* 3rd edition. Basingstoke: Palgrave Macmillan.

Bratton, J. and Gold, J. (2007) *Human Resource Management Theory and Practice*, 4th edition. Basingstoke: Palgrave Macmillan.

Braverman, H. (1974) *Labour and Monopoly Capital: The degradation of work in the twentieth century*. New York: Monthly Review Press.

Brefi Group website: http://www.brefigroup.co.uk [accessed 11 January 2005].

Brinkerhoff, R. O. (1987) *Achieving Results From Training*. San Francisco: Jossey-Bass.

Broad, M. L. and Newstrom, J. W. (1992) *Transfer of Training*. Reading, MA: Addison-Wesley.

Brooks, I. (2003) *Organisational Behaviour: Individuals, groups and organisation*, 2nd edition. Harlow: FT/Prentice Hall.

Brown, D. and Armstrong, M. (1999) *Paying for Contribution*. London: Kogan Page.

Brown, E. J. (2001) 'A study of the relationship between self-concept and management style: a perspective on individual managers'. Unpublished PhD thesis, University of Surrey.

Brumbach, G. B. (1988) 'Some ideas, issues and predictions about performance management', *Public Personnel Management*, Winter, pp387–402.

Buchanan, D. and Badham, R. (1999) *Power, Politics and Organizational Change: Winning the turf war game*. London: Sage.

Buchanan, D. and Huczynski, A. (2007) *Organizational Behaviour*, 6th edition. London: FT/ Prentice Hall.

Buchanan, D. A. and Wilson, B. (1996) 'Next patient please: the operating theatres problem at Leicester General Hospital NHS Trust', in J. Storey (ed.) *Cases in Human Resource and Change Management.* Oxford: Blackwell Business.

Buchanan, D., Claydon, T. and Doyle, M. (1999) 'Organization development and change: the legacy of the nineties', *Human Resource Management Journal*, Vol.9, No.2, pp20–37.

Buckley, R. and Caple, C. (2004) *The Theory and Practice of Training*. London: Kogan Page.

Butler, P. and Collins, N. (1995) 'Marketing public sector services: concepts and characteristics', *Journal of Marketing Management*, Vol.11, pp83–96.

Cassell, C., Nadin, S. and Gray, M. (2002) 'Exploring human resource management practices in small and medium-sized enterprises', *Personnel Review*, Vol.31, No.6, pp671–92.

Caulkin, S. (2003) 'How to catch a rising star', *The Observer* business pages, 9 November, p.15. London: Guardian Newspapers.

Chhokar, J. S., Brodbeck, F. C. and House, R. J. eds (2007) *Culture and Leadership Across the World.* New Jersey: Lawrence Earlbaum Associates.

Christopher, M., Payne, A. and Ballantyne, D. (1991) *Relationship Marketing*. Oxford: Butterworth-Heinemann.

Chryssochoou, X. (2004) *Cultural Diversity: Its social psychology*. Oxford: Blackwell.

CIPD (2001a) *The Case for Good People Management: A summary of research*. London: CIPD.

CIPD (2001b) *CIPD Professional Standards*. CIPD, London.

CIPD (2002) 'UK workforce is "one of the least committed in Europe"', *People Management*, Vol.12, September, p11.

CIPD (2003a) *Maximising employee potential and business performance: the role of high-performance working*. Report. December. London: CIPD.

CIPD (2003b) *Pressure of Work and the Psychological Contract*. London: CIPD.

CIPD (2003c) *Work–life Balance*. Fact sheet, April. London: CIPD.

CIPD (2003d) *Reward Management 2003: A survey of policy and practice*. London: CIPD.

CIPD (2003e) *People and Performance in Knowledge-Intensive Firms*. London: CIPD.

CIPD (2004a) *High-Performance Working*. Fact sheet. Available online at: www.cipd.co.uk/subjects/corp/strategy/general/highperfwk.htm [accessed 10 January 2005].

CIPD (2004b) *High-performance working*. Fact sheet, revised February. London: CIPD.

CIPD (2004c) *Leadership and Management Standards*, Final draft. Professional Standards Conference, June 2004.

CIPD (2004d) *Performance Management*. Fact sheet. London: CIPD.

CIPD (2004e) *Recruitment, Retention and Turnover, 2004. A survey of the UK and Ireland.* Report. London: CIPD.

CIPD (2004f) *Graphology*. Fact sheet. London: CIPD.

CIPD (2005) *Managing Change: The role of the psychological contract*. London: CIPD.

CIPD (2005) *Managing the psychological contract*. Fact sheet. London: CIPD.

CIPD (2005) *Performance Management Survey Report*. London: CIPD.

CIPD (2006) *Diversity: An overview*. Fact sheet. Available online at: www.cipd.co.uk/subjects/dvsequl/general/divover.htm?Issrchres=1 [accessed 8 May 2008].

CIPD (2007) *Annual Survey Report: Recruitment, Retention and Turnover*. London: CIPD.

CIPD (2007) *Human Capital Evaluation: Developing performance measures*. Human Capital Panel Report.

CIPD (2007) *Leadership and Management Standards*. Available for download from CIPD website at http://www.cipd.co.uk [accessed 21 April 2008].

CIPD (2008a) 'Flexible working "boosts staff performance"', *People Management*, 6 May.

CIPD (2008b) *Work–life balance*. Fact sheet, April. London: CIPD.

Clark, J. (1993) 'Full flexibility and self-supervision in an automated factory', in Clark, J. (ed.) *Human Resource Management and Technical Change*. London: Sage.

Clarke, C. and Pratt, S. (1985) 'Leadership's four-part progress', *Management Today*, March, pp84–6.

Clegg, S., Kornberger, M. and Pitsis, T. (2008) *Managing and Organizations*, 2nd edition. London: Sage.

Clutterbuck, D. (1998) 'Empowerment as a mutuality of benefit', *Human Resource Development International*, Vol.1, No.1, in Morrell, K. and Wilkinson, A. (2002) 'Empowerment: through the smoke and the mirrors', *Human Resource Development International*, Vol.5, No.1, pp119–30.

Collins, D. (1996) 'Control and isolation in the management of empowerment', *Empowerment in Organizations*, Vol.4, No.2, pp29–39.

Collis, D. J. and Montgomery, C. A. (1995) 'Competing on resources: strategy in the 1990s', *Harvard Business Review*, July–August 1995, pp118–28.

Confederation of British Industry (1979) 'Guidelines for action on employee involvement', in Farnham, D. (1993) *Employee Relations*. London: Institute of Personnel and Development.

Conger, J. (1999) 'Charisma and how to grow it', *Management Today*, December, pp78–81.

Conger, J. (2002) 'Danger of delusion', *Financial Times*, 29 November.

Constable, J. and McCormick, R. (1987) *The Making of British Managers*. London: British Institute of Management.

Cox, A., Zagelmeyer, S. and Marchington, M. (2006) 'Embedding employee involvement and participation at work', *Human Resource Management Journal*, Vol.16, No.3, pp250–67.

Coyle-Shapiro, J. and Kessler, I. (2000) 'Consequences of the psychological contract for the employment relationship: a large-scale survey', *Journal of Management Studies*, Vol.37, Issue 7, p.903.

Crail, M. (2007) 'Online recruitment delivers more applicants and wins vote of most employers', *Personnel Today*, 20 November. Available online at: www.personneltoday.com [accessed 16 May 2008].

Crane, A. and Matten, D. (2006) *Business Ethics*, 2nd edition. Oxford: Oxford University Press.

Crook, C. (2005) 'The good company', *Economist*, 22 January, pp3–4.

Cully, M., Woodland, S. and O'Reilly, A. (1999) *Britain at Work, As Depicted by the 1998 Workplace Employee Relations Survey*. London: Routledge.

Cunningham, I. and Hyman, J. (1996) 'Empowerment: the right medicine for improving employee commitment and morale in the NHS?', *Health Manpower Management*, Vol.22, No.6, pp14–24.

Czerny, A. (2005) 'People strategy toolkit for RBS', *People Management*, January, p.9.

Daniels, K. and Macdonald, L. (2005) *Equality, Diversity and Discrimination*. London: CIPD.

Davenport, T. H. (1993) *Process Innovation: Re-engineering work through information technology*. Boston, MA: Harvard Business School Press.

De George, R. T. (1999) *Business Ethics*, 5th edition. New Jersey: Prentice Hall.

Delery, J. and Doty, H. (1996) 'Modes of theorizing in strategic human resource management', *Academy of Management Journal*, Vol.39, No.4, pp802–35.

Denham, N., Ackers, P. and Travers, C. (1997) 'Doing yourself out of a job? How middle managers cope with empowerment', *Employee Relations*, Vol.19, No.2, pp147–59.

Donaldson, T. and Preston, L. (1995) 'The stakeholder theory of the corporation: concepts, evidence and implications', *Academy of Management Review*, Vol.5, pp265–9.

Dowling, P. J., Festing, M. and Engle, A. D. (2008) *International Human Resource Management*, 5th edition. London: Thomson.

Doyle, P. (2000) *Value-Based Marketing*. Chichester: John Wiley.

Drucker, P. F. (1993) *Post-Capitalist Society*. Oxford: Butterworth-Heinemann.

DTI (2005) *High Performance Work Practices: Linking strategy and skills to performance outcomes*. London: DTI in association with the CIPD.

Dyer, L. and Shafer, R. (1999) 'Creating organizational agility: implications for strategic human resource management', in Wright, P., Dyer, L. and Boudreau, J. (eds) *Research in Personnel and Human Resource Management* (Supplement 4: Strategic human resources management in the twenty-first century). Stamford, CT: JAI Press.

Easterby-Smith, M. (1986) *Evaluation of Management Education, Training and Development*. Aldershot: Gower.

Eglin, R. (2004) 'Cash is not king in holding on to staff', *Sunday Times* appointments, 15 February, p.7. London: Times Newspapers.

Eglin, R. (2004) *Sunday Times*, 5 September.

Eisenhardt, K. and Bourgeois, L. J. (1988) 'Politics of strategic decision-making in high velocity environments: towards a mid-range theory', *Academy of Management Journal*, Vol.31, No.4, pp737–70.

Elliott, L. (2004) 'Job flexibility can tie you up in knots', *Guardian Weekly*, 25–31 March, p16.

Etzioni, A. (1975) *A Comparative Analysis of Complex Organizations: On power, involvement and their correlates*, revised edition. London: Free Press.

Evans, J. (2008) 'Leaders need to be humble, not heroes' *People Management Online*, 17 April 2008 http://www.peoplemanagement.co.uk accessed 18 April 2008

European Institute for Managing Diversity (2004) updated from: http://www.iegd.org/ English/ chartFrames.htm [accessed 16 December 2004].

Farnham, D. (1993) *Employee Relations*. London: Institute of Personnel and Development.

Farnham, D. and Stevens, A. (2000). 'Developing and implementing competence-based recruitment and selection in a social services department', *International Journal of Public Sector Management*, Vol.13, No.4, pp369–82.

Fisher, C. and Lovell, A. (2003) *Business Ethics and Values*. Harlow: FT/Prentice Hall.

Fletcher, C. (2004) *Appraisal and Feedback: Making performance review work*. London: CIPD.

Fletcher, C. and Williams, R. (1996) 'Performance management, job satisfaction and organisational commitment', *British Journal of Management*, Vol.7, pp169–79.

Fletcher, C. (2007) *Appraisal, Feedback and Development: Making performance review work*, 4th edition. London: Taylor & Francis

Foot, M. and Hook, C. (2005) *Introducing Human Resource Management*, 4th edition. Harlow: FT/Prentice Hall.

Fowler, A. (1990) 'Performance management: the MBO of the '90s?', *Personnel Management*, July, pp47–54.

Francis, H. and Keegan, A. (2006) 'The changing face of HRM: in search of balance', *Human Resource Management Journal*, Vol.16, No.3: pp231–49.

Frank, E. (1991) 'The UK's management charter initiative: the first three years', *Journal of European Industrial Training*, Vol.17, No.1, pp9–11.

French, J. and Raven, B. (1968) 'The bases of social power', in Cartwright, D. and Zander, A. (eds) *Group Dynamics: Research and theory*. London: Harper & Row.

French, R. (2007) *Cross-Cultural Management in Work Organisations*. London: CIPD.

French, R., Rayner, C., Rees, G. and Rumbles, S. (2008) *Organizational Behaviour*. Chichester: John Wiley & Sons.

Friedman, M. (1970) 'The social responsibility of business is to increase its profits', *New York Times* Magazine, 13 September, pp32ff.

Furnham, A. (2005) 'Where egos dare', *People Management*, Vol.11, No.3, pp40–2.

Garcia, M. F., Posthuma, R. A. and Colella, A. (2008) 'Fit perceptions and the employment interview: the role of similarity, liking and expectations', *Journal of Occupational and Organizational Psychology*, Vol.81, No.2, pp173–89.

Gennard, J. and Judge, G. (2005) *Employee Relations*. London: CIPD.

Gilliland, S. W. (1993) 'The perceived fairness of selection systems: an organizational justice perspective', *Academy of Management Review*, Vol.18, pp694–734.

Gilmore, S. E. and Williams, S. (2003) 'Constructing the HR professional: a critical analysis of the Chartered Institute of Personnel and Development's professional project'. Third International Critical Management Studies Conference, Lancaster University Management School.

Gilmore, S. E. and Williams, S. (2007) 'Conceptualising the "personnel professional": a critical analysis of the Chartered Institute of Personnel and Development's professional qualification scheme', *Personnel Review*, Vol.36, No.3, pp398–414.

Godard, J. (2004) 'A critical assessment of the high-performance paradigm', *British Journal of Industrial Relations*, Vol.42, No.2, pp25–52.

Godard, J. and Delaney, J. (2000) 'Reflection on the "high performance" paradigm's implications for industrial relations as a field', *Industrial and Labor Relations Review*, Vol.53 No.3, pp482–502.

Goldthorpe, J. H., Lockwood, D., Bechhofer, F. and Platt, J. (1968) *The Affluent Worker: Attitudes and behaviour*. Cambridge: Cambridge University Press.

Grahl, J. and Teague, P. (1991) 'Industrial relations trajectories and European human resource management', in Brewster, C. and Tyson, S. (eds) *International Comparisons in Human Resource Management*. London: Pitman.

Greasley, K., Bryman, A., Dainty, A., Price, A., Naismith, N. and Soetanto, R. (2008) 'Understanding empowerment from an employee perspective: what does it mean and do they want it?', *Team Performance Management*, Vol.14 No.1/2, pp39–55.

Grey, C. and Garsten, C. (2001) 'Trust, control and post-bureaucracy', *Organization Studies*, Vol.22, No.2, pp229–50.

Grey, C. (2005) *A Very Short, Fairly Interesting and Reasonably Cheap Book About Studying Organizations*. London: Sage

Grint, K. (1997) *Leadership: Classical, contemporary and critical approaches*. Oxford: Oxford University Press.

Guest, D. (1986) 'Worker participation and personnel policy in the UK: some case studies', *International Labour Review*, Vol.125, No.6, pp406–27.

Guest, D. (1995) 'Human resource management, trade unions and industrial relations', in Storey, J. (ed.) *Human Resource Management*. London: Routledge.

Guest, D. (1997) 'Human resource management and performance: a review of the research agenda', *International Journal of Human Resource Management*, Vol.8, No.3, pp263–76.

Guest, D. (1998) 'Is the psychological contract worth taking seriously?', *Journal of Organizational Behaviour*, Vol.19, pp649–64.

Guest, D. (1999) 'Human resource management – the workers' verdict', *Human Resource Management Journal*, Vol.9, No.3: pp5–25.

Guest, D. (2001) 'Human resource management, trade unions and industrial relations', in Storey, J. (ed.) *Human Resource Management: A critical text*. London: Thomson Learning.

Hackman, J. R. and Oldham, G. R. (1980) *Work Redesign*. New York: Addison-Wesley.

Hales, C. (2000) 'Management and empowerment programmes', *Work, Employment and Society*, Vol.14, No.3, September, p502.

Hamblin, A. C. (1974) *Evaluation and Control of Training*. Maidenhead: McGraw-Hill.

Hambrick, D., Nadler, D. and Tushman, M. (1998) *Navigating Change: How CEOs, top team and boards steer transformation*, Boston, MA: Harvard University Press.

Hamel, G. and Prahalad, G. K. (1994) *Competing for the Future*. Boston, MA: Harvard Business School Press.

Hammer, M. and Champy, J. (1993) *Re-engineering the Corporation: A manifesto for business revolution*. London: Nicholas Brealey.

Handy, C. (1976) *Understanding Organisations*. London: Penguin Books.

Handy, C. B. (1984) *The Future of Work*. Oxford: Blackwell.

Handy, C. (1987) *The Making of Managers*. London: National Economic Development Office.

Handy, C. (1989) *The Age of Unreason*. London: Business Books.

Harris, H., Brewster, C. and Sparrow, P. (2003) *International Human Resource Management*. London: CIPD.

Harrison, R. (1997) *Employee Development*. London: Institute of Personnel and Development.

Harrison, R. (2005) *Learning and Development* (3rd edition). London: CIPD.

Harrison, R. and Kessels, J. (2004) *Human Resource Development in a Knowledge Economy*. Basingstoke: Palgrave Macmillan.

Hasson, J. (2007) 'Blogging for talent', *HR Magazine*, Vol.52, No.10, pp65–8.

Hays-Thomas, R, (2004) 'Why now? The contemporary focus on managing diversity', in Stockdale, M. S. and Crosby, F. J. (eds) *The Psychology and Management of Workplace Diversity*. Oxford: Blackwell Publishing.

Heneman, R. L. (1992) *Merit Pay: Linking pay increases to performance ratings*. Reading, MA: Addison-Wesley.

Herriot, P. and Pemberton, C. (1995) *New Deals*. Chichester: John Wiley.

Hersey, P., Blanchard, K. and Johnson, D. (2001) *Management of Organisational Behaviour: Leading human resources*, 8th edition. London: Prentice Hall.

Herzberg, F. (1968) 'One more time: how do you motivate your employees?', *Harvard Business Review*, January–February, pp109–20.

Hiltrop, J.-M. (1996) 'Managing the changing psychological contract', *Employee Relations*, Vol.18, No.1, pp36–49.

Hofstede, G. (1991) *Cultures and Organizations*. Maidenhead: McGraw-Hill.

Hofstede, G. (2001) *Culture's Consequences: Comparing values, behaviours, institutions and organizations across nations*. London: Sage.

Holbeche, L. (2008) 'Where is Leadership Going?' *Impact* CIPD Issue 22 February: pp16-17

Holden, N. (2002) *Cross-Cultural Management: A knowledge management perspective*. Harlow: Pearson.

Hooley, G., Broderick, A. and Möller, K. (1998) 'Competitive positioning and the resource-based view of the firm', *Journal of Strategic Marketing*, Vol.6, pp97–115.

Hooley, G. J., Piercy, N. F. and Nicolaud, B. (2008) *Marketing Strategy and Competitive Positioning*, 4th edition. Harlow: FT/Prentice Hall.

Huczynski, A. and Buchanan, D. (2006) *Organisational Behaviour; an Introductory Text* (6th edition). Harlow: Pearson Education.

Huczynski, A. and Buchanan, D. (2007) *Organisational Behaviour: An introductory text*, 6th edition. Harlow: Pearson Education.

Humble, J. (1972) *Management by Objectives*. London: Management Publications.

Hunt, B. (2007) 'Managing equality and cultural diversity in the health workforce', *Journal of Clinical Nursing*, Vol.16, pp2252–9.

Huselid, M. (1995) 'The impact of human resource management practices on turnover, productivity and corporate financial performance', *Academy of Management Journal*, Vol.38, No.3, pp635–72.

Hutchinson, S. and Purcell, J. (2003) *Bringing Policies to Life: The vital role of front-line managers in people managemen*t. London: CIPD.

Hutton, W. (2004) 'Got those old blue-collar blues', *The Observer*, 22 August.

Ichniowski, C., Kochan, T. A., Levine, D., Olson, C. and Strauss, G. (1996) 'What works at work: overview and assessment', *Industrial Relations*, Vol.35, No.3, pp299–333.

IDS (2006) *Online Recruitment.* IDS study 819, April. London: Incomes Data Services.

Iles, P., Forster, A. and Tinline, G. (1996) 'The changing relationships between work commitment, personal flexibility and employability: an evaluation of a field experiment in executive development', *Journal of Managerial Psychology*, Vol.11, No.8, pp18–34.

Institute of Personnel Management (1992) *Performance Management in the UK: An analysis of the issues*. London: Institute of Personnel Management.

International Labour Organisation website: http://www.ilo.org/public/english/employment/skills/workplace

Investors in People website: http://www.iipuk.co.uk [accessed 18 April 2008].

Janis, I. L. (1972) *Victims of Groupthink*. Boston: Houghton Mufflin Company

Jehn, K. (1994) 'Enhancing effectiveness: an investigation of advantages and disadvantages of value-based intragroup conflict optimising performance by conflict stimulation', *International Journal of Conflict Management*, Vol.5, No.3, pp223–38.

Johnson, G. and Scholes, K. (2002) *Exploring Corporate Strategy*, 6th edition. London: FT/Pitman.

Johnson, G., Scholes, K. and Whittington, R. (2007) *Exploring Corporate Strategy: Texts and cases*, 7th edition. London, FT/Pitman.

Jones, T. W. (1995) 'Performance management in a changing context', *Human Resource Management*, Fall, pp425–42.

Judge, T. A. and Cable, D. M. (1997) 'Applicant personality, organisational culture and organisation attraction', *Personnel Psychology*, Vol.50, No.2, pp359–94.

Kakabadse, A., Myers, A. and McMahon, T. (1997) 'Top management styles in Europe: implications for business and cross-national teams', in Grint, K. (1997) *Leadership: Classical, contemporary and critical approaches*. Oxford: Oxford University Press.

Kandola, R. and Fullerton, J. (1998) *Diversity in Action: Managing the mosaic*. London: CIPD.

Kang, D. and Stewart, J. (2007) 'Leader-member exchange (LMX) theory of leadership and HRD' *Leadership and Organization Development Journal*, Vol.28, No.6 pp531-551.

Kaplan R.S. and Norton D. P. (1996) *The Balanced Scorecard: translating strategy into action.* Boston Mass: Harvard Business School Press.

Karami, A., Analoui, F. and Cusworth, J. (2004) 'Strategic human resource management and the resource-based approach: the evidence from British manufacturing industry', *Management Research News*, Vol.27, No.6, pp50–68.

Kay, J. (1993) *Foundations of Corporate Success*. Oxford: Oxford University Press.

Kersley, B., Alpin, C., Forth, J., Bryson, A., Bewley, H., Dix, G. and Oxenbridge, S. (2006) *Inside the Workplace: Findings from the 2004 WERS survey*. London: Routledge.

Kessler, I. and Coyle-Shapiro, J. (1998) 'Restructuring the employment relationship in Surrey County Council', *Employee Relations*, Vol.20, No.4, pp365–82.

Kessler, I. and Purcell, J. (1992) 'Performance-related pay: objectives and application', *Human Resource Management Journal*, Vol.2, No.3, Spring, pp6–33.

Kessler I. and Purcell J. (1995) 'Individualism and collectivism in theory and practice: management style and the design of pay systems', in Edwards P. (ed.) *Industrial Relations Theory and Practice in Britain*. Oxford: Blackwell.

Kim, W. C. and Mauborgne, R. (1997) 'Fair process: managing in the knowledge economy', *Harvard Business Review*, July–August, pp65–75.

Kirkpatrick, D. L. (1967) 'Evaluation of training', in Craig, R. L. and Bittel, L. R. (eds) *Training and Development Handbook*. New York: McGraw-Hill.

Klagge, J. (1998) 'The empowerment squeeze – views from the middle management position', *Journal of Management Development*, Vol.17, No.8, pp548–58.

Klein, K. J. and Harrison, D. A. (2007) 'On the diversity of diversity: tidy logic, messier realities', *Academy of Management Perspectives*, Vol.21, Issue 4, pp26–33.

Kohn, A. (1993) 'Why incentive plans cannot work', *Harvard Business Review*, September–October, pp54–63.

Kolb, D. G. (2003) 'Seeking continuity amidst organizational change: a storytelling approach', *Journal of Management Inquiry*, Vol.12, No.2, 180–3.

Kreitner, R. (2001) *Management*, 6th edition. Boston: Houghton Mifflin.

Kreitner, R. and Kinicki, A. (2001) *Organizational Behaviour*, 5th edition. New York: McGraw-Hill.

Lane, C. and Bachman, R. (1998) *Trust Within and Between Organizations: Conceptual issues and empirical applications*. Oxford: Oxford University Press.

Lashley, C. (1995) 'Towards an understanding of employee empowerment in hospitality services', *International Journal of Contemporary Hospitality Management*, Vol.7, No.1, pp27–32.

Leach, D. and Wall, T. (2004) *What is – job design?* Sheffield: Institute of Work Psychology.

Leanna, C. and Barry, B. (2000) 'Stability and change as simultaneous experiences in organizational life', *Academy of Management Review*, Vol.25, No.4, pp753–9.

Learning and Teaching Support Network website: http://www.hlst.ltsn.ac.uk/ resources/ empowerment.html#2 [accessed 13 September 2004].

Lee, R. (1996) 'The "pay forward" view of training', *People Management*, Vol.2, No.3, pp30–2.

Legge, K. (1978) *Power, Innovation and Problem-Solving in Personnel Management*. London: McGraw-Hill.

Legge, K. (2001) 'Silver bullet or spent round? Assessing the meaning of the high commitment management/performance relationship', in Storey, J. (ed.) *Human Resource Management: A critical text*, 2nd edition. Thomson Learning, London.

Legge, K. (2005) *Human Resource Management; Rhetorics and realities*, 2nd edition. Basingstoke: Palgrave Macmillan.

Leitch (2006) Leitch Report: http://www.dcsf.gov.uk/furthereducation/index.cfm?fuseaction=content.view&categoryID=21&contentID=37 [accessed 24 January 09]

Leopold, J., Harris, L. and Watson, T. (2005) *The Strategic Managing of Human Resources*. Harlow: FT/Prentice Hall.

Levinson, H. (1970) 'Management by whose objectives?', *Harvard Business Review*, July–August, pp125–34.

Levinson, H. (1976) 'Appraisal of what performance?', *Harvard Business Review*, July–August, pp30–46.

Lewin, D. (2001) 'IR and HR perspectives on workplace conflict: what can each learn from the other?', *Human Resource Management Review*, Winter, Vol.11, No.4, pp453–85.

Linstead, S., Fulop, S. and Lilley, S. (2004) *Management and Organisation: A critical text*. Basingstoke: Palgrave Macmillan.

Locke, E. A. and Latham, G. P. (1990) *A Theory of Goal Setting and Task Performance*. Englewood Cliffs, NJ: Prentice Hall.

Macdonald, L. (2004) *Managing Equality, Diversity and the Avoidance of Discrimination*. London: CIPD.

MacDuffie, J. P. (1995) 'Human resource bundles and manufacturing performance: organizational logic and flexible production systems in the world auto industry', *Industrial and Labour Relations Review*, Vol.48, No.2, pp195–221.

Mackay, C. J., Cousins, R. and Kelly, P. J. (2004) 'Management standards and work-related stress in the UK: policy background and science', *Work and Stress*, Vol.18, No.2, pp91–112.

Mackie, J. L. (1977) *Ethics – Inventing Right and Wrong*. Harmondsworth: Penguin.

Maguire, H. (2002) 'Psychological contracts: are they still relevant?', *Career Development International*, Vol.7, No.3, pp167–80.

Mahoney, J. (1994) 'How to be ethical: ethics resource management', in Harvey, B. (ed.) *Business Ethics – A European Approach*. Hemel Hempstead: Prentice Hall.

Maitland, A. (2003) 'Clearing up after the visionaries: an interview with Stephen Cooper', *Financial Times*, 30 January, p12.

Malone, S. A. (2003) *Learning about Learning*. London: CIPD.

Management Standards Centre website: http://www.management-standards.org [accessed 18 April 2008].

Marchington, M. (2001) 'Employee involvement at work', in Storey, J. (ed.) *Human Resource Management: A critical text*. London: Thomson Learning.

Marchington, M., Grimshaw, D., Rubery, G. and Willmott, H. (2005) *Fragmenting Work: Blurring organizational boundaries and disordering hierarchies*. Oxford: Oxford University Press.

Market Research Society website: www.mrs.org.uk.

Marks, A. (2001) 'Developing a multiple foci conceptualization of the psychological contract', *Employee Relations*, Vol.23, No.5, pp454–69.

Marks & Spencer (2008) *About Plan A*. Company website: http://plana.marksandspencer.com [accessed 18 April 2008].

Marsden, D. and French, S. (1998) *What a Performance: Performance-related pay in the public services*. London: Centre for Economic Performance.

Maslow, A. (1943) 'A theory of human motivation', *Psychological Review*, Vol.50, No.4, pp370–96.

Mathur, S. S. (1992) 'Talking straight about competitive strategy', *Journal of Marketing Management*, Vol.8, pp199–217.

Mathur, S. S. and Kenyon, A. (2001) *Creating Value*, 2nd edition. Oxford: Butterworth-Heinemann.

McDonald, D. and Makin, P. (2000) 'The psychological contract, organisational commitment and job satisfaction of temporary staff', *Leadership and Organization Development Journal*, Vol.21, No.2, pp84–91.

Millward, N., Bryson, A. and Forth, J. (2000) 'All change at work: British employment relations 1980–1998 as portrayed by the Workplace Industrial Relations Series', in Blyton, P. and Turnbull, P. (2004) *The Dynamics of Employee Relations*, 3rd edition. Basingstoke: Palgrave Macmillan.

Mohrman, A. M. and Mohrman, S. A. (1995) 'Performance management is "running the business"', *Compensation and Benefits Review*, July–August, pp69–75.

Montanari, J. R. and Bracker, J. S. (1986) 'The strategic management process at the public planning unit level', *Strategic Management Journal*, Vol.7, No.3, pp251–65.

Morehead, A., Steele, M. and Alexander, M. (1997) *Changes at Work: The 1995 Australian Workplace Industrial Relations Survey*. Reading, MA: Addison-Wesley/Longman.

Morgan, G. (1997) *Images of Organization*. London: Sage.

Mullins, L. J. (2005) *Management and Organisational Behaviour* (7th edition). Harlow: Prentice Hall.

Mullins, L. J. (2007) *Management and Organisational Behaviour*, 8th edition. London: FT/ Prentice Hall.

Mumford, E. (1995) 'Contracts, complexity and contradictions: the changing employment relationship', *Personnel Review*, Vol.24, No.8, pp54–70.

Murphy, N. (2008) 'Trends in recruitment methods in 2006 and 2007', *IRS Employment Review*, Issue 893. Available online at: www.xperthr.co.uk [accessed 16 May 2008].

Murray-West, R. (2002) 'Sunderland car workers are Europe's most productive', *Daily Telegraph*, 9 July.

Newell, S., Robertson, M. and Scarbrough, H. (2002) *Managing Knowledge Work*. Basingstoke: Palgrave Macmillan.

Ngai, E. W. T., Law, C. C. H., Chan, S. C. H. and Wat, F. K. T. (2008) 'The importance of the Internet to human resource practitioners in Hong Kong', *Personnel Review*, Vol.37, No.1/2, pp66–84.

Nohria, N., Groysberg, B. and Lee, L.-E. (2008) 'Employee Motivation: a powerful new model', Harvard Business Review, July-August, p.82.

Nonaka, I and Takeuchi, H. (1995) *The Knowledge-Creating Company*. Oxford: Oxford University Press.

Noon, M. and Blyton, P. (2002) *The Realities of Work*, 2nd edition. Basingstoke: Palgrave Macmillan.

Nye, J. S. (2008) *The Powers to Lead; Soft, Hard, and Smart.* Oxford: Oxford University Press

Page, S. E. (2007) 'Making the difference: applying a logic of diversity', *Academy of Management Perspectives*, Vol.21, Issue 4, pp6–20.

Patterson, M., West, M., Lawthorn, R. and Nickell, S. (1997) 'Impact of people management practices on business performance', *Issues in People Management*, IPD, London.

Perkins, S. J. and Shortland, S. M. (2006) *Strategic International Human Resource Management*, 2nd edition. London: Kogan Page.

Peston, R. (2007) *Rose Goes Green in Pursuit of Profit*. BBC News website, 15 January, at http:// news.bbc.co.uk [accessed 18 April 2008].

Pettigrew, A. (1985) *The Awakening Giant: Continuity and change at ICI*. Oxford: Blackwell.

Perry, M. (2001) 'Flexibility Pays', Accountancy Age, 6 December, pp15-18, in (2002) *Human Resource Management International Digest*, Vol.10, No.4, pp13-15.

Pfeffer, J. (1994) *Competitive Advantage Through People*. Boston, MA: Harvard Business School Press.

Pfeffer, J. (1998) *Building Profits While Putting People First*. New York: Harper & Row.

Phillips, J. J. (1992) *Handbook of Training Evaluation and Measurement*. Houston: Gulf.

Pilbeam S. and Corbridge M. (2006) *People Resourcing – Contemporary HRM in practice*, 3rd edition. Harlow: FT/Prentice Hall.

Pollert, A. (1991) 'The orthodoxy of flexibility', in Pollert, A. *Farewell to Flexibility?* Oxford: Blackwell, pp3–31.

Pollitt, D. (2003) 'Shift-pattern switch improves staff turnover and recruitment at Seeboard', *Human Resource Management International Digest*, Vol.11, No.1, pp12–14.

Porter, L. and Lawler, E. (1968) *Managerial Attitudes and Performance*. Homewood, IL: Dorsey.

Porter, M. (1980) *Competitive Strategies: Technologies for analysing industries and firms*. New York: Free Press.

Porter, M. (1985) *Competitive Advantage: Creating and sustaining superior performance*. New York: Free Press.

Prahalad, C. K. and Hamel, G. (1990) 'The core competence of the corporation', *Harvard Business Review*, Vol.68, No.3, pp79–91.

Price, A. (2004) *Human Resource Management in a Business Context*, 2nd edition. London: Thomson Publishing.

Purcell, J. and Hutchinson, S. (2007) 'Front-line managers as agents in the HRM–performance causal chain: theory, analysis and evidence', *Human Resource Management Journal*, Vol.17, No.1, pp3–20.

Purcell, J. and Sisson, K. (1983) 'Strategies and practice: the management of industrial relations', in Bain, G. S. (ed.) *Industrial Relations in Britain*. Oxford: Blackwell.

Purcell, J., Kinnie, N. and Hutchinson, S. (2003) 'Open-minded', *People Management*, 15 May, pp30–3.

Purcell, J., Kinnie, N., Hutchinson, S., Rayton, B. and Swart, J. (2003) *Understanding the People and Performance Link: Unlocking the black box*. London: CIPD.

Quine, L. (1999) 'Workplace bullying in an NHS Trust', *British Medical Journal*, Vol.318, pp228–32.

Rajan, A. (2002) 'The meaning of leadership in 2002', *Professional Manager*, March, p33.

Redman, T. and Wilkinson, A. (2006) *Contemporary Human Resource Management: Texts and cases*, 2nd edition. Harlow: FT/Prentice Hall.

Reid, M. A., Barrington, H. and Brown, M. (2004) *Human Resource Development: Beyond training interventions*. London: CIPD.

Reilly, P., Tamkin, P. and Broughton, A. (2007) *The Changing HR Function: Transforming HR?* Research into Practice report. London: CIPD.

Ritzer, G. (1993) *The McDonaldization of Society: An investigation into the changing character of contemporary social life*. Thousand Oaks, CA: Pine Forge Press.

Robbins, S. P. (2005) *Organizational Behaviour*, 11th edition. Harlow: Pearson/Prentice Hall.

Rodgers, K. (2003) 'Closing the gap', *Personnel Today*, 28 January, at www.personneltoday.com [accessed 21 February 2005].

Rodrigues, C. A. (1988) 'Identifying the right leader for the right situation', *Personnel*, September, pp43–6.

Rosener, J. (1990) 'Ways women lead', *Harvard Business Review*, November–December, pp119–25.

Rosset, A. (1997) 'That was a great class but …', *Training and Development*, Vol.5, No.7, pp18–25.

Rousseau, D. (1995) *Psychological Contracts in Organizations: Understanding written and unwritten agreements*. London: Sage.

Rousseau, D. (1998) 'The problem of the psychological contract', *Journal of Organizational Behaviour*, Vol.19, pp665–71.

Rousseau, D. (2001) 'Schema, promise and mutuality: the building blocks of the psychological contract', *Journal of Occupational and Organizational Psychology*, Vol.74, pp511–41.

Rousseau, D. (2004) 'Psychological contracts in the workplace: understanding the ties that motivate', *Academy of Management Executive*, Vol.18, pp120–7.

Rynes, S. L., Giluk, T. L. and Brown, K. G. (2007) 'The very separate worlds of academic and practitioner periodicals in human resource management: implications for evidence-based management', *Academy of Management Journal*, Vol.50, Issue 5, pp987–1008.

Sadler-Smith, E., Down, S. and Field, J. (1999) 'Adding value to HRD: evaluation, Investors in People and small firm training', *Human Resource Development International*, Vol.2, No.4, pp369–90.

Sako, M. (1992) *Price, Quality and Trust: Inter-firm relations in Britain and Japan*. Cambridge: Cambridge University Press.

Salinger, R. D. and Deming, B. S. (1982) 'Practical strategies for evaluating training', *Training and Development Journal*, August, pp20–9.

Sanders, K. and Schyns, B. (2006) 'Trust, conflict and cooperative behaviour: considering reciprocity within organizations', *Personnel Review*, Vol.35, pp508–18.

Scarbrough, H. (1998) 'The unmaking of management? Change and continuity in British management in the 1990s', *Human Relations*, Vol.51, No.6, pp691–715.

Schein, E. A. (1978), *Careers Dynamics: Matching the individual and organizational needs*. Reading, MA: Addison-Wesley.

Schein, E. (1984) 'Coming to a new awareness of organizational culture', *Sloan Management Review*, Vol.25, No.2, pp3–16.

Schneider, S. C. and Barsoux, J. (2003) *Managing Across Cultures*, 2nd edition. Harlow: FT/Prentice Hall.

Schultz, T. W. (1961) 'Investment in human capital', *American Economic Review*, Vol.51, March, pp1–17.

Schwartz, S. H. (1999) 'A theory of cultural values and some implications for work', *Applied Psychology: An International Review*, Vol.48, No.1, pp23–47.

Searle, R. (2003) *Selection and Recruitment: A critical text*. Milton Keynes: Palgrave Macmillan in association with The Open University.

Semler, R. (1993) *Maverick: The success story behind the world's most unusual workplace*. London: Arrow Books.

Senge, P. (1990) *The Fifth Discipline*. London: Century Business.

Sennett, R. (1998) *The Corrosion of Character: The personal consequences of work in the new capitalism*. London: Norton.

Shapiro, G. (2000) 'Employee involvement: opening the diversity Pandora's Box?', *Personnel Review*, Vol.29, No.3, April, pp304–23.

Sheth, J. N. and Sharma, A. (2008) 'The impact of the product to service shift in industrial markets and the evolution of the sales organization', *Industrial Marketing Management*, Vol.37, No.3, pp260–9.

Sisson, K. (1994) *Personnel Management: A comprehensive guide to theory and practice in Britain*, 2nd edition. Oxford: Blackwell.

Slotte, V, Tynjälä, P. and Hytönen, T. (2004) 'How do HRD practitioners describe learning at work?', *Human Resource Development International*, Vol.7, No.4, pp481–99.

Sternberg, E. (2000) *Just Business*, 2nd edition. Oxford: Oxford University Press.

Stewart, J. (1999) *Employee Development Practice*. London: Financial Times/Pitman Publishing.

Storey, J. (1989) 'From personnel management to human resource management', in Storey, J. (ed.) *New Perspectives on Human Resource Management*. London: Routledge.

Sun, H., Hui, I. K. and Tam, A. Y. K. (2000) 'Employee involvement and quality management', *The TQM Magazine*, Vol.12, No.5, May, pp350–4.

Sung, J. and Ashton, D. (2005) *High Performance Work Practices: Linking strategy and skills to performance outcomes*. London: DTI.

Sweeney, P. D., McFarlin, D. B. and Interrieden, E. J. (1990) 'Using relative deprivation theory to explain satisfaction with income and pay level: a multi-study examination', *Academy of Management Journal*, Vol.33, pp423–36.

Szivas, E. (1997) 'A study of labour mobility into tourism: the case of Hungary'. Unpublished PhD thesis, University of Surrey, Guildford.

Tamkin, P., Barber, L. and Hirsh, W. (1995) *Personal Development Plans: Case studies of practice*. Brighton: Institute for Employment Studies.

Tannenbaum, R. and Schmidt, W. H. (1973) 'How to choose a leadership pattern', *Harvard Business Review*, May–June, pp162–80.

Taylor, F. W. (1911) *Principles of Scientific Management*. New York: Harper.

Taylor, R. (2002) 'The future of work–life balance', *Human Resource Management International Digest*, Vol.10, No.4, pp13–15.

Tesco (2008) Tesco.com website [accessed 13 September 2004; 16 February 2005; 4 May 2008].

Thompson, P. and McHugh, D. (2002) *Work Organisations: A critical introduction*, 3rd edition. Basingstoke: Palgrave Macmillan.

Tichy, N. M. and Devanna, M. A. (1986) *The Transformational Leader*. Chichester: John Wiley & Sons.

Torrington, D. Hall, L, and Taylor, S. (2002) *Human Resource Management* (5th edition). Harlow: FT Prentice Hall

Torrington, D., Hall, L. and Taylor, D. (2008) *Human Resource Management*, 7th edition. Harlow: FT/Prentice Hall.

Townley, B. (1994) *Reframing Human Resource Management*. London: Sage.

Toynbee, P. (2008) 'MPs must fulfil Labour's pledge to low-paid and temporary workers', *The Guardian*, 22 February, p.33.

Trompenaars, F. (1996) 'Resolving international conflict: culture and business strategy', *Business Strategy Review*, Vol.7, No.3, pp51–68.

Ulrich, D. (1997) *Human Resource Champions: The next agenda for adding value and delivering results*. Boston, MA: Harvard University Press.

Ulrich, D. (1998) 'A new mandate for human resources', *Harvard Business Review*, January–February, 124–34.

Ulrich, D. and Brockbank, W. (2005) *The HR Value Proposition*. Boston, MA: Harvard University Press.

Von Bergen, C. W., Soper, B. and Parnell, J. A. (2005) 'Workplace diversity and organisational performance', *Equal Opportunties International,* Vol.24, No.3/4; electronic copy.

Walton, J. (1999) *Strategic Human Resource Development*. Harlow: FT/Prentice Hall.

Warr, P., Bird, M. and Rackham, N. (1978) *Evaluation of Management Training*. London: Gower.

Watson, T. J. (2006) *Organising and Managing Work,* 2nd edition. Harlow: FT/Prentice Hall.

Weber, M. (1947) *The Theory of Social and Economic Organization* (translated by Henderson, A. M. and Parsons, T.). Oxford: Oxford University Press.

Whitford, A. (2003) 'Why you can't ignore Internet recruitment: one-stop guide', Reed Business Information. Available online at: www.xperthr.co.uk [accessed 16 May 2008].

Wignall, A. (2004) 'Work in progresss', [Professor P. Nolan quoted], *The Guardian*, 21 September.

Wilkinson, A. (1998) 'Empowerment: theory and practice', *Personnel Review*, Vol.27, No.1, pp40–56.

Wilkinson, G. and Monkhouse, E. (1994) 'Strategic planning in public sector organisations', *Executive Development*, Vol.7, No.6, pp16–19.

William, N. (2008) *Competency-based interviews and online psychometric tests are best for choosing candidates*. Personnel Today 10 March 2008 [Accessed online 07 May 08].

Williams, R. S. (1998) *Performance Management: Perspectives on employee performance*. London: International Thomson Business Press.

Williams, S. and Adam-Smith, D. (2005) *Contemporary Employment Relations: A critical introduction*. Oxford: Oxford University Press.

Wilson, F. L. (2004) *Organizational Behaviour and Work: A critical introduction*. Oxford: Oxford University Press.

Winstanley, D. and Stuart-Smith, K. (1996) 'Policing performance: the ethics of performance management', *Personnel Review*, Vol.25, No.6, pp66–84.

Wood, S. and de Menezes, L. (1998) 'High commitment management in the UK: evidence from the Workplace Industrial Relations Survey and Employers' Manpower and Skills Practices Survey', *Human Relations*, Vol.51, No.4, pp501–31.

Wood, S. J. and Wall, T. D. (2007) 'Work enrichment and employee voice in human resource management–performance studies', *International Journal of Human Resource Management*, Vol.18, No.7, pp1335–72.

Work Foundation (2003) *The Missing Link: From productivity to performance*. Work and enterprise panel of inquiry. London: The Work Foundation.

Worrall, L., Collinge, C. and Bill, T. (1998) 'Managing strategy in local government', *International Journal of Public Sector Management*, Vol.11, No.6, pp 472–93.

Yukl, G. (2006) *Leadership in Organisations*, 6th edition. London: Prentice Hall.

Zigurs, I. (2003) 'Leadership in Virtual teams: Oxymoron or Opportunity?' *Organizational Dynamics*, Vol.31 Issue 4 pp339-351.

Index

The CIPD would like to thank the following members of the CIPD Publishing editorial board for their help and advice:

- Caroline Hook, Huddersfield University Business School
- Edwina Hollings, Staffordshire University Business School
- Pauline Dibben, Sheffield University Business School
- Simon Gurevitz, University of Westminster Business School
- Barbara Maiden, University of Wolverhampton Business School
- Wendy Yellowley and Marilyn Farmer, Buckinghamshire New University School of Business and Management